CREATED BY **JOSS WHEDON**

JORDIE **BELLAIRE** DAVID **LÓPEZ** RAÚL **ANGULO**

Buffy the Vampire Slayer™

VOLUME THREE **FROM BENEATH YOU**

A **BUFFY** + **ANGEL** EVENT

HELLMOUTH

Published by
BOOM! STUDIOS

Series Designer
Michelle Ankley

Collection Designer
Scott Newman

Assistant Editor
Gavin Gronenthal

Associate Editor
Jonathan Manning

Editor
Jeanine Schaefer

Special Thanks to **Sierra Hahn**, **Dafna Pleban**,
Becca J. Sadowsky, and **Nicole Spiegel**,
& **Carol Roeder** at Twentieth Century Fox.

Ross Richie CEO & Founder
Joy Huffman CFO
Matt Gagnon Editor-in-Chief
Filip Sablik President, Publishing & Marketing
Stephen Christy President, Development
Lance Kreiter Vice President, Licensing & Merchandising
Arune Singh Vice President, Marketing
Bryce Carlson Vice President, Editorial & Creative Strategy
Kate Henning Director, Operations
Spencer Simpson Director, Sales
Scott Newman Manager, Production Design
Elyse Strandberg Manager, Finance
Sierra Hahn Executive Editor
Jeanine Schaefer Executive Editor
Dafna Pleban Senior Editor
Shannon Watters Senior Editor
Eric Harburn Senior Editor
Matthew Levine Editor
Sophie Philips-Roberts Associate Editor
Amanda LaFranco Associate Editor
Jonathan Manning Associate Editor
Gavin Gronenthal Assistant Editor

Gwen Waller Assistant Editor
Allyson Gronowitz Assistant Editor
Ramiro Portnoy Assistant Editor
Shelby Netschke Editorial Assistant
Michelle Ankley Design Coordinator
Marie Krupina Production Designer
Grace Park Production Designer
Chelsea Roberts Production Designer
Samantha Knapp Production Design Assistant
José Meza Live Events Lead
Stephanie Hocutt Digital Marketing Lead
Esther Kim Marketing Coordinator
Cat O'Grady Digital Marketing Coordinator
Breanna Sarpy Live Events Coordinator
Amanda Lawson Marketing Assistant
Holly Aitchison Digital Sales Coordinator
Morgan Perry Retail Sales Coordinator
Megan Christopher Operations Coordinator
Rodrigo Hernandez Operations Coordinator
Zipporah Smith Operations Assistant
Jason Lee Senior Accountant
Sabrina Lesin Accounting Assistant

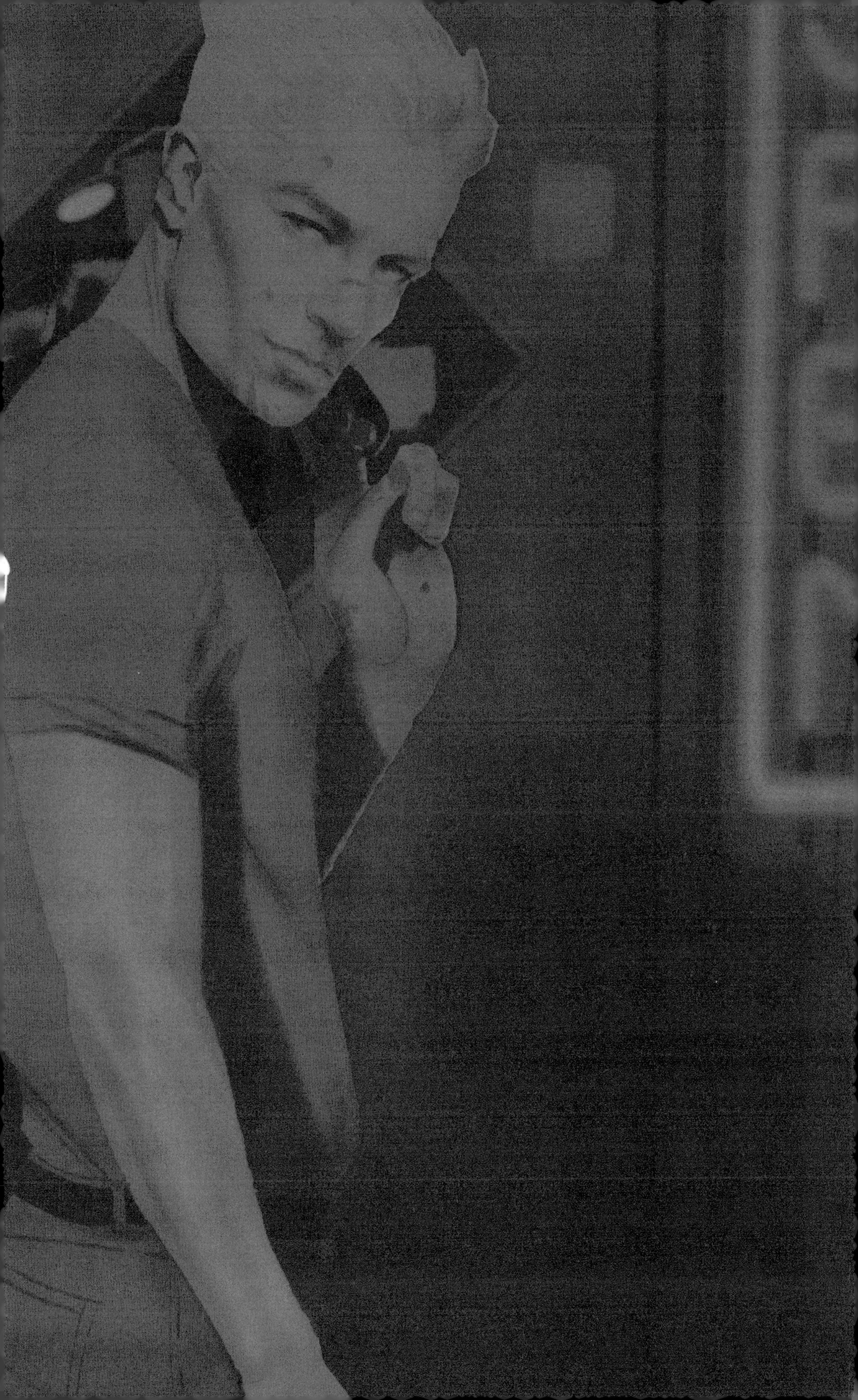

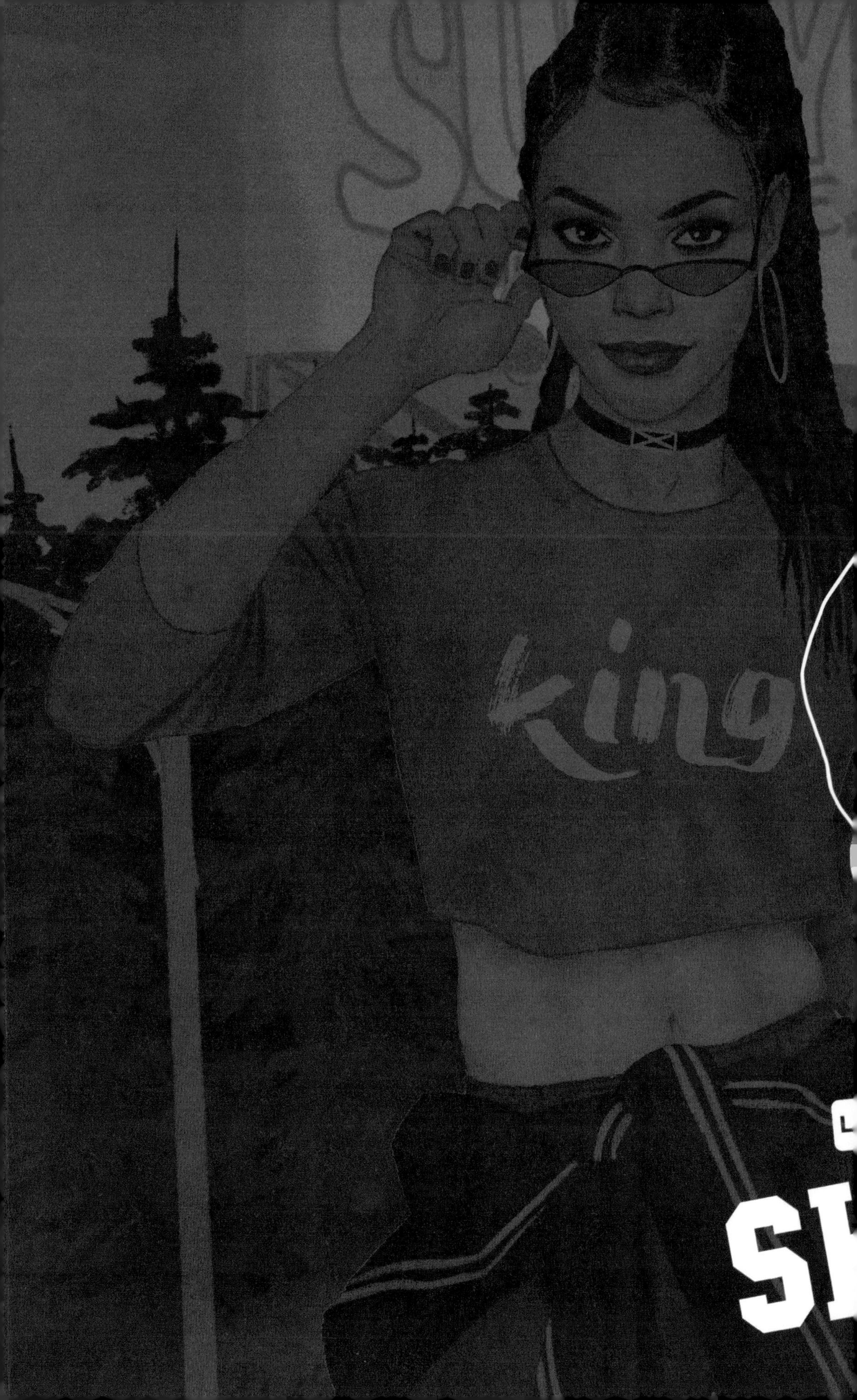
king

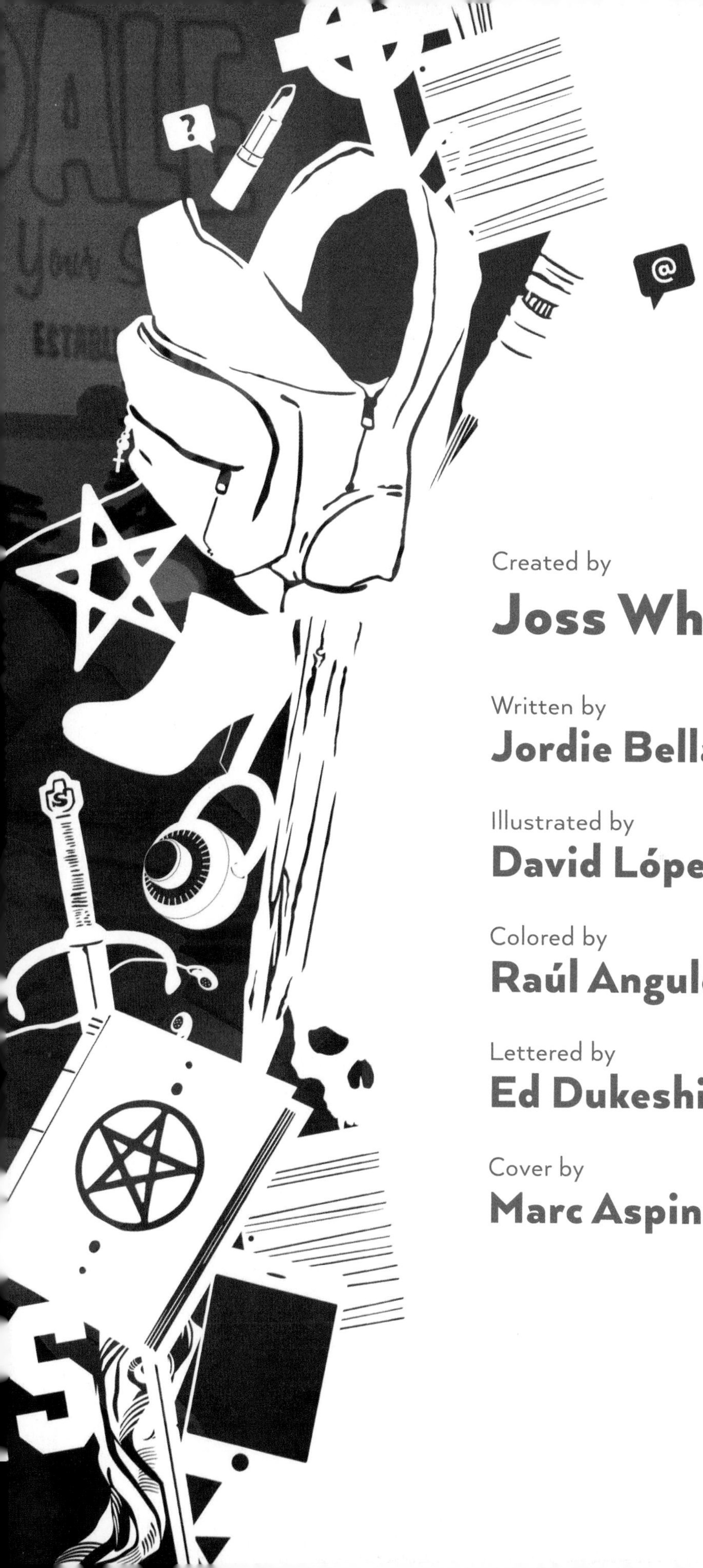

Created by
Joss Whedon

Written by
Jordie Bellaire

Illustrated by
David López

Colored by
Raúl Angulo

Lettered by
Ed Dukeshire

Cover by
Marc Aspinall

CHAPTER NINE

Issue Nine Cover by **Marc Aspinall**

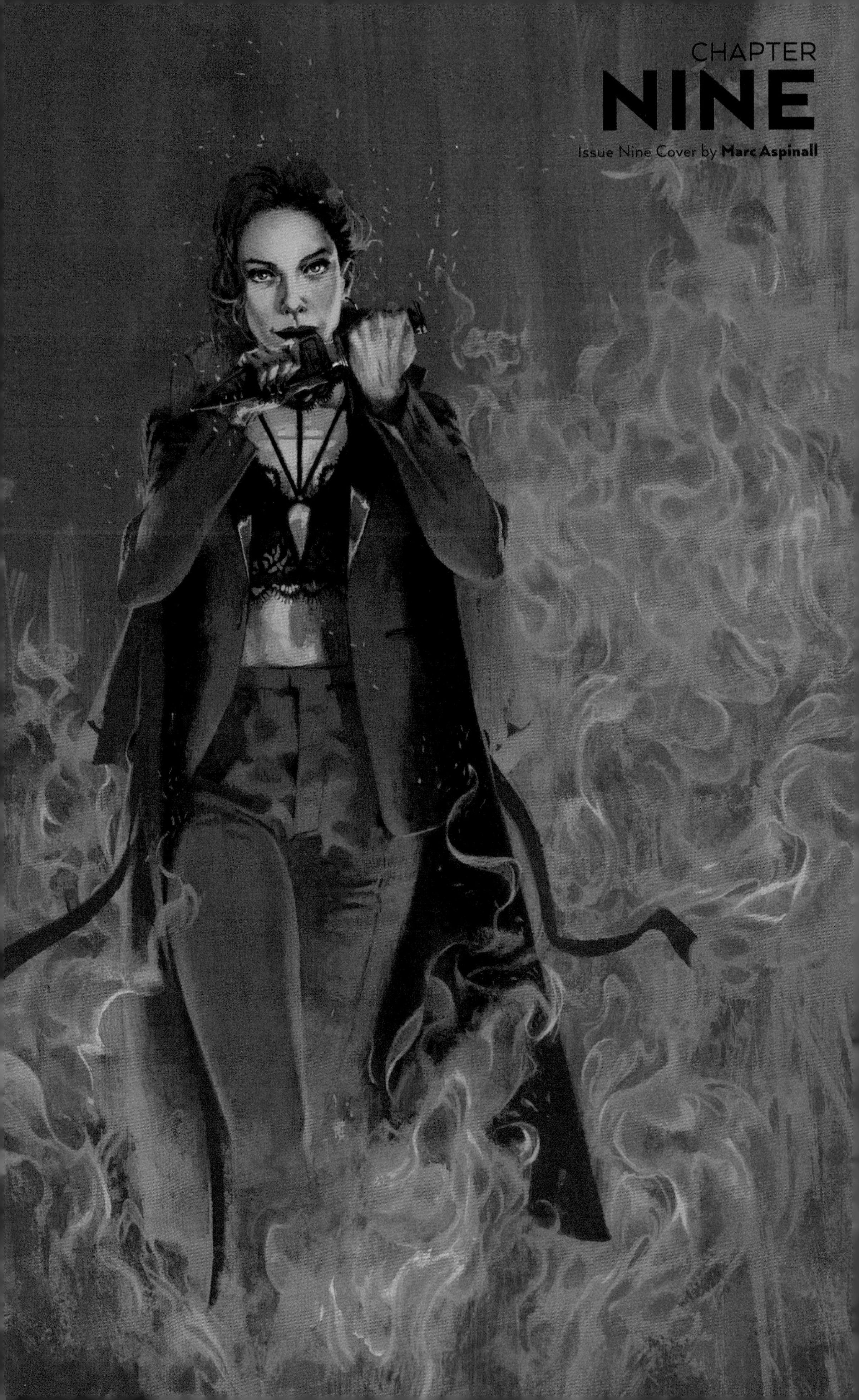

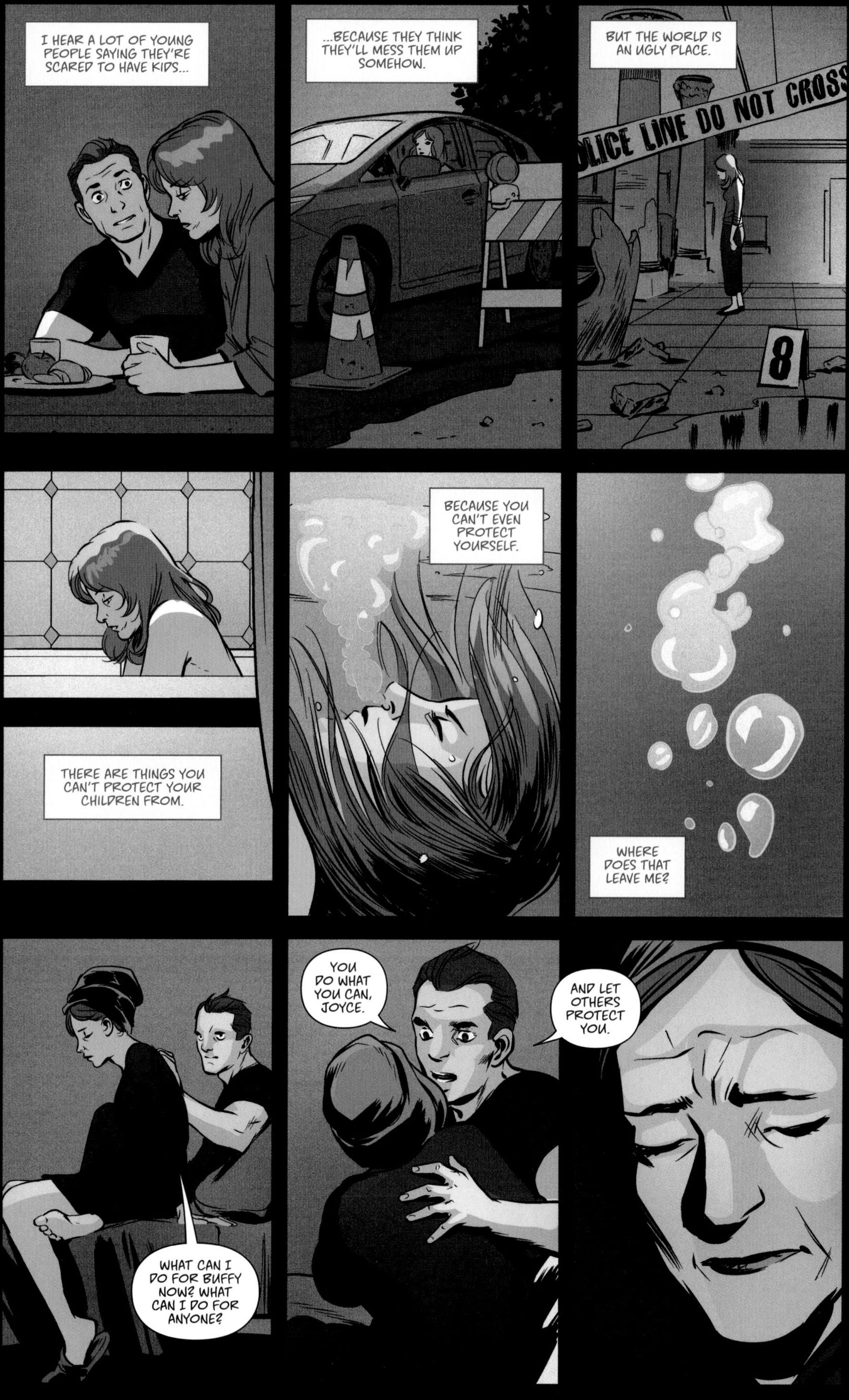
I HEAR A LOT OF YOUNG PEOPLE SAYING THEY'RE SCARED TO HAVE KIDS...
...BECAUSE THEY THINK THEY'LL MESS THEM UP SOMEHOW.
BUT THE WORLD IS AN UGLY PLACE.
POLICE LINE DO NOT CROSS
8
THERE ARE THINGS YOU CAN'T PROTECT YOUR CHILDREN FROM.
BECAUSE YOU CAN'T EVEN PROTECT YOURSELF.
WHERE DOES THAT LEAVE ME?
WHAT CAN I DO FOR BUFFY NOW? WHAT CAN I DO FOR ANYONE?
YOU DO WHAT YOU CAN, JOYCE.
AND LET OTHERS PROTECT YOU.

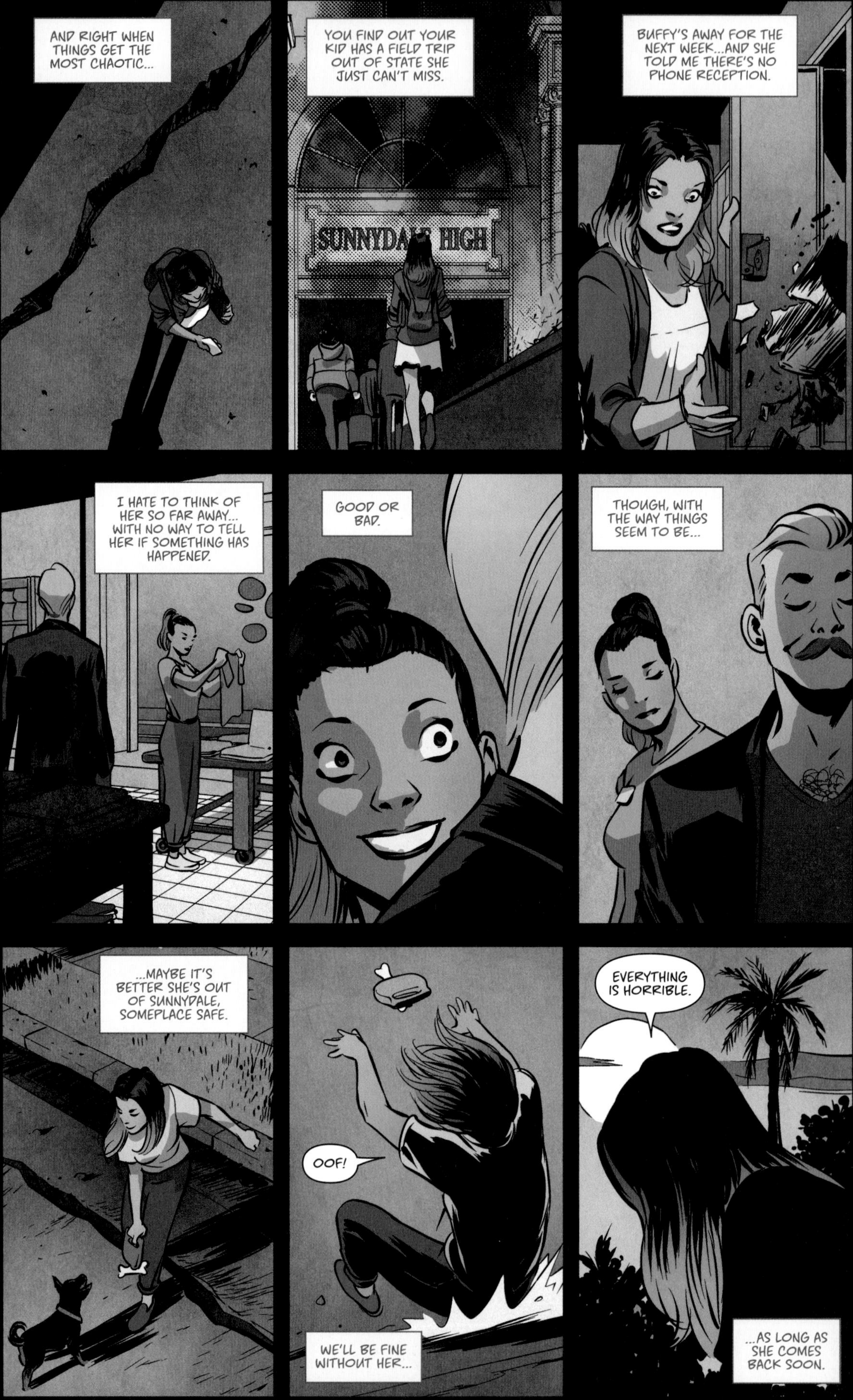
AND RIGHT WHEN THINGS GET THE MOST CHAOTIC...
YOU FIND OUT YOUR KID HAS A FIELD TRIP OUT OF STATE SHE JUST CAN'T MISS.
SUNNYDALE HIGH
BUFFY'S AWAY FOR THE NEXT WEEK...AND SHE TOLD ME THERE'S NO PHONE RECEPTION.
I HATE TO THINK OF HER SO FAR AWAY... WITH NO WAY TO TELL HER IF SOMETHING HAS HAPPENED.
GOOD OR BAD.
THOUGH, WITH THE WAY THINGS SEEM TO BE...
...MAYBE IT'S BETTER SHE'S OUT OF SUNNYDALE, SOMEPLACE SAFE.
OOF!
WE'LL BE FINE WITHOUT HER...
EVERYTHING IS HORRIBLE.
...AS LONG AS SHE COMES BACK SOON.

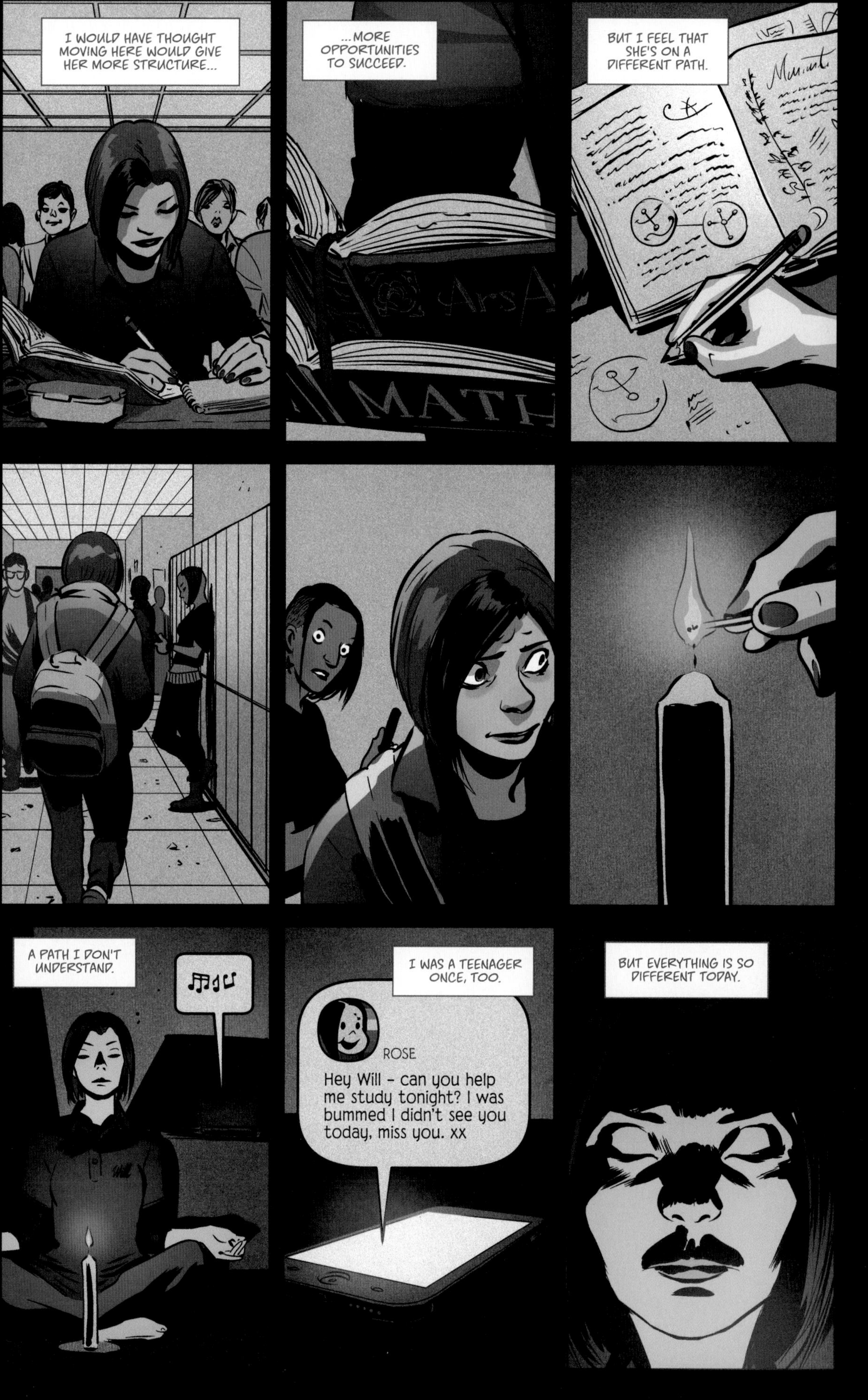
I WOULD HAVE THOUGHT MOVING HERE WOULD GIVE HER MORE STRUCTURE...
...MORE OPPORTUNITIES TO SUCCEED.
MATH
BUT I FEEL THAT SHE'S ON A DIFFERENT PATH.
A PATH I DON'T UNDERSTAND.
I WAS A TEENAGER ONCE, TOO.
ROSE
Hey Will - can you help me study tonight? I was bummed I didn't see you today, miss you. xx
BUT EVERYTHING IS SO DIFFERENT TODAY.

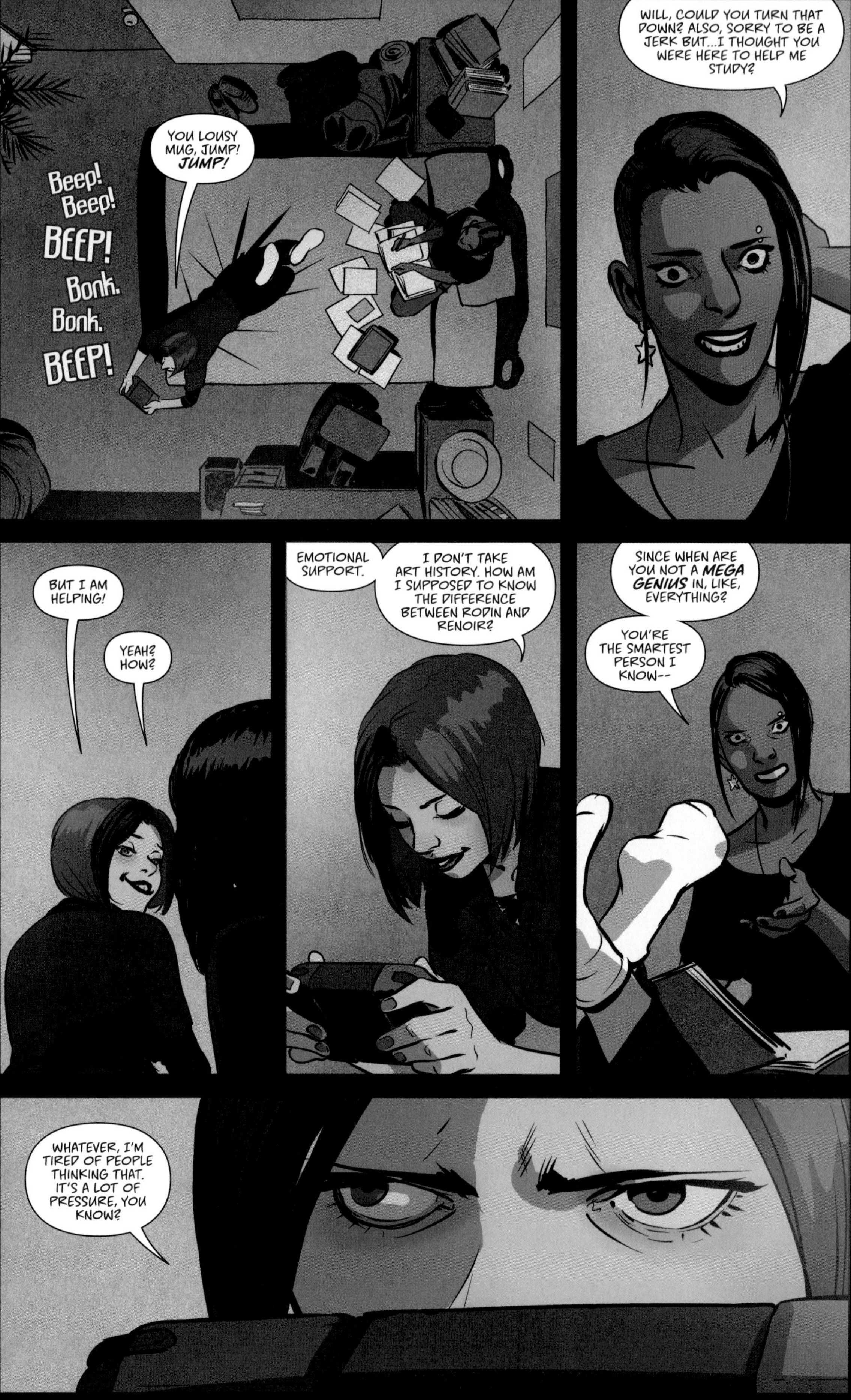
YOU LOUSY MUG, JUMP! *JUMP!*
Beep! Beep! BEEP! Bonk. Bonk. BEEP!
WILL, COULD YOU TURN THAT DOWN? ALSO, SORRY TO BE A JERK BUT...I THOUGHT YOU WERE HERE TO HELP ME STUDY?
BUT I AM HELPING!
YEAH? HOW?
EMOTIONAL SUPPORT.
I DON'T TAKE ART HISTORY. HOW AM I SUPPOSED TO KNOW THE DIFFERENCE BETWEEN RODIN AND RENOIR?
SINCE WHEN ARE YOU NOT A **MEGA GENIUS** IN, LIKE, EVERYTHING?
YOU'RE THE SMARTEST PERSON I KNOW--
WHATEVER, I'M TIRED OF PEOPLE THINKING THAT. IT'S A LOT OF PRESSURE, YOU KNOW?

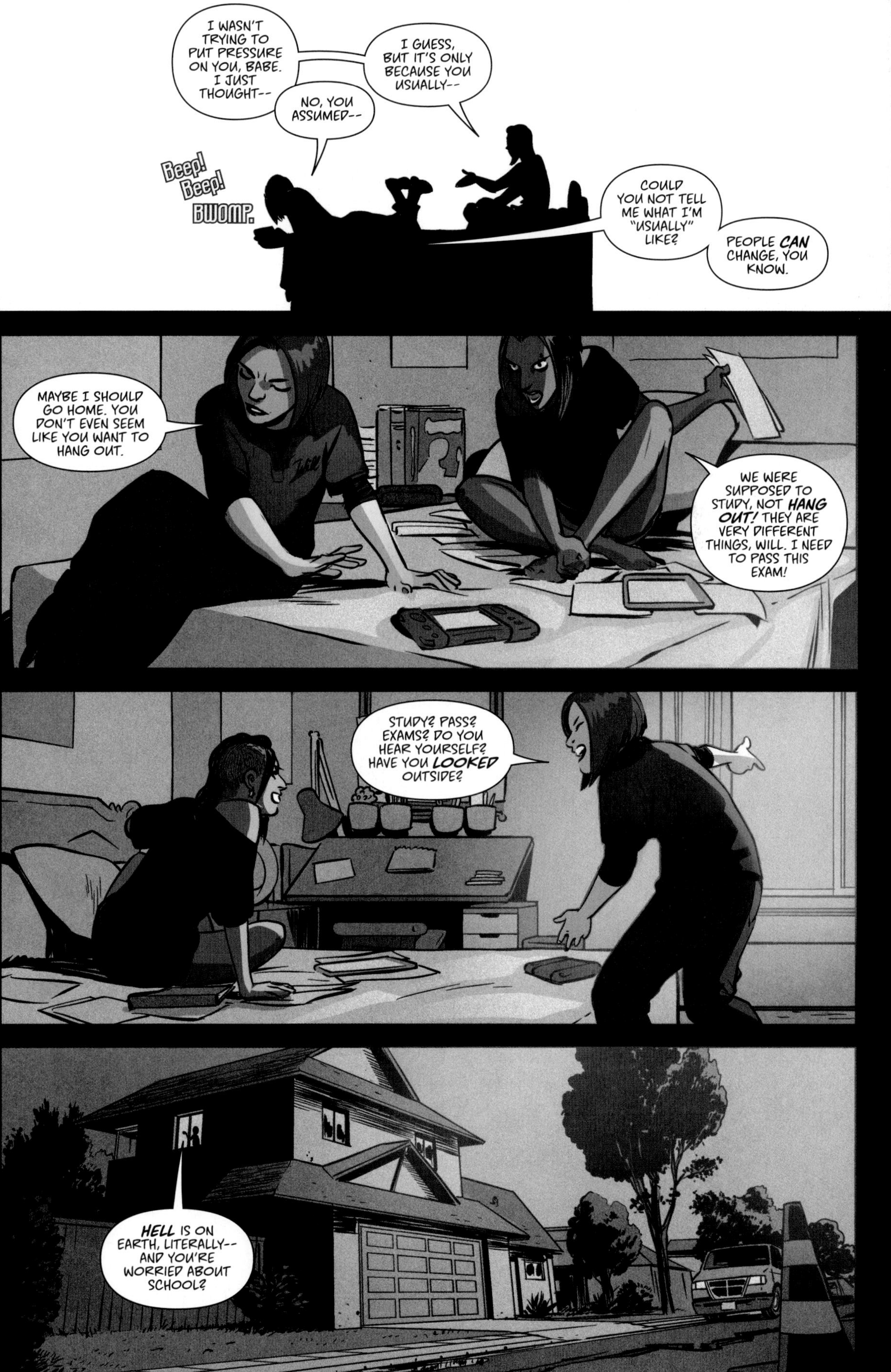
I WASN'T TRYING TO PUT PRESSURE ON YOU, BABE. I JUST THOUGHT--
I GUESS, BUT IT'S ONLY BECAUSE YOU USUALLY--
NO, YOU ASSUMED--
Beep! Beep!
BWOMP.
COULD YOU NOT TELL ME WHAT I'M "USUALLY" LIKE?
PEOPLE CAN CHANGE, YOU KNOW.
MAYBE I SHOULD GO HOME. YOU DON'T EVEN SEEM LIKE YOU WANT TO HANG OUT.
WE WERE SUPPOSED TO STUDY, NOT HANG OUT! THEY ARE VERY DIFFERENT THINGS, WILL. I NEED TO PASS THIS EXAM!
STUDY? PASS? EXAMS? DO YOU HEAR YOURSELF? HAVE YOU LOOKED OUTSIDE?
HELL IS ON EARTH, LITERALLY-- AND YOU'RE WORRIED ABOUT SCHOOL?

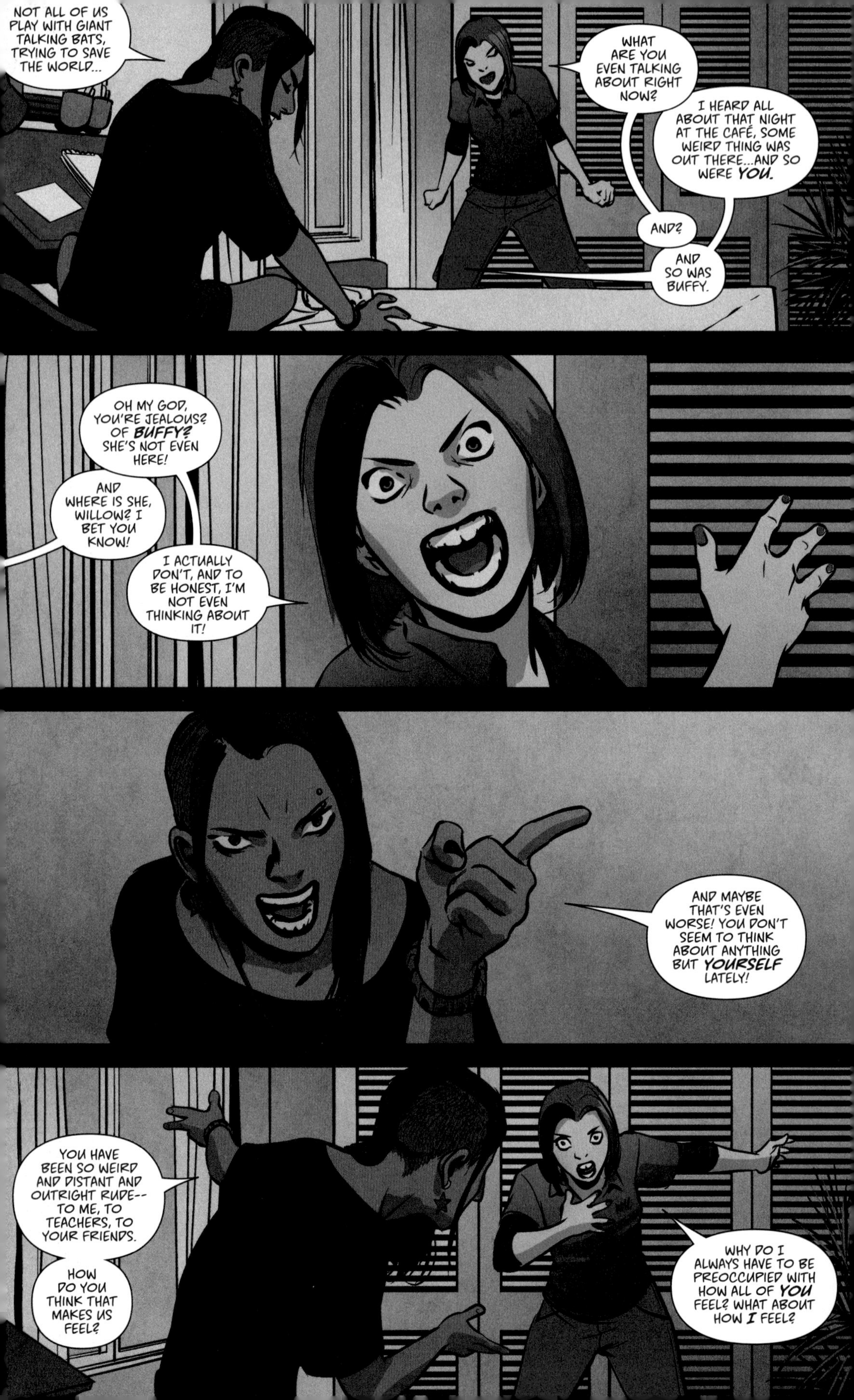
NOT ALL OF US PLAY WITH GIANT TALKING BATS, TRYING TO SAVE THE WORLD...
WHAT ARE YOU EVEN TALKING ABOUT RIGHT NOW?
I HEARD ALL ABOUT THAT NIGHT AT THE CAFÉ, SOME WEIRD THING WAS OUT THERE...AND SO WERE YOU.
AND?
AND SO WAS BUFFY.
OH MY GOD, YOU'RE JEALOUS? OF BUFFY? SHE'S NOT EVEN HERE!
AND WHERE IS SHE, WILLOW? I BET YOU KNOW!
I ACTUALLY DON'T, AND TO BE HONEST, I'M NOT EVEN THINKING ABOUT IT!
AND MAYBE THAT'S EVEN WORSE! YOU DON'T SEEM TO THINK ABOUT ANYTHING BUT YOURSELF LATELY!
YOU HAVE BEEN SO WEIRD AND DISTANT AND OUTRIGHT RUDE--TO ME, TO TEACHERS, TO YOUR FRIENDS.
HOW DO YOU THINK THAT MAKES US FEEL?
WHY DO I ALWAYS HAVE TO BE PREOCCUPIED WITH HOW ALL OF YOU FEEL? WHAT ABOUT HOW I FEEL?

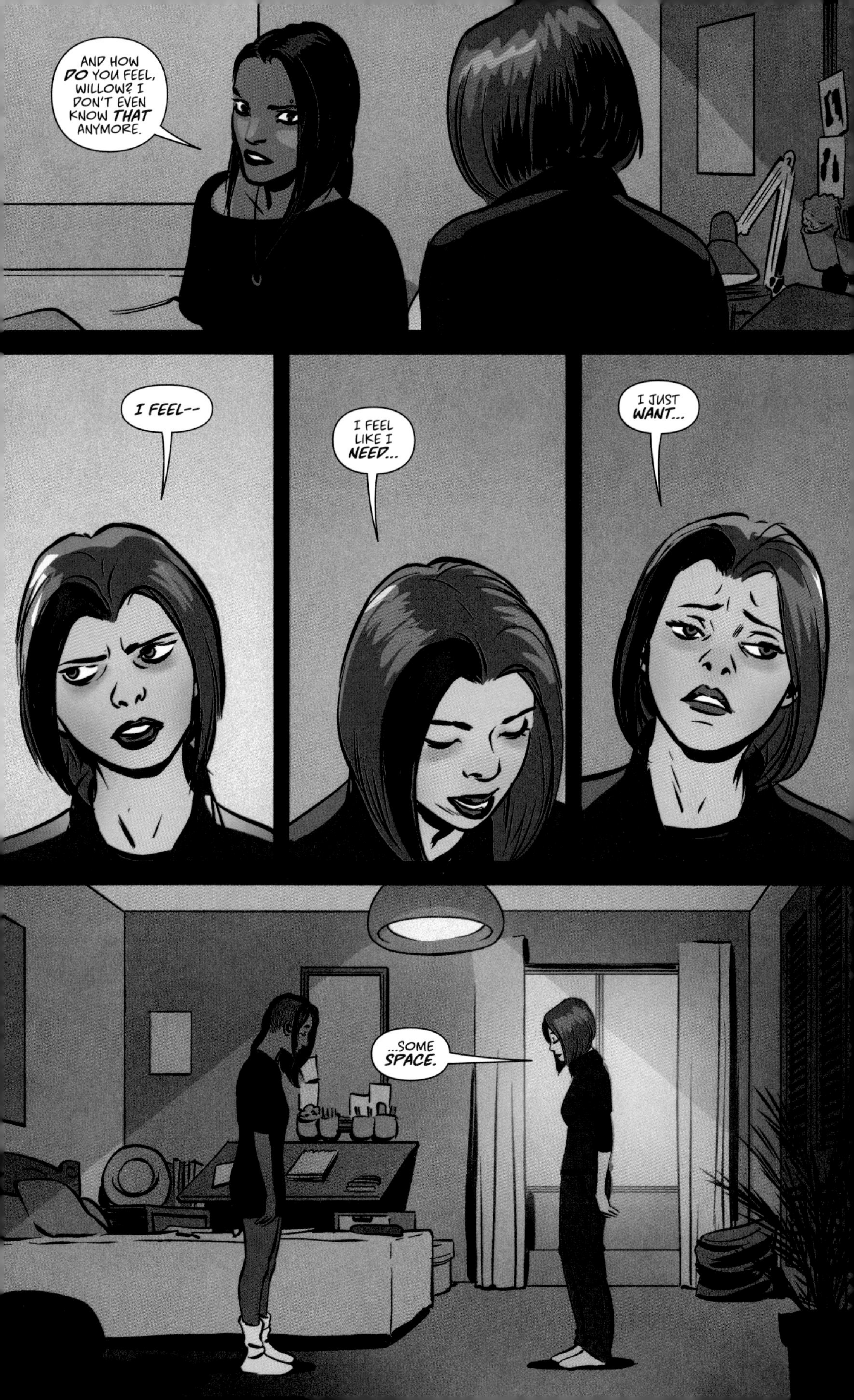
AND HOW DO YOU FEEL, WILLOW? I DON'T EVEN KNOW THAT ANYMORE.
I FEEL--
I FEEL LIKE I NEED...
I JUST WANT...
...SOME SPACE.

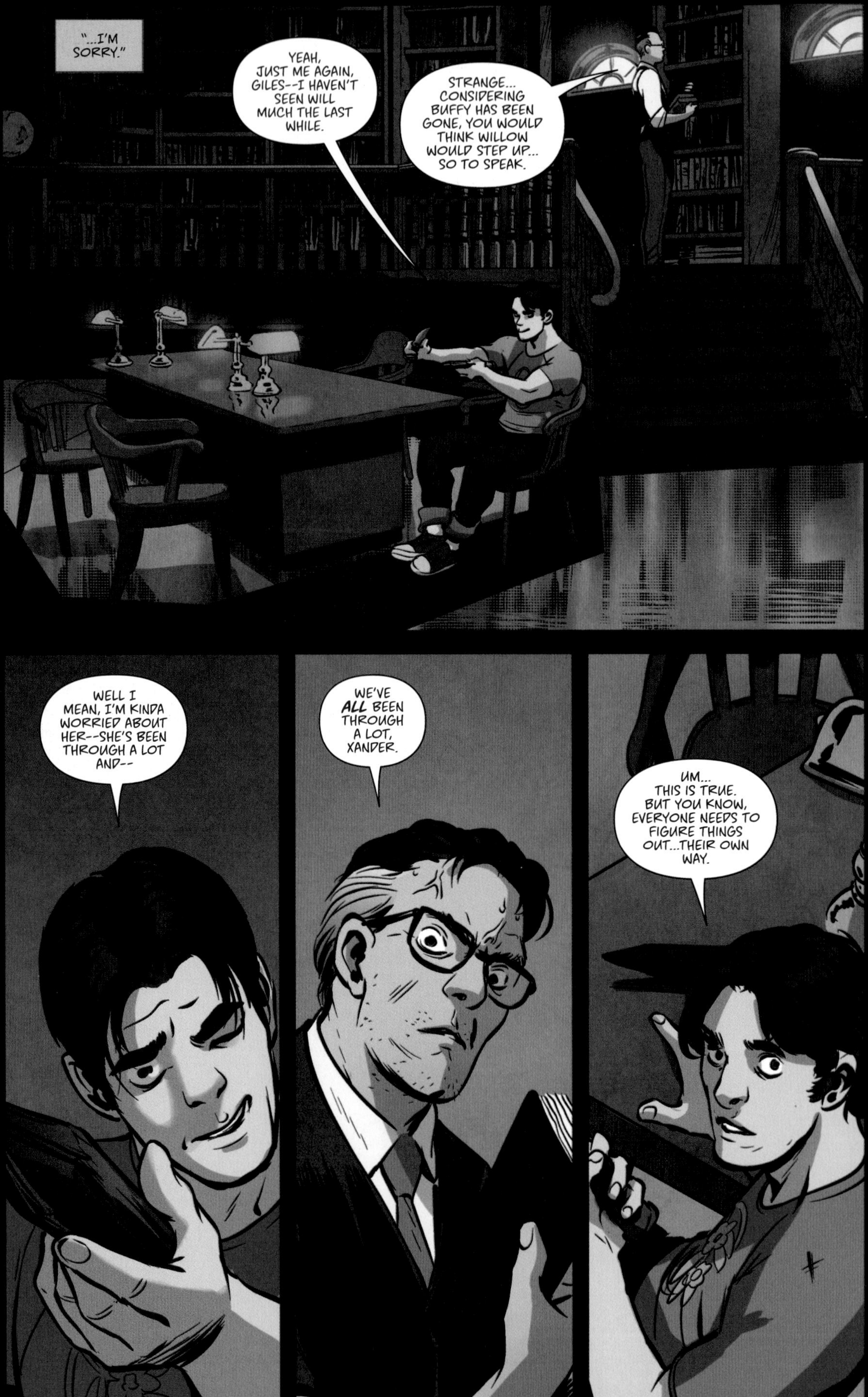
"...I'M SORRY."
YEAH, JUST ME AGAIN, GILES--I HAVEN'T SEEN WILL MUCH THE LAST WHILE.
STRANGE... CONSIDERING BUFFY HAS BEEN GONE, YOU WOULD THINK WILLOW WOULD STEP UP... SO TO SPEAK.
WELL I MEAN, I'M KINDA WORRIED ABOUT HER--SHE'S BEEN THROUGH A LOT AND--
WE'VE ALL BEEN THROUGH A LOT, XANDER.
UM... THIS IS TRUE. BUT YOU KNOW, EVERYONE NEEDS TO FIGURE THINGS OUT...THEIR OWN WAY.

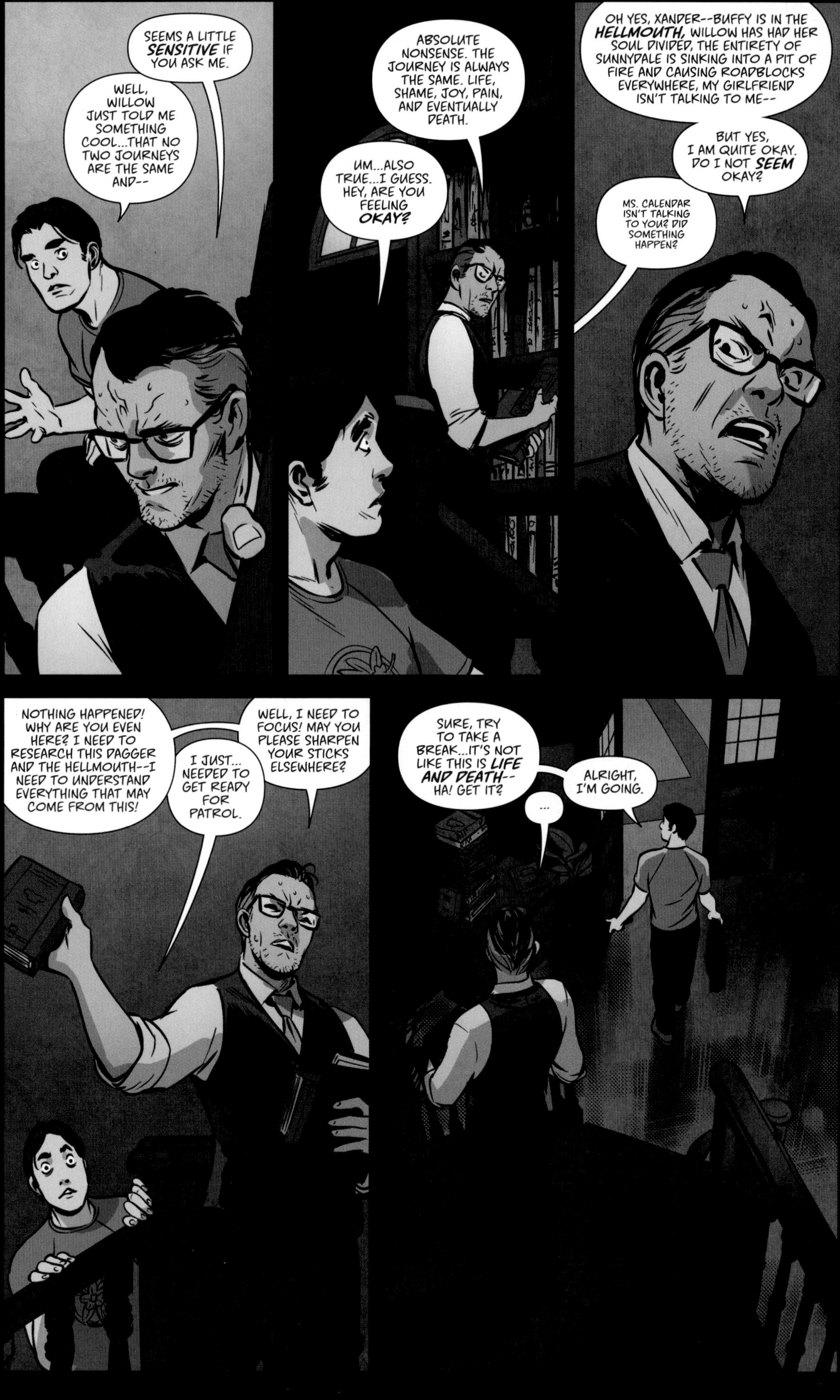
SEEMS A LITTLE SENSITIVE IF YOU ASK ME.
WELL, WILLOW JUST TOLD ME SOMETHING COOL...THAT NO TWO JOURNEYS ARE THE SAME AND--
ABSOLUTE NONSENSE. THE JOURNEY IS ALWAYS THE SAME. LIFE, SHAME, JOY, PAIN, AND EVENTUALLY DEATH.
UM...ALSO TRUE...I GUESS. HEY, ARE YOU FEELING OKAY?
OH YES, XANDER--BUFFY IS IN THE HELLMOUTH, WILLOW HAS HAD HER SOUL DIVIDED, THE ENTIRETY OF SUNNYDALE IS SINKING INTO A PIT OF FIRE AND CAUSING ROADBLOCKS EVERYWHERE, MY GIRLFRIEND ISN'T TALKING TO ME--
BUT YES, I AM QUITE OKAY. DO I NOT SEEM OKAY?
MS. CALENDAR ISN'T TALKING TO YOU? DID SOMETHING HAPPEN?
NOTHING HAPPENED! WHY ARE YOU EVEN HERE? I NEED TO RESEARCH THIS DAGGER AND THE HELLMOUTH--I NEED TO UNDERSTAND EVERYTHING THAT MAY COME FROM THIS!
I JUST... NEEDED TO GET READY FOR PATROL.
WELL, I NEED TO FOCUS! MAY YOU PLEASE SHARPEN YOUR STICKS ELSEWHERE?
SURE, TRY TO TAKE A BREAK...IT'S NOT LIKE THIS IS LIFE AND DEATH-- HA! GET IT?
...
ALRIGHT, I'M GOING.

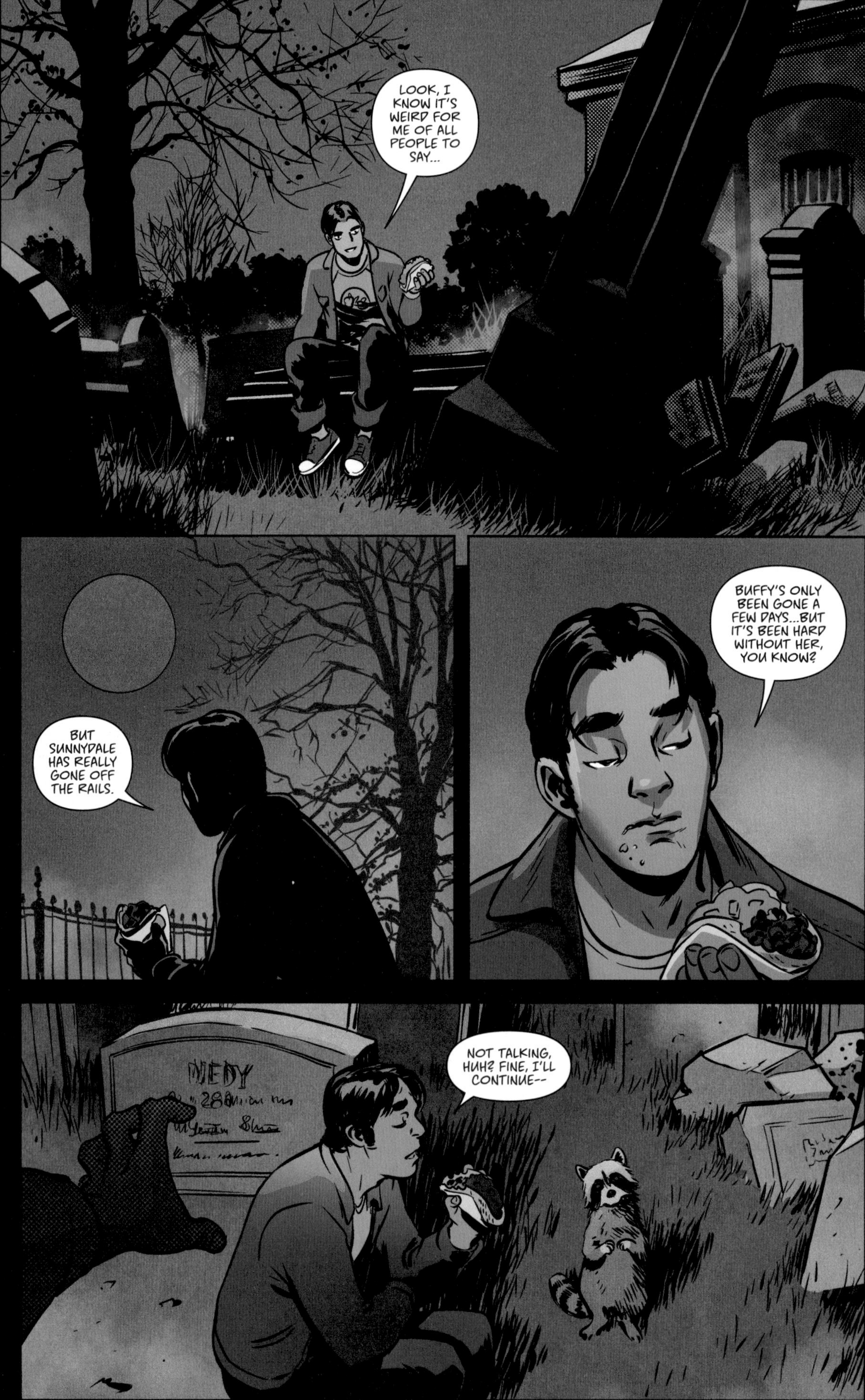
LOOK, I KNOW IT'S WEIRD FOR ME OF ALL PEOPLE TO SAY...
BUT SUNNYDALE HAS REALLY GONE OFF THE RAILS.
BUFFY'S ONLY BEEN GONE A FEW DAYS...BUT IT'S BEEN HARD WITHOUT HER, YOU KNOW?
NOT TALKING, HUH? FINE, I'LL CONTINUE--

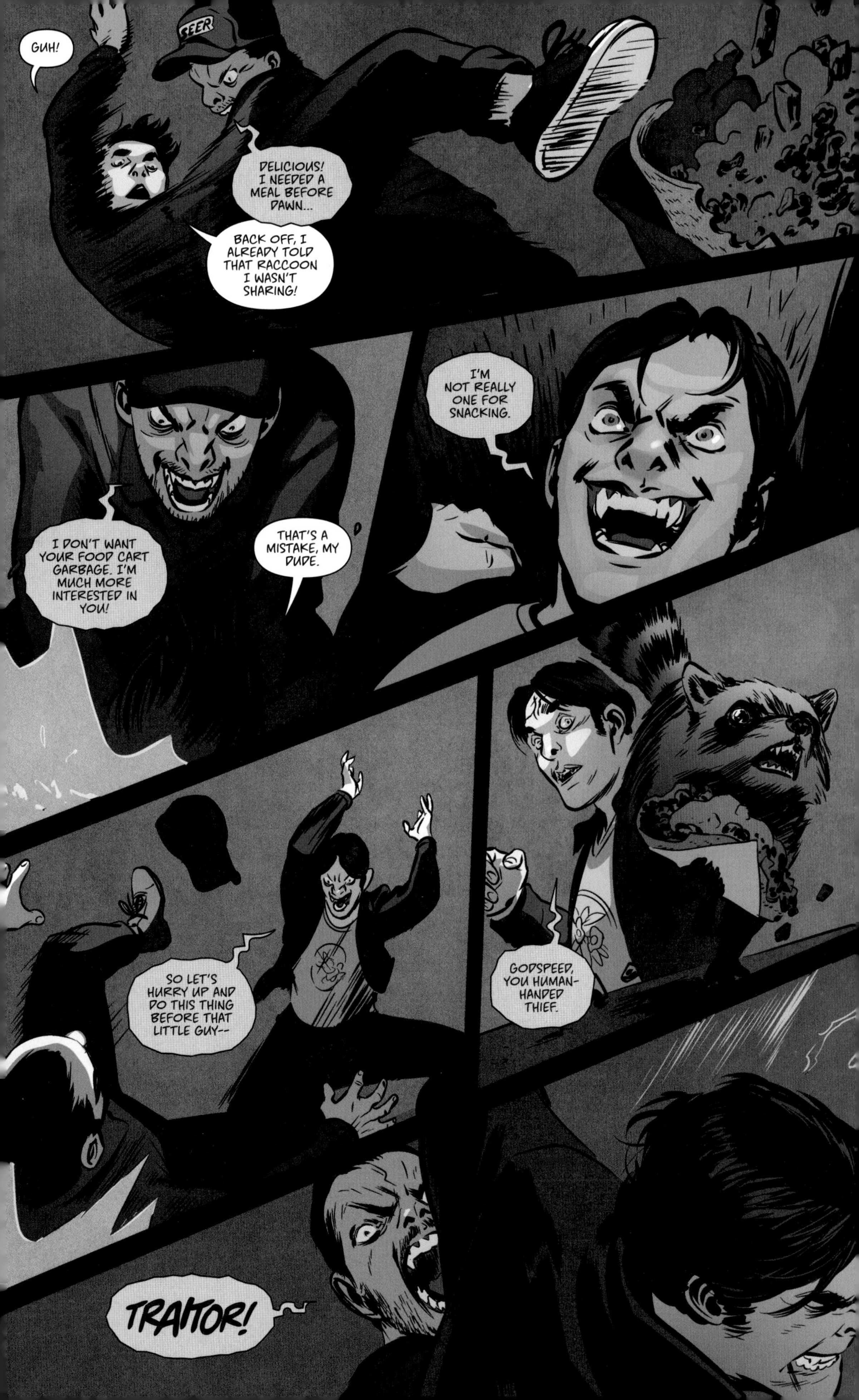
GUH!
SEER
DELICIOUS! I NEEDED A MEAL BEFORE DAWN...
BACK OFF, I ALREADY TOLD THAT RACCOON I WASN'T SHARING!
I'M NOT REALLY ONE FOR SNACKING.
I DON'T WANT YOUR FOOD CART GARBAGE. I'M MUCH MORE INTERESTED IN YOU!
THAT'S A MISTAKE, MY DUDE.
GODSPEED, YOU HUMAN-HANDED THIEF.
SO LET'S HURRY UP AND DO THIS THING BEFORE THAT LITTLE GUY--
TRAITOR!

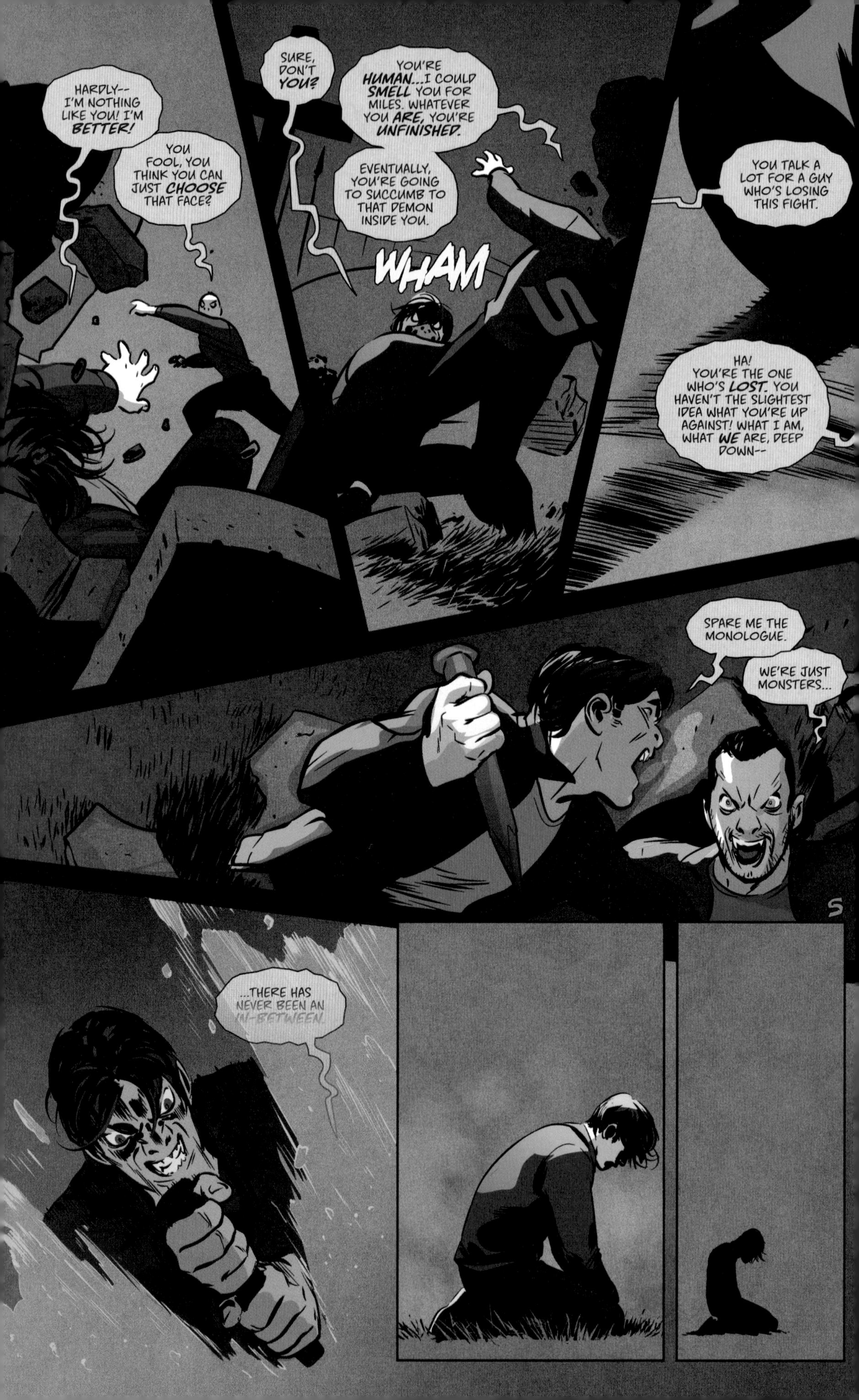
HARDLY-- I'M NOTHING LIKE YOU! I'M BETTER!
YOU FOOL, YOU THINK YOU CAN JUST CHOOSE THAT FACE?
SURE, DON'T YOU?
YOU'RE HUMAN... I COULD SMELL YOU FOR MILES. WHATEVER YOU ARE, YOU'RE UNFINISHED.
EVENTUALLY, YOU'RE GOING TO SUCCUMB TO THAT DEMON INSIDE YOU.
WHAM
YOU TALK A LOT FOR A GUY WHO'S LOSING THIS FIGHT.
HA! YOU'RE THE ONE WHO'S LOST. YOU HAVEN'T THE SLIGHTEST IDEA WHAT YOU'RE UP AGAINST! WHAT I AM, WHAT WE ARE, DEEP DOWN--
SPARE ME THE MONOLOGUE.
WE'RE JUST MONSTERS...
...THERE HAS NEVER BEEN AN IN-BETWEEN.

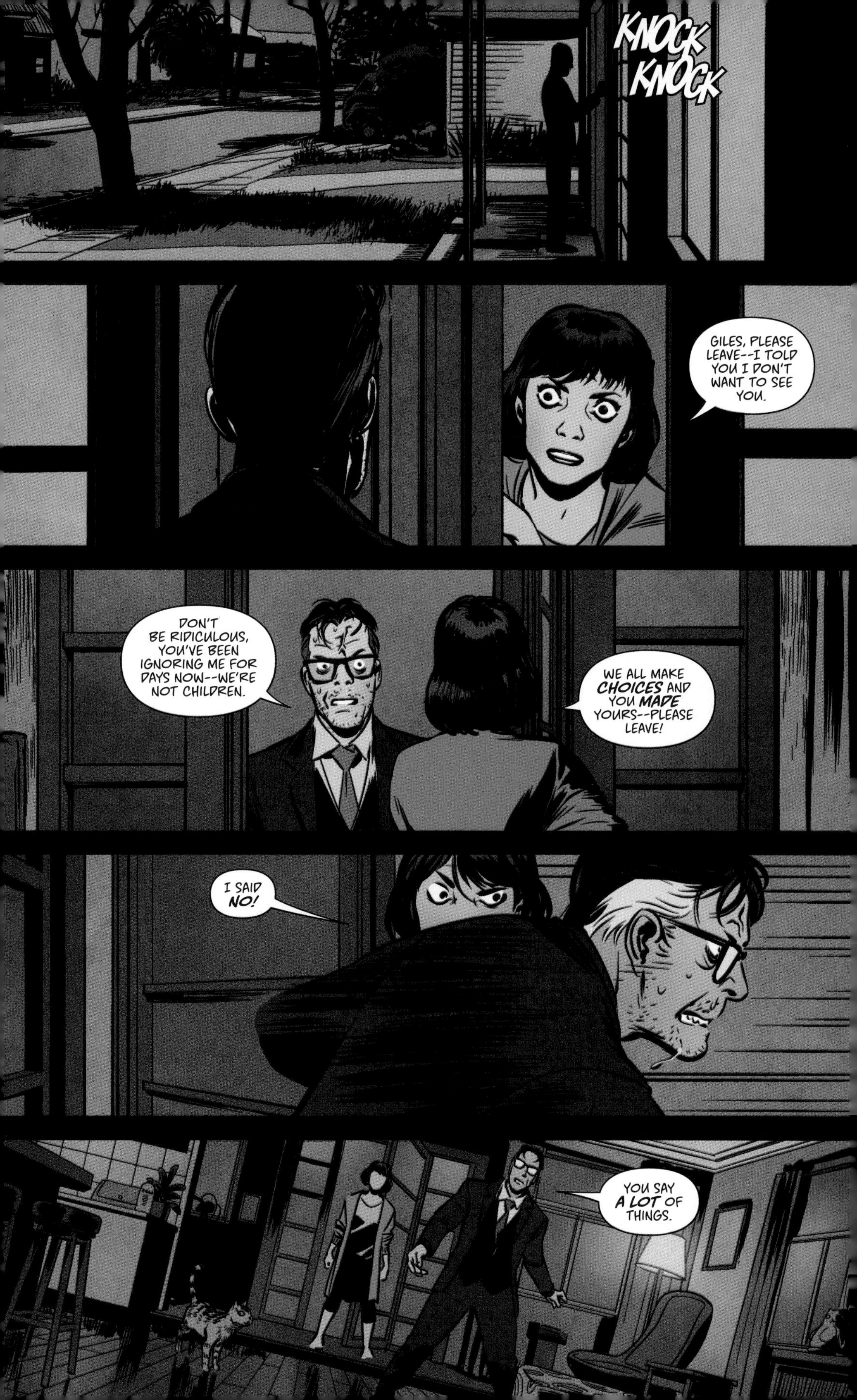
KNOCK KNOCK
GILES, PLEASE LEAVE--I TOLD YOU I DON'T WANT TO SEE YOU.
DON'T BE RIDICULOUS, YOU'VE BEEN IGNORING ME FOR DAYS NOW--WE'RE NOT CHILDREN.
WE ALL MAKE CHOICES AND YOU MADE YOURS--PLEASE LEAVE!
I SAID NO!
YOU SAY A LOT OF THINGS.

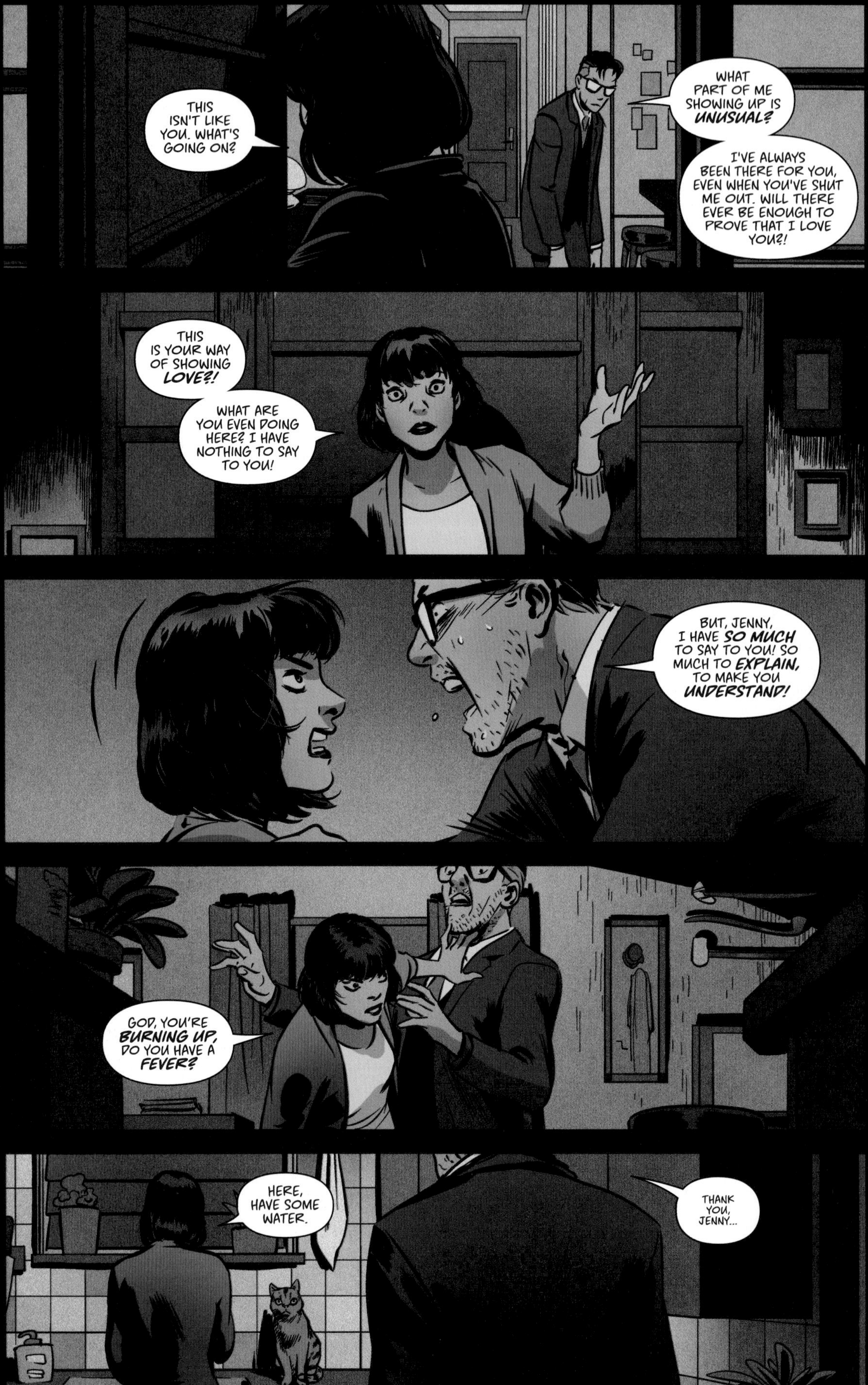
THIS ISN'T LIKE YOU. WHAT'S GOING ON?
WHAT PART OF ME SHOWING UP IS UNUSUAL?
I'VE ALWAYS BEEN THERE FOR YOU, EVEN WHEN YOU'VE SHUT ME OUT. WILL THERE EVER BE ENOUGH TO PROVE THAT I LOVE YOU?!
THIS IS YOUR WAY OF SHOWING LOVE?!
WHAT ARE YOU EVEN DOING HERE? I HAVE NOTHING TO SAY TO YOU!
BUT, JENNY, I HAVE SO MUCH TO SAY TO YOU! SO MUCH TO EXPLAIN, TO MAKE YOU UNDERSTAND!
GOD, YOU'RE BURNING UP, DO YOU HAVE A FEVER?
HERE, HAVE SOME WATER.
THANK YOU, JENNY...

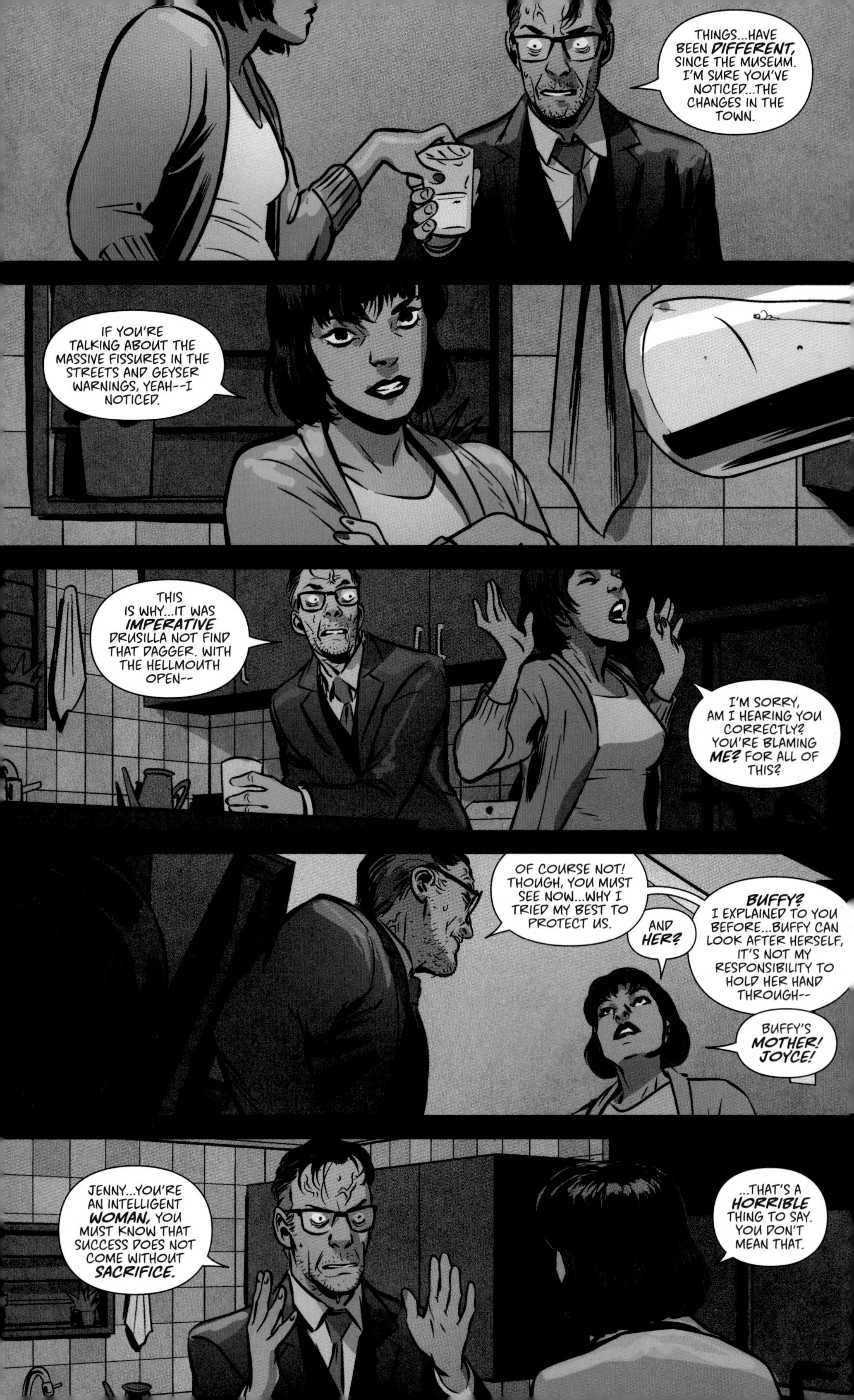

THINGS...HAVE BEEN **DIFFERENT,** SINCE THE MUSEUM. I'M SURE YOU'VE NOTICED...THE CHANGES IN THE TOWN.
IF YOU'RE TALKING ABOUT THE MASSIVE FISSURES IN THE STREETS AND GEYSER WARNINGS, YEAH--I NOTICED.
THIS IS WHY...IT WAS **IMPERATIVE** DRUSILLA NOT FIND THAT DAGGER. WITH THE HELLMOUTH OPEN--
I'M SORRY, AM I HEARING YOU CORRECTLY? YOU'RE BLAMING **ME?** FOR ALL OF THIS?
OF COURSE NOT! THOUGH, YOU MUST SEE NOW...WHY I TRIED MY BEST TO PROTECT US.
AND **HER?**
BUFFY? I EXPLAINED TO YOU BEFORE...BUFFY CAN LOOK AFTER HERSELF, IT'S NOT MY RESPONSIBILITY TO HOLD HER HAND THROUGH--
BUFFY'S **MOTHER! JOYCE!**
JENNY...YOU'RE AN INTELLIGENT **WOMAN,** YOU MUST KNOW THAT SUCCESS DOES NOT COME WITHOUT **SACRIFICE.**
...THAT'S A **HORRIBLE** THING TO SAY. YOU DON'T MEAN THAT.

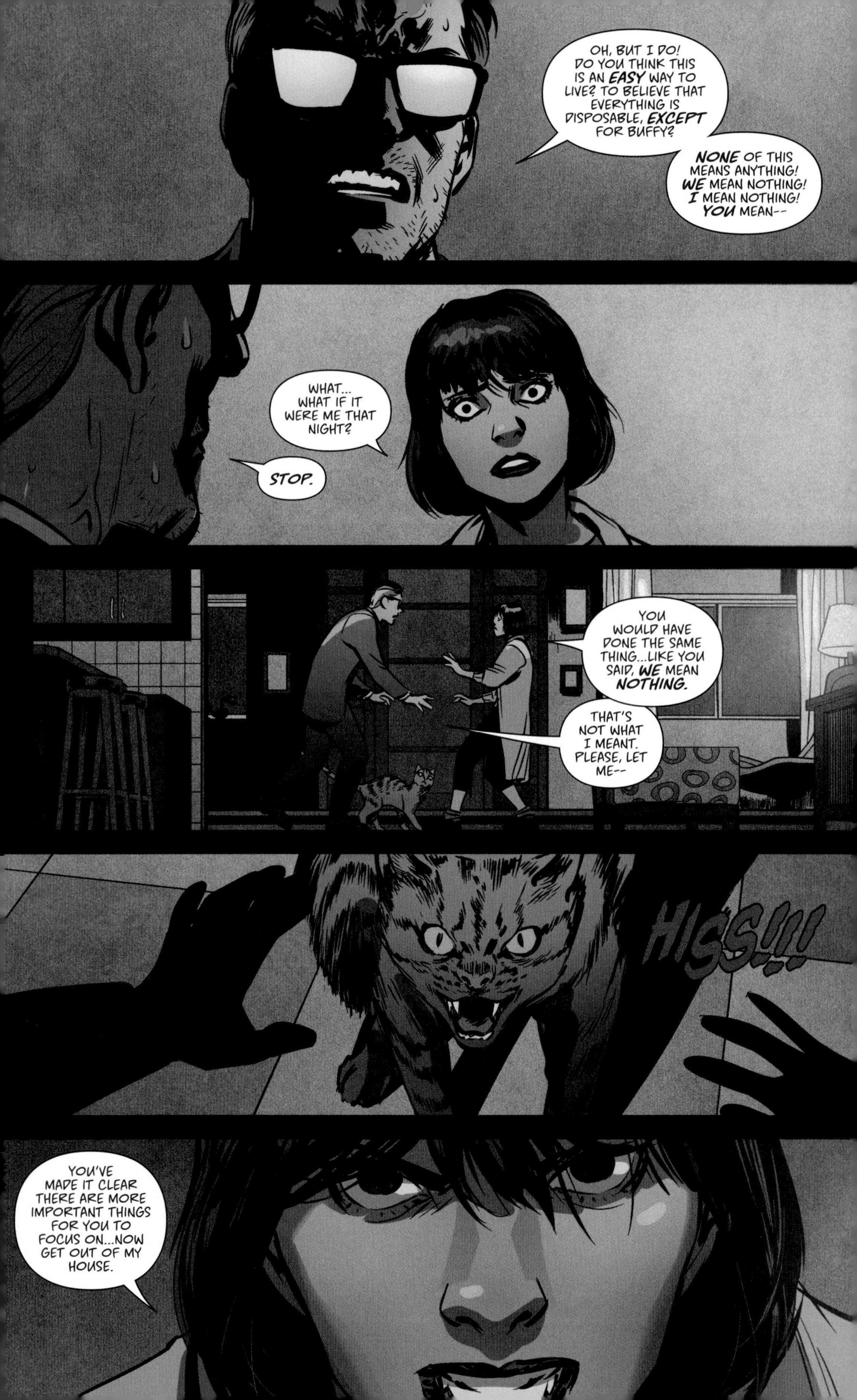
OH, BUT I DO! DO YOU THINK THIS IS AN EASY WAY TO LIVE? TO BELIEVE THAT EVERYTHING IS DISPOSABLE, EXCEPT FOR BUFFY?
NONE OF THIS MEANS ANYTHING! WE MEAN NOTHING! I MEAN NOTHING! YOU MEAN--
WHAT... WHAT IF IT WERE ME THAT NIGHT?
STOP.
YOU WOULD HAVE DONE THE SAME THING...LIKE YOU SAID, WE MEAN NOTHING.
THAT'S NOT WHAT I MEANT. PLEASE, LET ME--
HISS!!!
YOU'VE MADE IT CLEAR THERE ARE MORE IMPORTANT THINGS FOR YOU TO FOCUS ON...NOW GET OUT OF MY HOUSE.

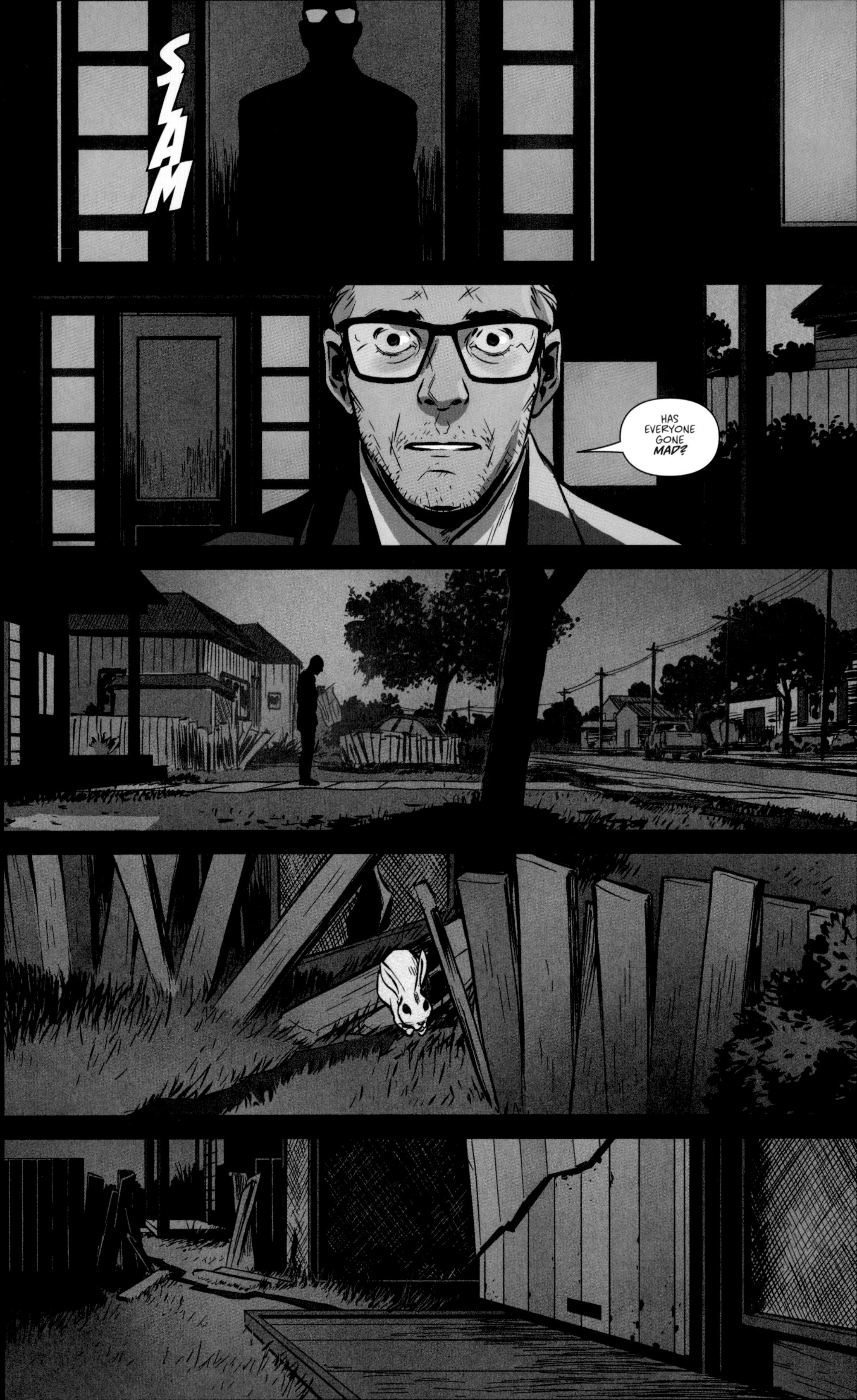
SLAM
HAS EVERYONE GONE MAD?

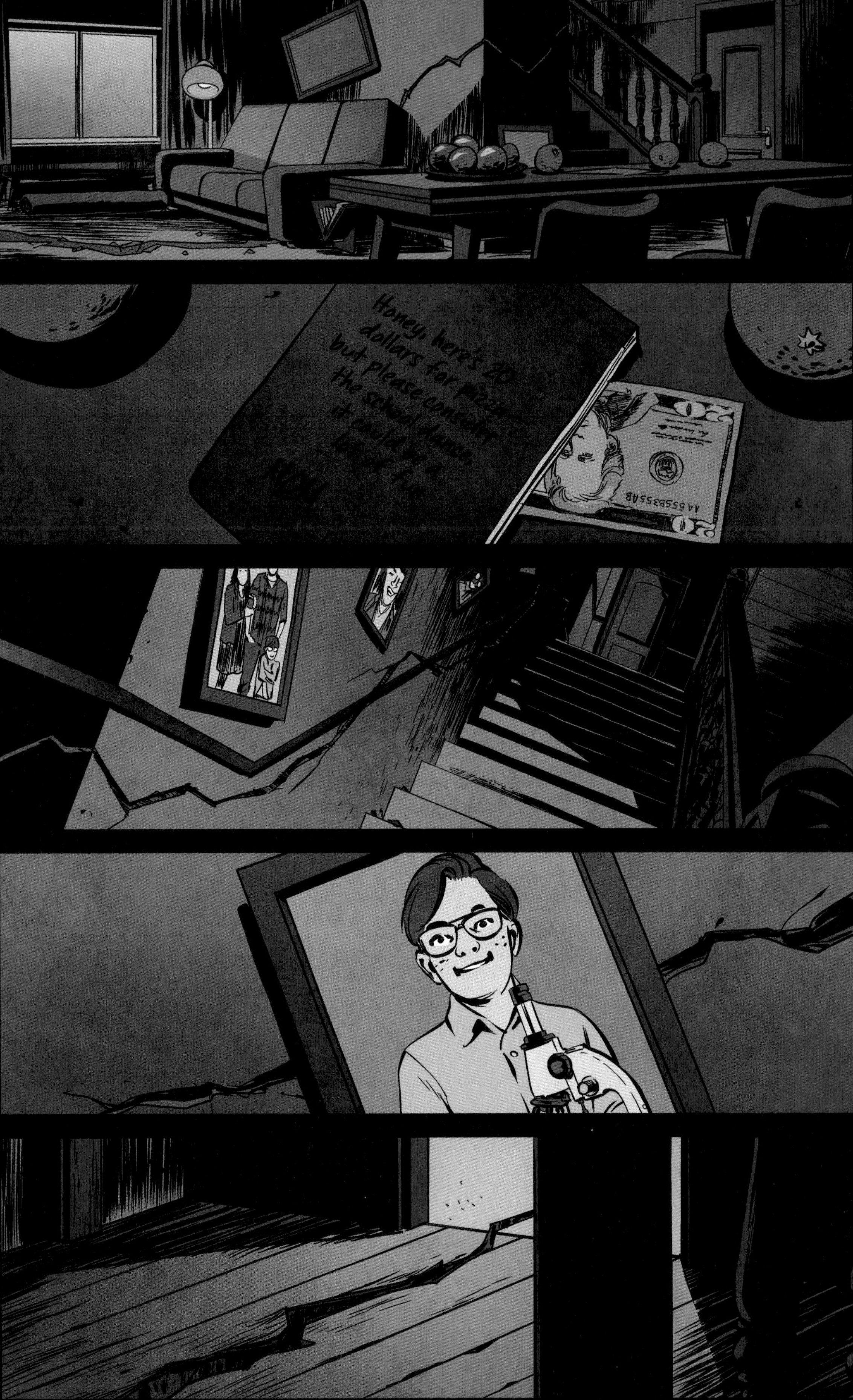
Honey, here's 20
dollars for pizza
but please consider
the school dance,
it could be a

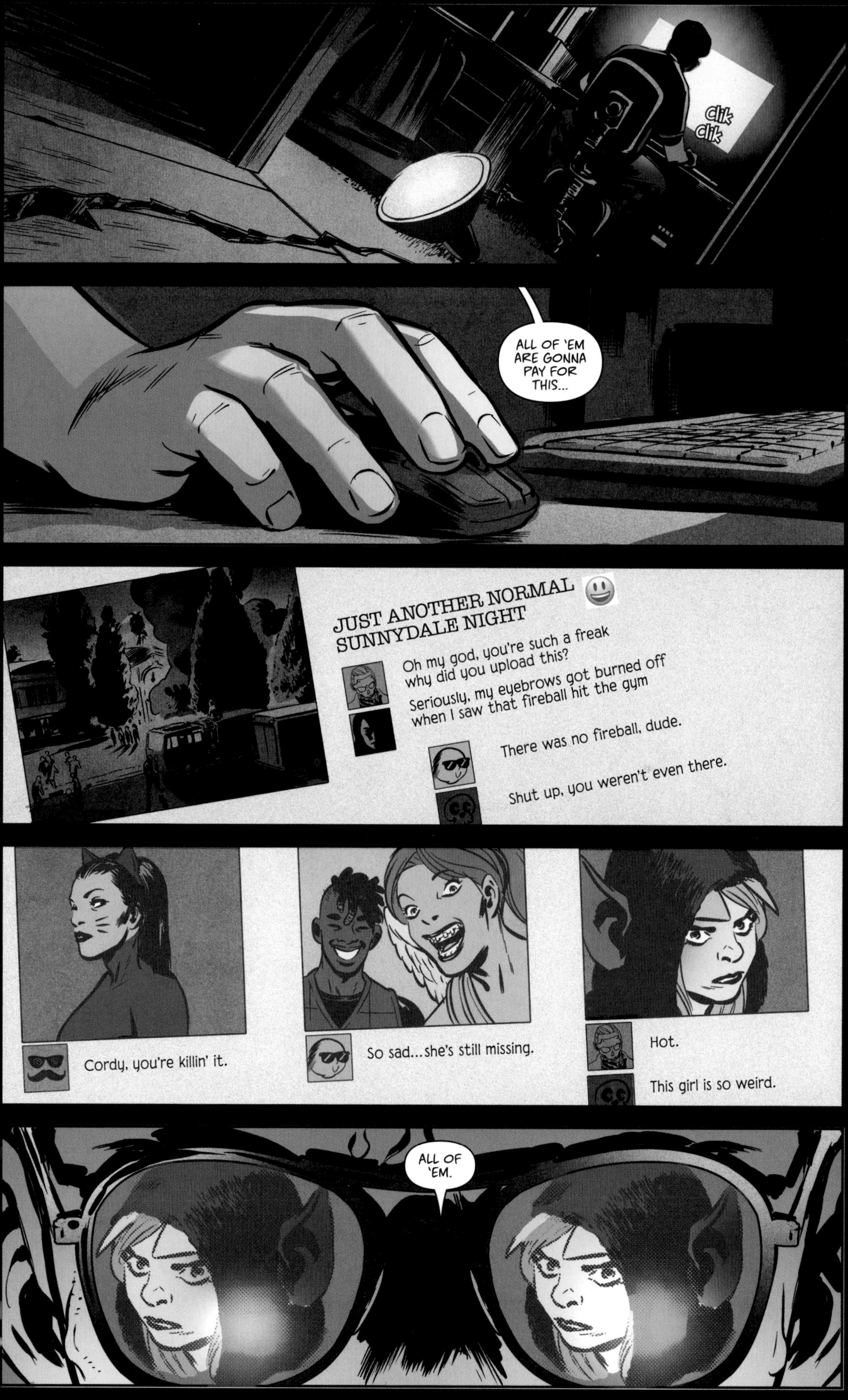

Clik
Clik
ALL OF 'EM ARE GONNA PAY FOR THIS...
JUST ANOTHER NORMAL SUNNYDALE NIGHT
Oh my god, you're such a freak why did you upload this?
Seriously, my eyebrows got burned off when I saw that fireball hit the gym
There was no fireball, dude.
Shut up, you weren't even there.
Cordy, you're killin' it.
So sad...she's still missing.
Hot.
This girl is so weird.
ALL OF 'EM.

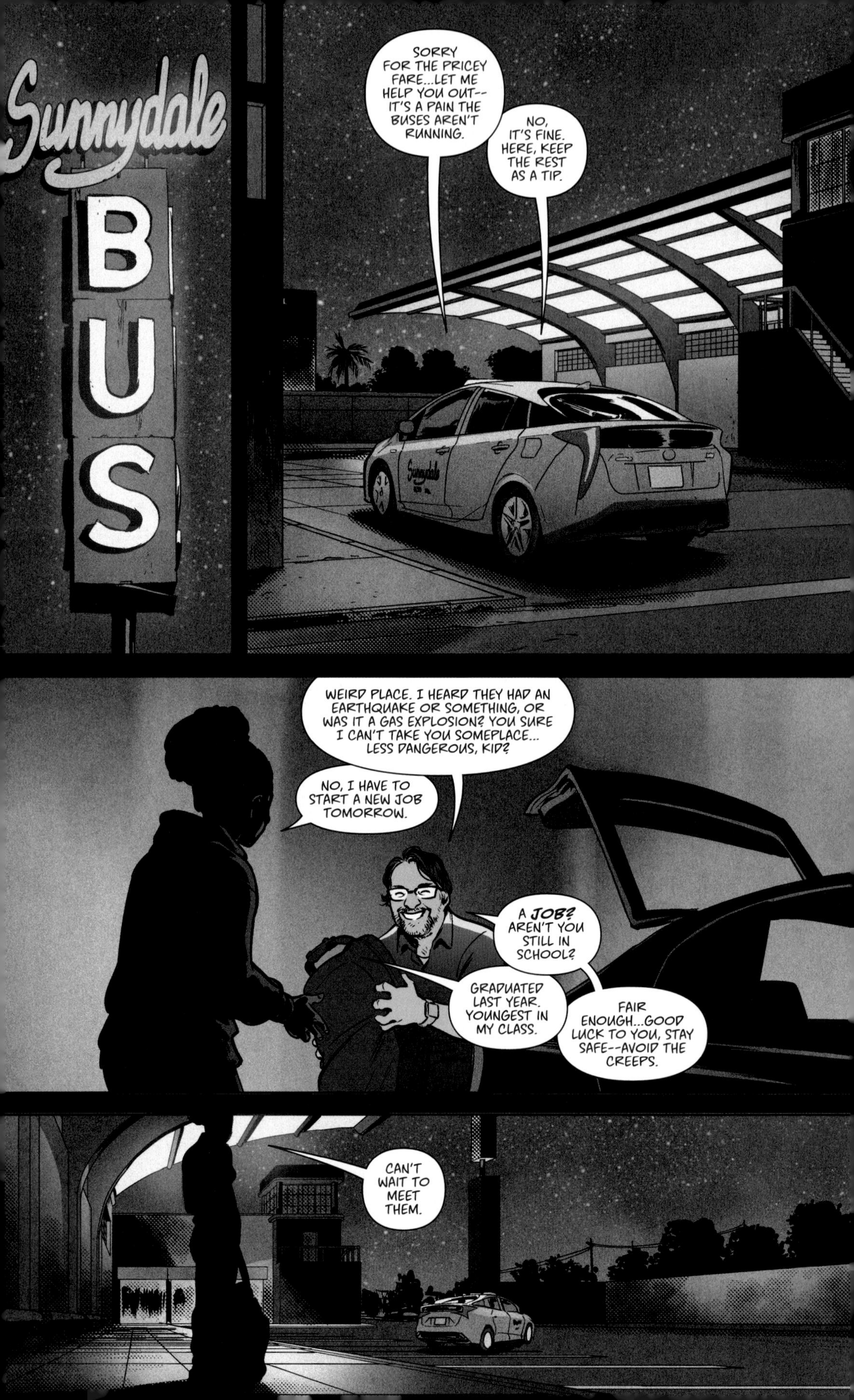
Sunnydale
BUS
SORRY FOR THE PRICEY FARE...LET ME HELP YOU OUT--IT'S A PAIN THE BUSES AREN'T RUNNING.
NO, IT'S FINE. HERE, KEEP THE REST AS A TIP.
WEIRD PLACE. I HEARD THEY HAD AN EARTHQUAKE OR SOMETHING, OR WAS IT A GAS EXPLOSION? YOU SURE I CAN'T TAKE YOU SOMEPLACE... LESS DANGEROUS, KID?
NO, I HAVE TO START A NEW JOB TOMORROW.
A ***JOB?*** AREN'T YOU STILL IN SCHOOL?
GRADUATED LAST YEAR. YOUNGEST IN MY CLASS.
FAIR ENOUGH...GOOD LUCK TO YOU, STAY SAFE--AVOID THE CREEPS.
CAN'T WAIT TO MEET THEM.

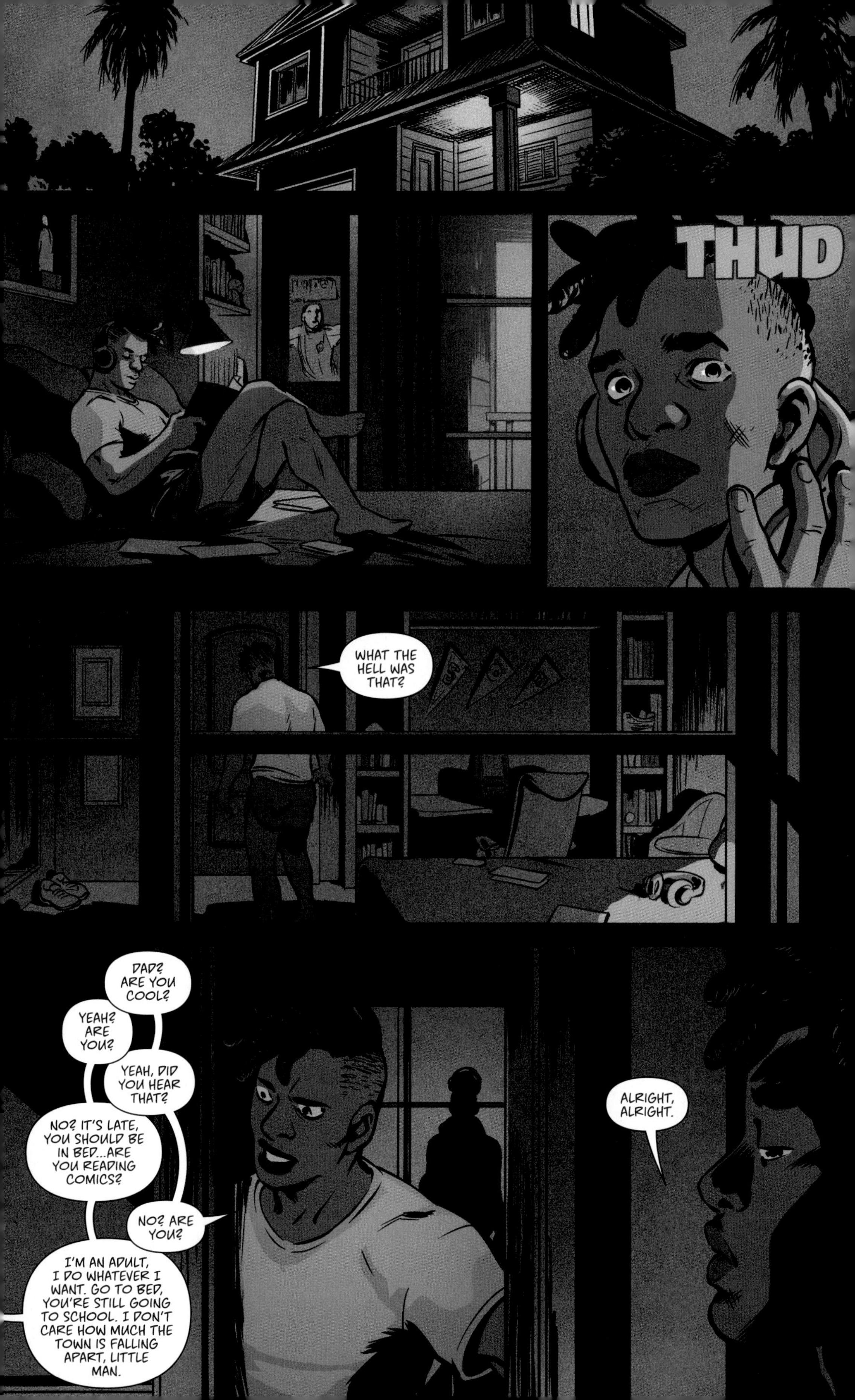
THUD
WHAT THE HELL WAS THAT?
DAD? ARE YOU COOL?
YEAH? ARE YOU?
YEAH, DID YOU HEAR THAT?
NO? IT'S LATE, YOU SHOULD BE IN BED...ARE YOU READING COMICS?
NO? ARE YOU?
I'M AN ADULT, I DO WHATEVER I WANT. GO TO BED, YOU'RE STILL GOING TO SCHOOL. I DON'T CARE HOW MUCH THE TOWN IS FALLING APART, LITTLE MAN.
ALRIGHT, ALRIGHT.

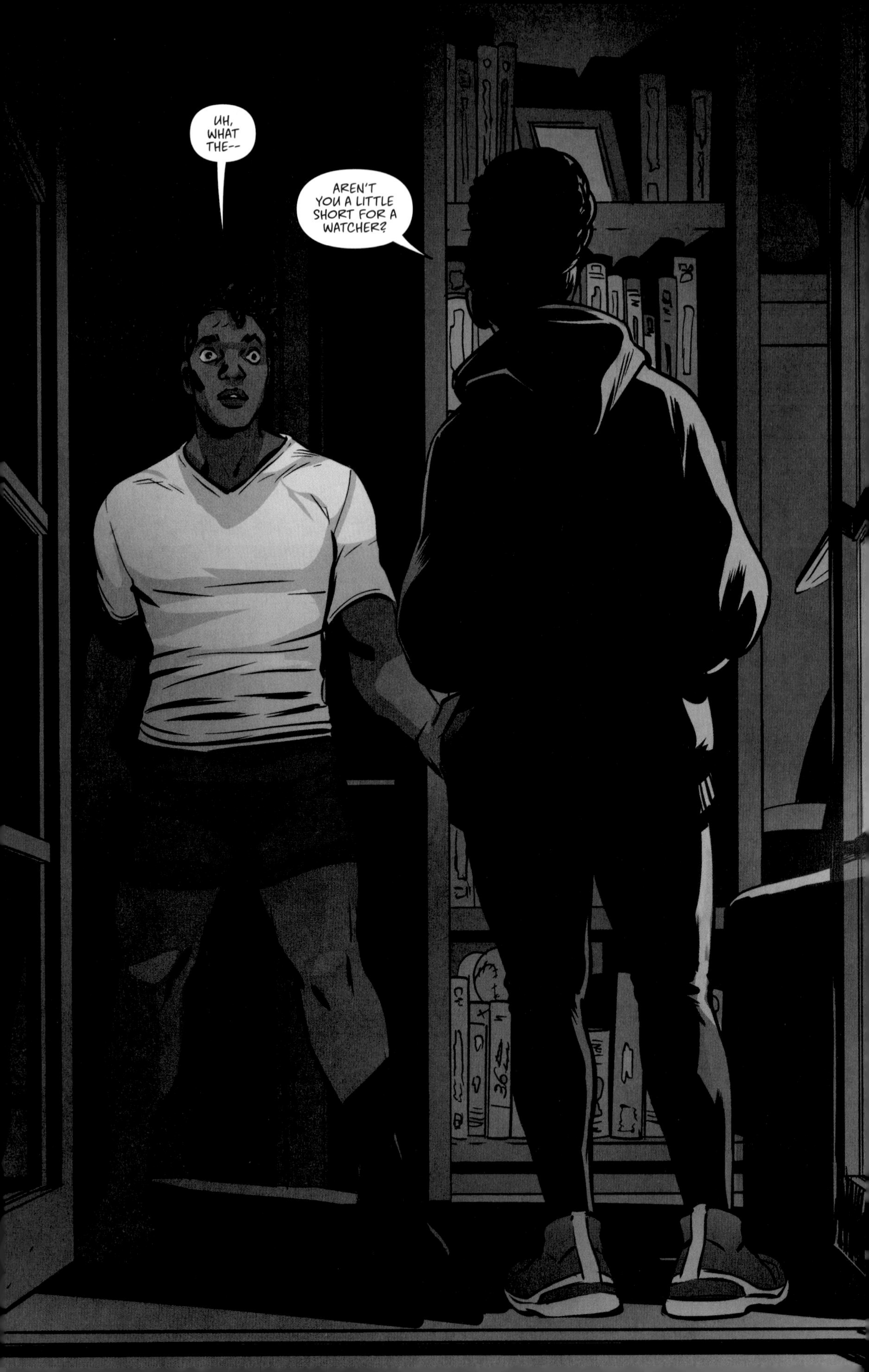
UH, WHAT THE--
AREN'T YOU A LITTLE SHORT FOR A WATCHER?

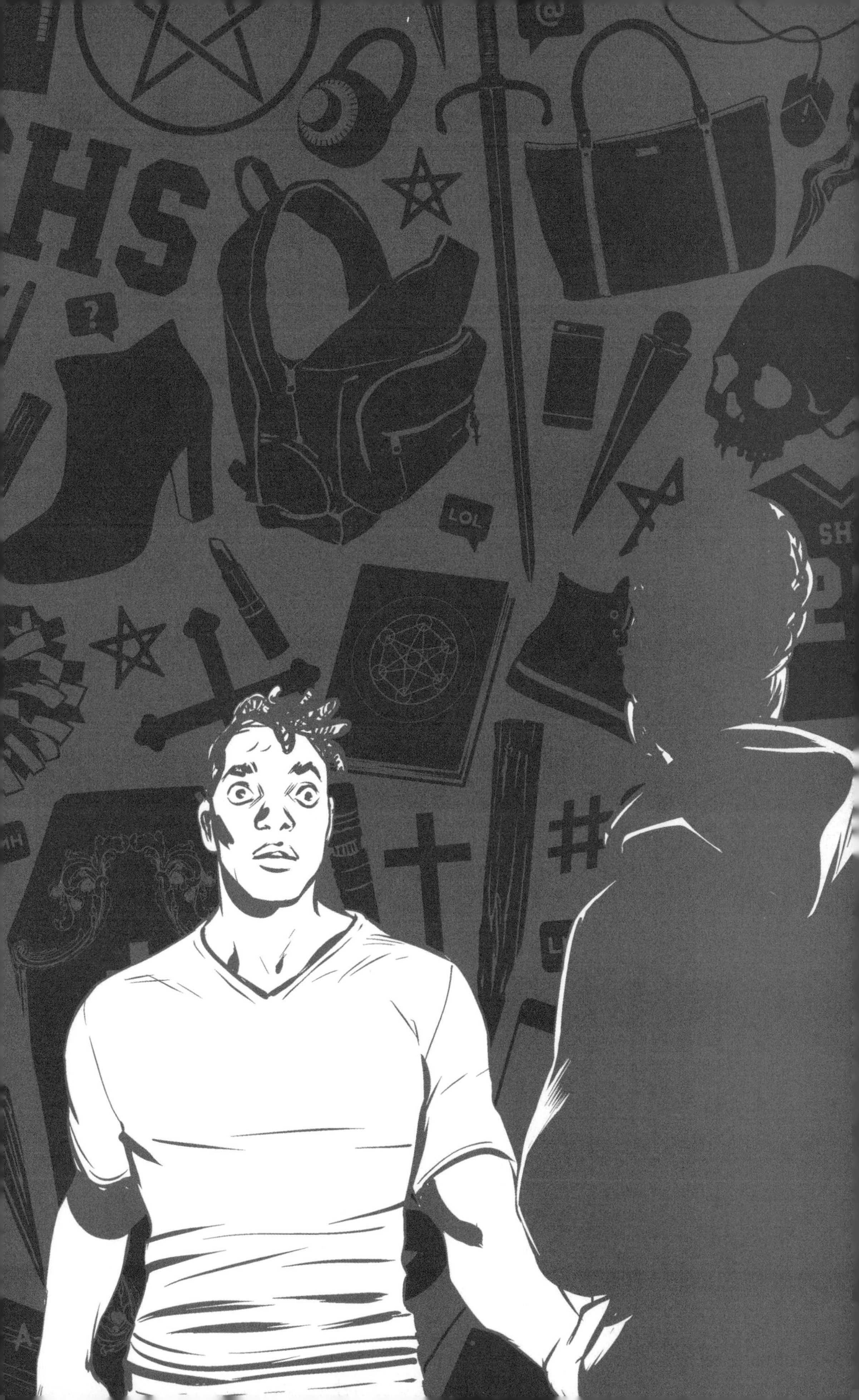
LOL

CHAPTER TEN

Issue Ten Cover by **Marc Aspinall**

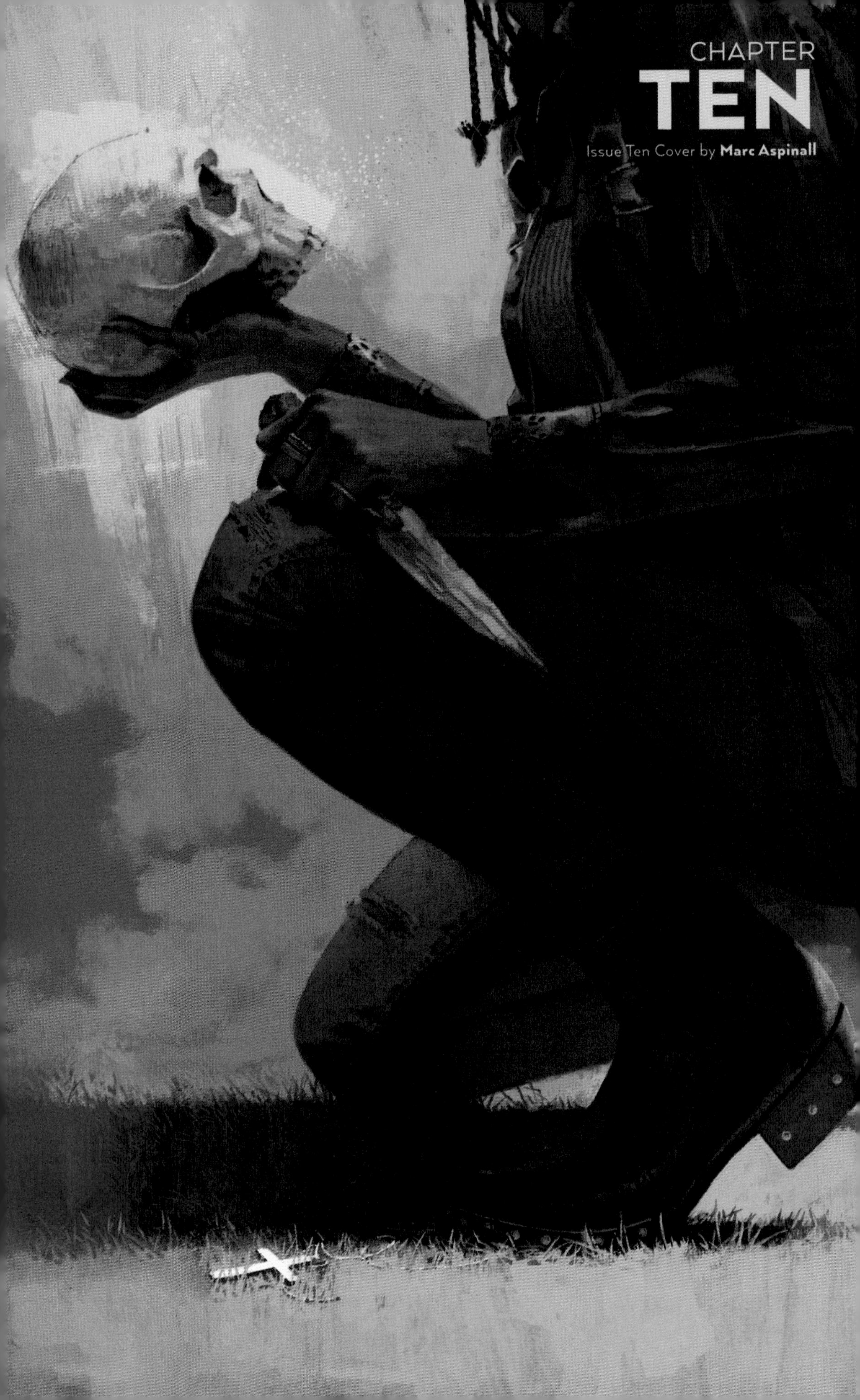

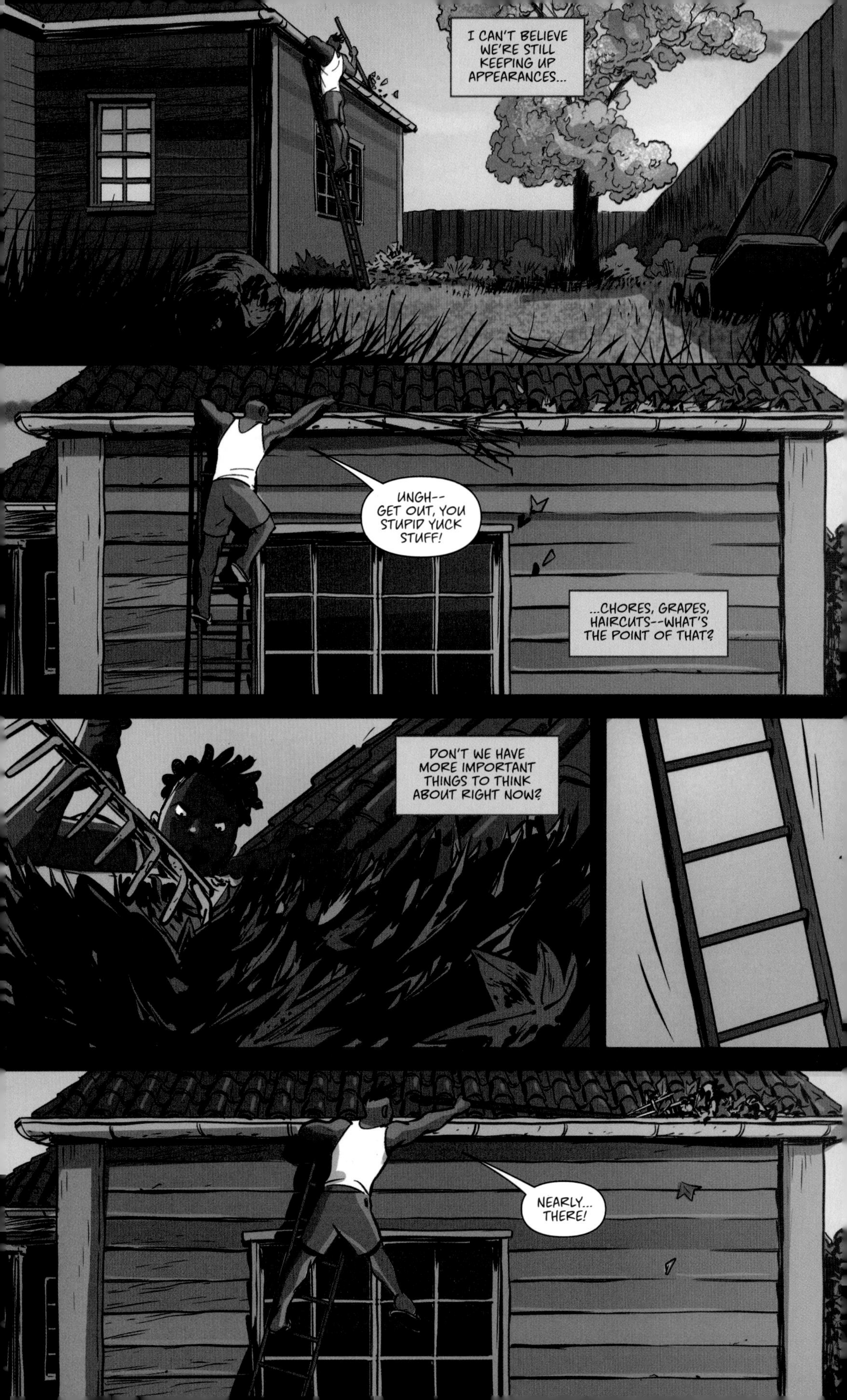
I CAN'T BELIEVE WE'RE STILL KEEPING UP APPEARANCES...
UNGH-- GET OUT, YOU STUPID YUCK STUFF!
...CHORES, GRADES, HAIRCUTS--WHAT'S THE POINT OF THAT?
DON'T WE HAVE MORE IMPORTANT THINGS TO THINK ABOUT RIGHT NOW?
NEARLY... THERE!

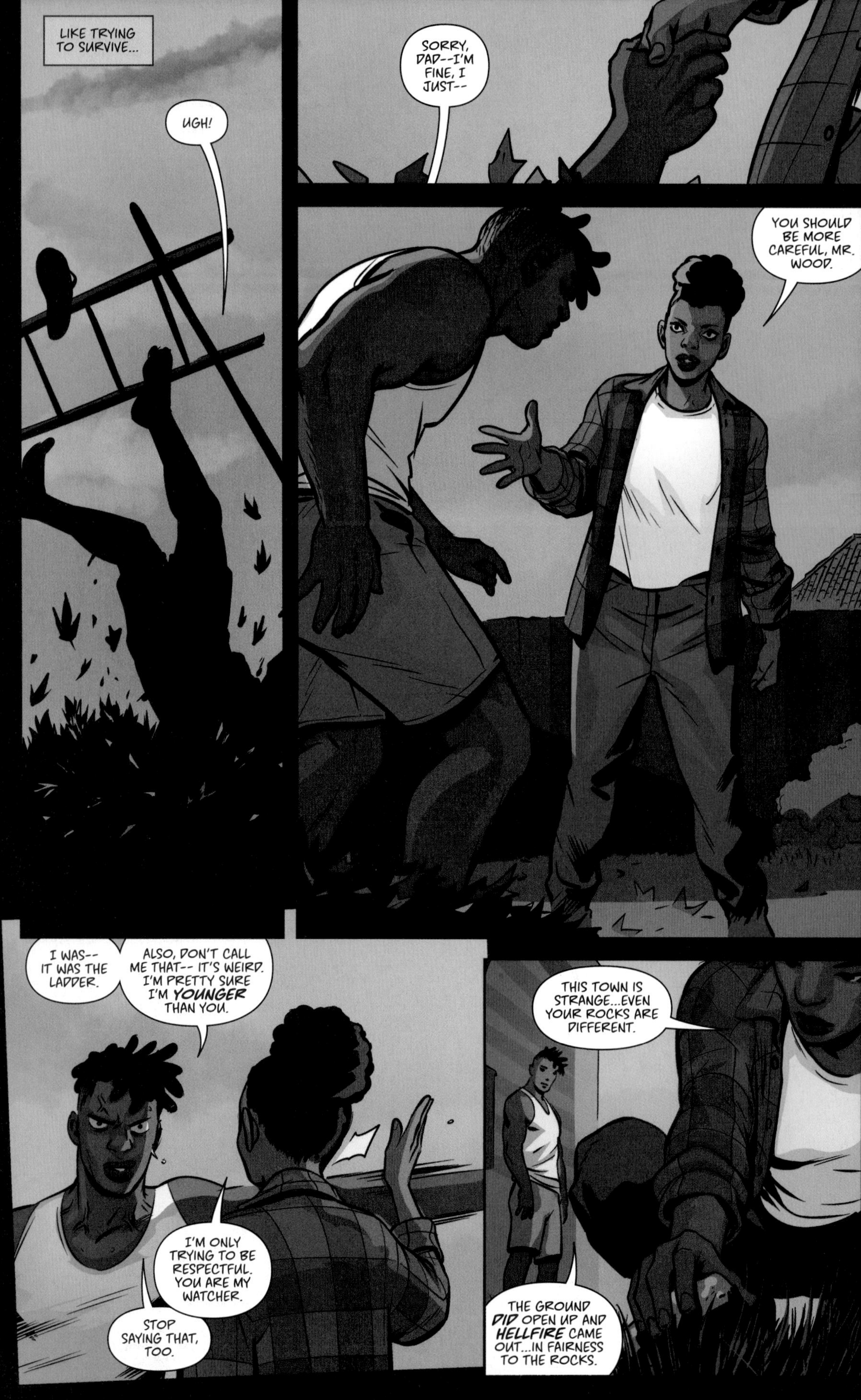
LIKE TRYING TO SURVIVE...
UGH!
SORRY, DAD--I'M FINE, I JUST--
YOU SHOULD BE MORE CAREFUL, MR. WOOD.
I WAS-- IT WAS THE LADDER.
ALSO, DON'T CALL ME THAT-- IT'S WEIRD. I'M PRETTY SURE I'M YOUNGER THAN YOU.
I'M ONLY TRYING TO BE RESPECTFUL. YOU ARE MY WATCHER.
STOP SAYING THAT, TOO.
THIS TOWN IS STRANGE...EVEN YOUR ROCKS ARE DIFFERENT.
THE GROUND DID OPEN UP AND HELLFIRE CAME OUT...IN FAIRNESS TO THE ROCKS.

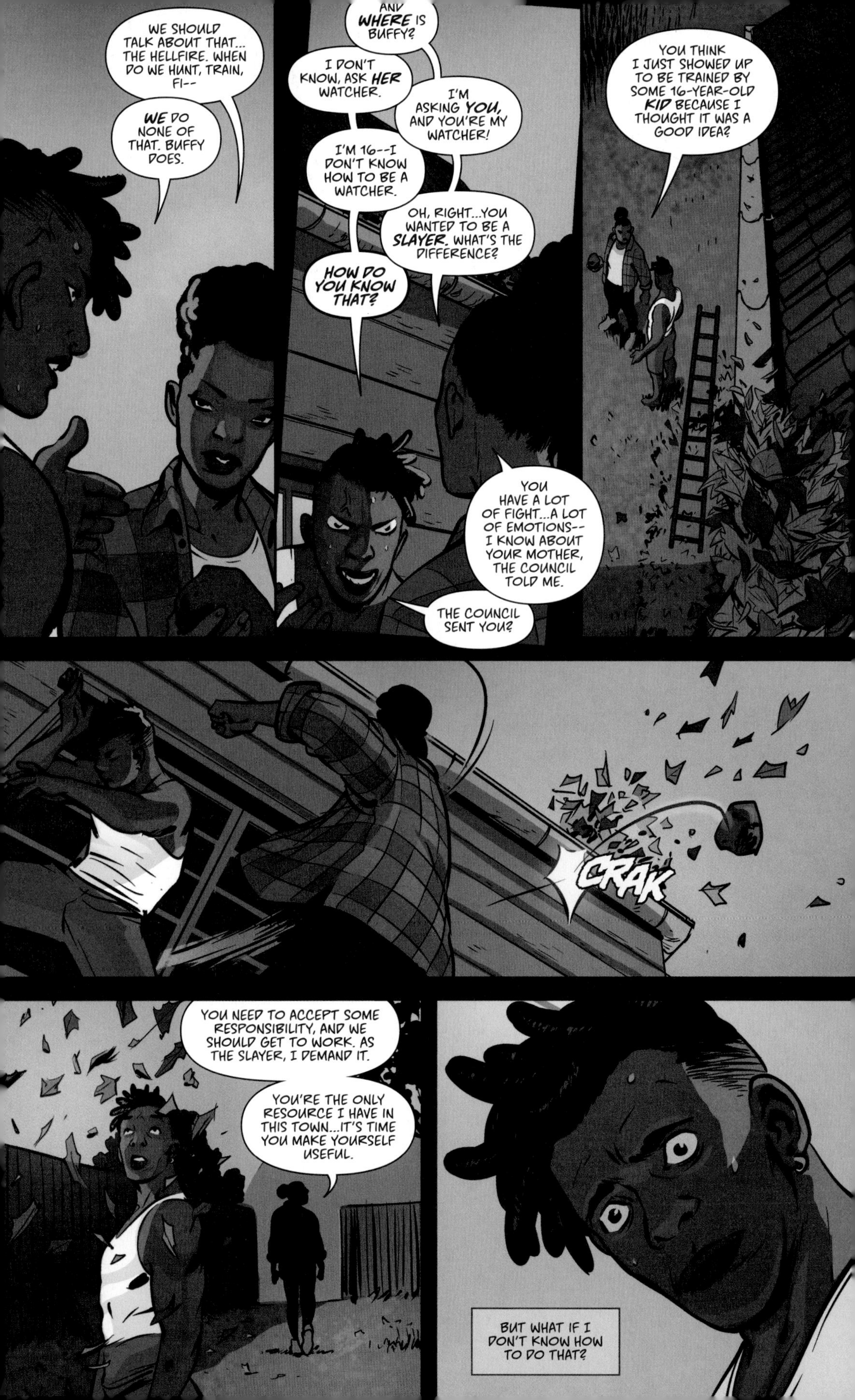
WE SHOULD TALK ABOUT THAT... THE HELLFIRE. WHEN DO WE HUNT, TRAIN, FI--
WE DO NONE OF THAT. BUFFY DOES.
AND WHERE IS BUFFY?
I DON'T KNOW, ASK HER WATCHER.
I'M ASKING YOU, AND YOU'RE MY WATCHER!
I'M 16--I DON'T KNOW HOW TO BE A WATCHER.
OH, RIGHT...YOU WANTED TO BE A SLAYER. WHAT'S THE DIFFERENCE?
HOW DO YOU KNOW THAT?
YOU HAVE A LOT OF FIGHT...A LOT OF EMOTIONS--I KNOW ABOUT YOUR MOTHER, THE COUNCIL TOLD ME.
THE COUNCIL SENT YOU?
YOU THINK I JUST SHOWED UP TO BE TRAINED BY SOME 16-YEAR-OLD KID BECAUSE I THOUGHT IT WAS A GOOD IDEA?
CRAK
YOU NEED TO ACCEPT SOME RESPONSIBILITY, AND WE SHOULD GET TO WORK. AS THE SLAYER, I DEMAND IT.
YOU'RE THE ONLY RESOURCE I HAVE IN THIS TOWN...IT'S TIME YOU MAKE YOURSELF USEFUL.
BUT WHAT IF I DON'T KNOW HOW TO DO THAT?

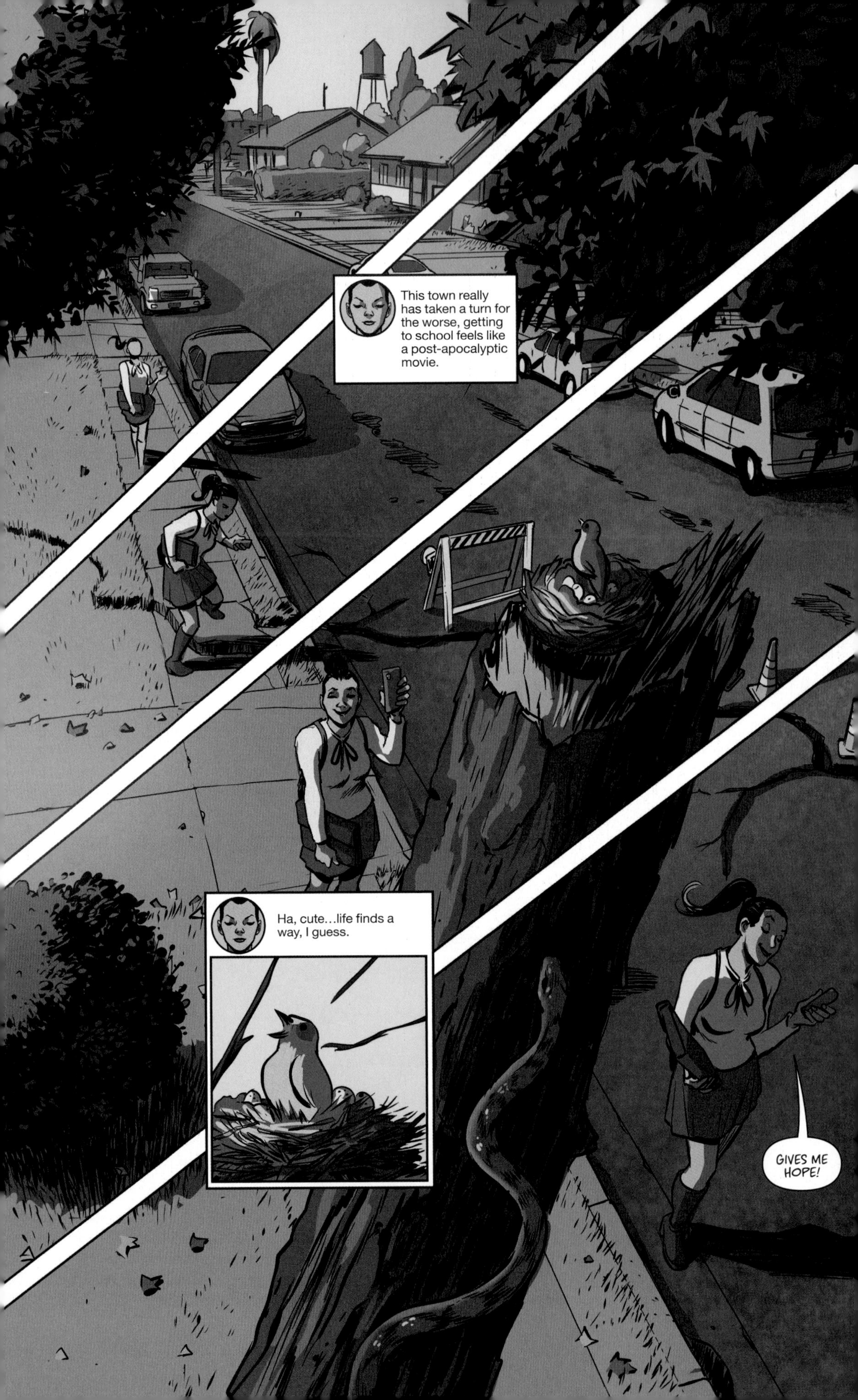
This town really has taken a turn for the worse, getting to school feels like a post-apocalyptic movie.
Ha, cute...life finds a way, I guess.
GIVES ME HOPE!

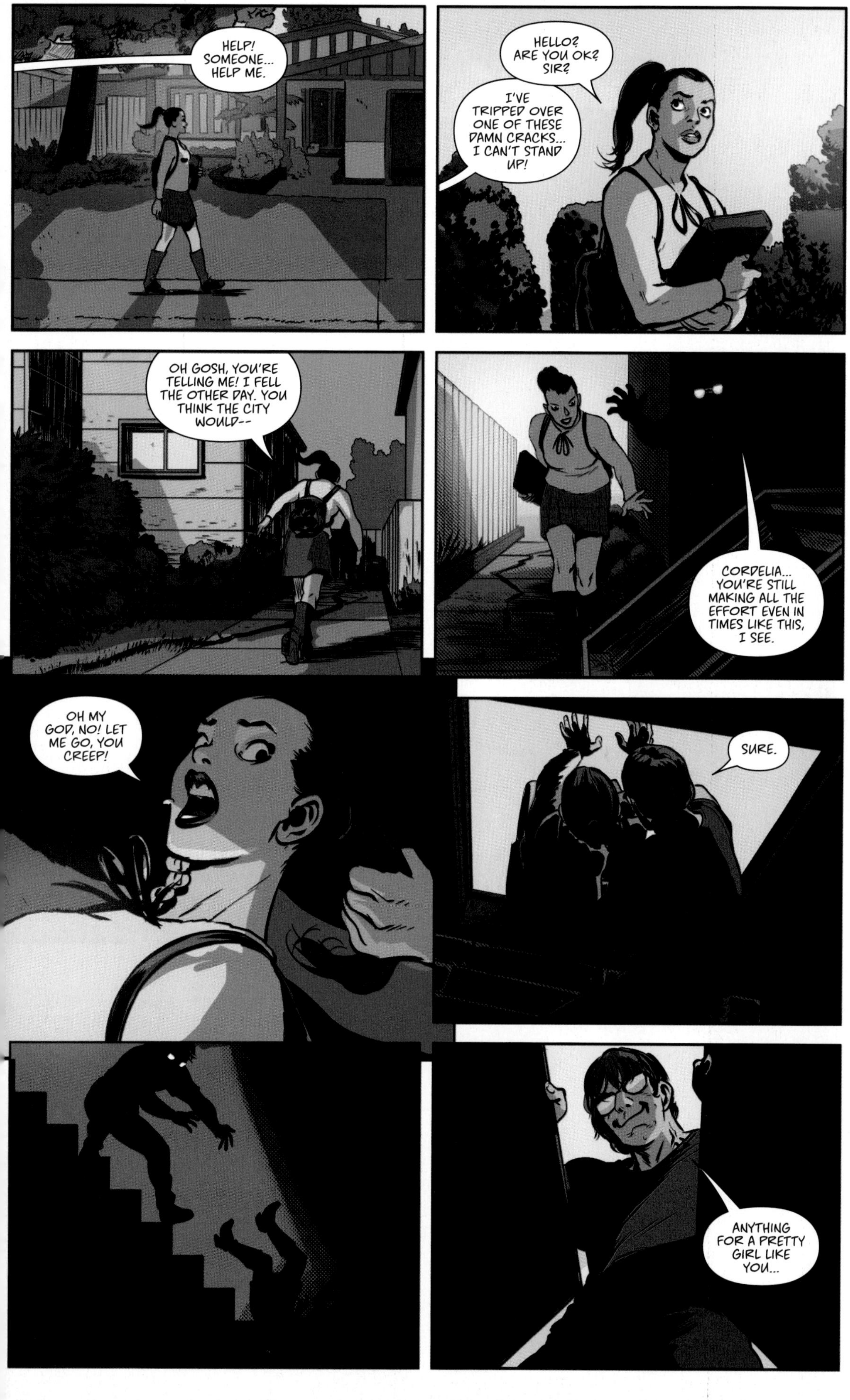
HELP! SOMEONE... HELP ME.
HELLO? ARE YOU OK? SIR?
I'VE TRIPPED OVER ONE OF THESE DAMN CRACKS... I CAN'T STAND UP!
OH GOSH, YOU'RE TELLING ME! I FELL THE OTHER DAY. YOU THINK THE CITY WOULD--
CORDELIA... YOU'RE STILL MAKING ALL THE EFFORT EVEN IN TIMES LIKE THIS, I SEE.
OH MY GOD, NO! LET ME GO, YOU CREEP!
SURE.
ANYTHING FOR A PRETTY GIRL LIKE YOU...

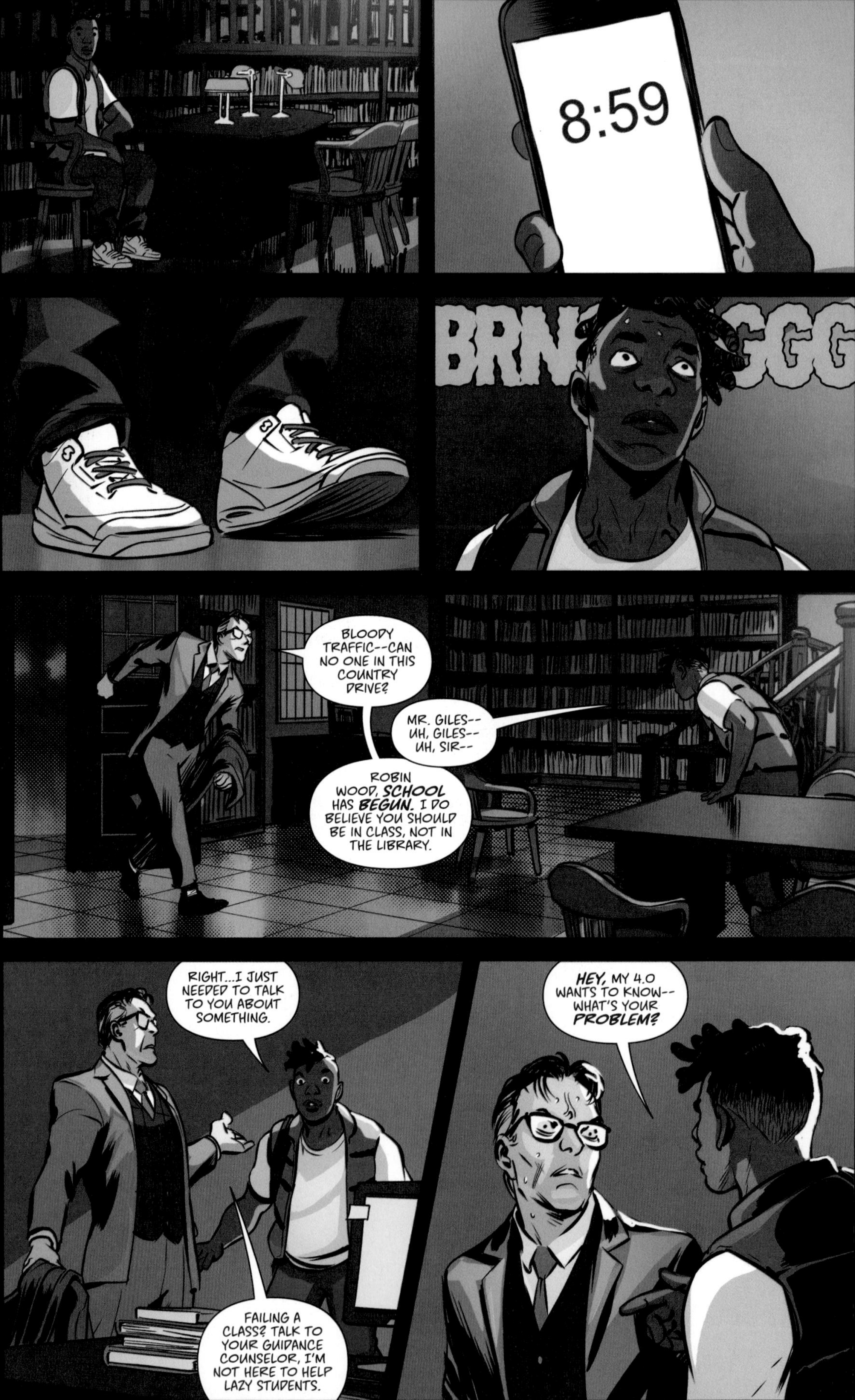
8:59
BRNGGG
BLOODY TRAFFIC--CAN NO ONE IN THIS COUNTRY DRIVE?
MR. GILES--UH, GILES--UH, SIR--
ROBIN WOOD, SCHOOL HAS BEGUN. I DO BELIEVE YOU SHOULD BE IN CLASS, NOT IN THE LIBRARY.
RIGHT...I JUST NEEDED TO TALK TO YOU ABOUT SOMETHING.
FAILING A CLASS? TALK TO YOUR GUIDANCE COUNSELOR, I'M NOT HERE TO HELP LAZY STUDENTS.
HEY, MY 4.0 WANTS TO KNOW--WHAT'S YOUR PROBLEM?

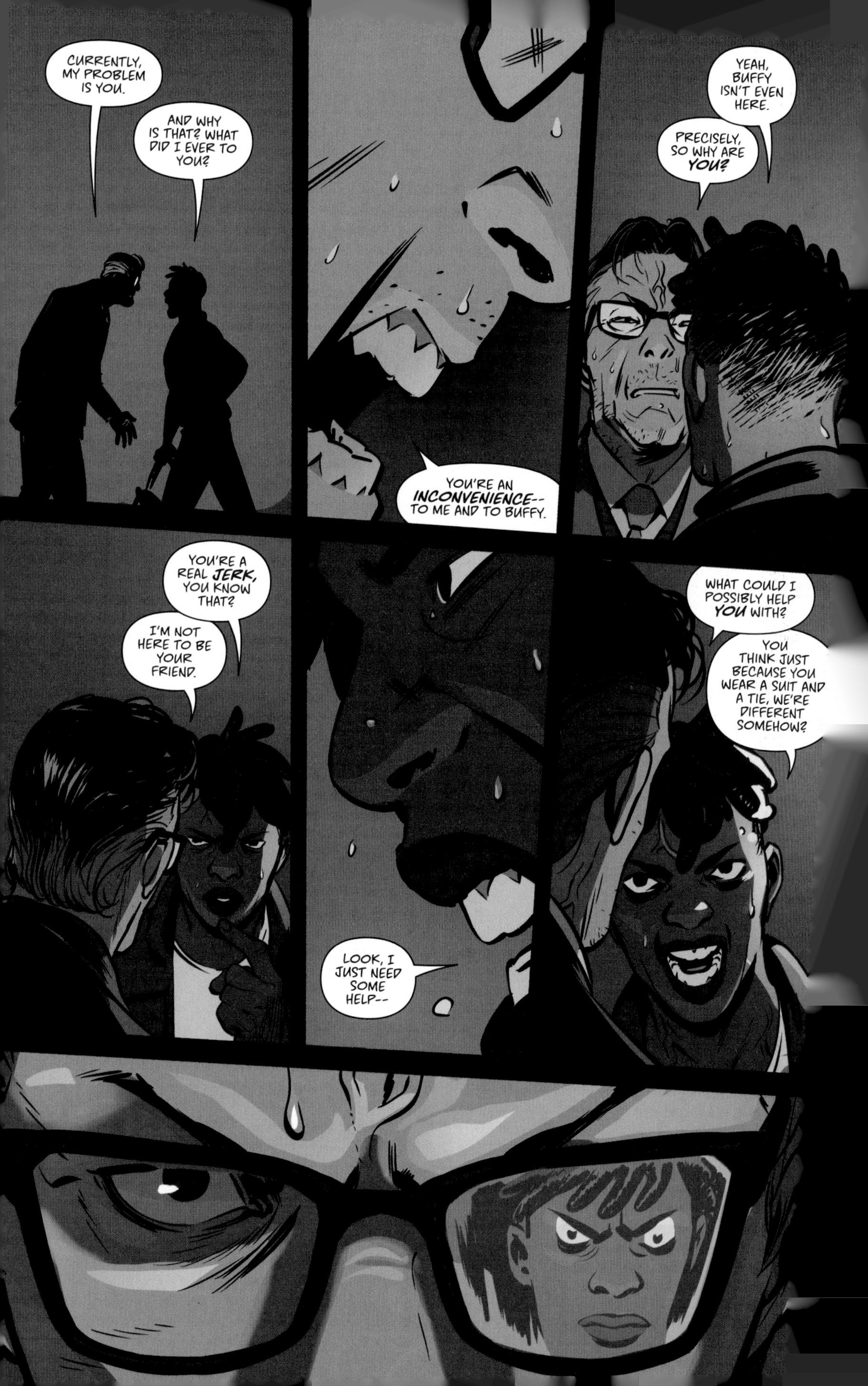
CURRENTLY, MY PROBLEM IS YOU.
AND WHY IS THAT? WHAT DID I EVER TO YOU?
YOU'RE AN INCONVENIENCE-- TO ME AND TO BUFFY.
YEAH, BUFFY ISN'T EVEN HERE.
PRECISELY, SO WHY ARE YOU?
YOU'RE A REAL JERK, YOU KNOW THAT?
I'M NOT HERE TO BE YOUR FRIEND.
LOOK, I JUST NEED SOME HELP--
WHAT COULD I POSSIBLY HELP YOU WITH?
YOU THINK JUST BECAUSE YOU WEAR A SUIT AND A TIE, WE'RE DIFFERENT SOMEHOW?

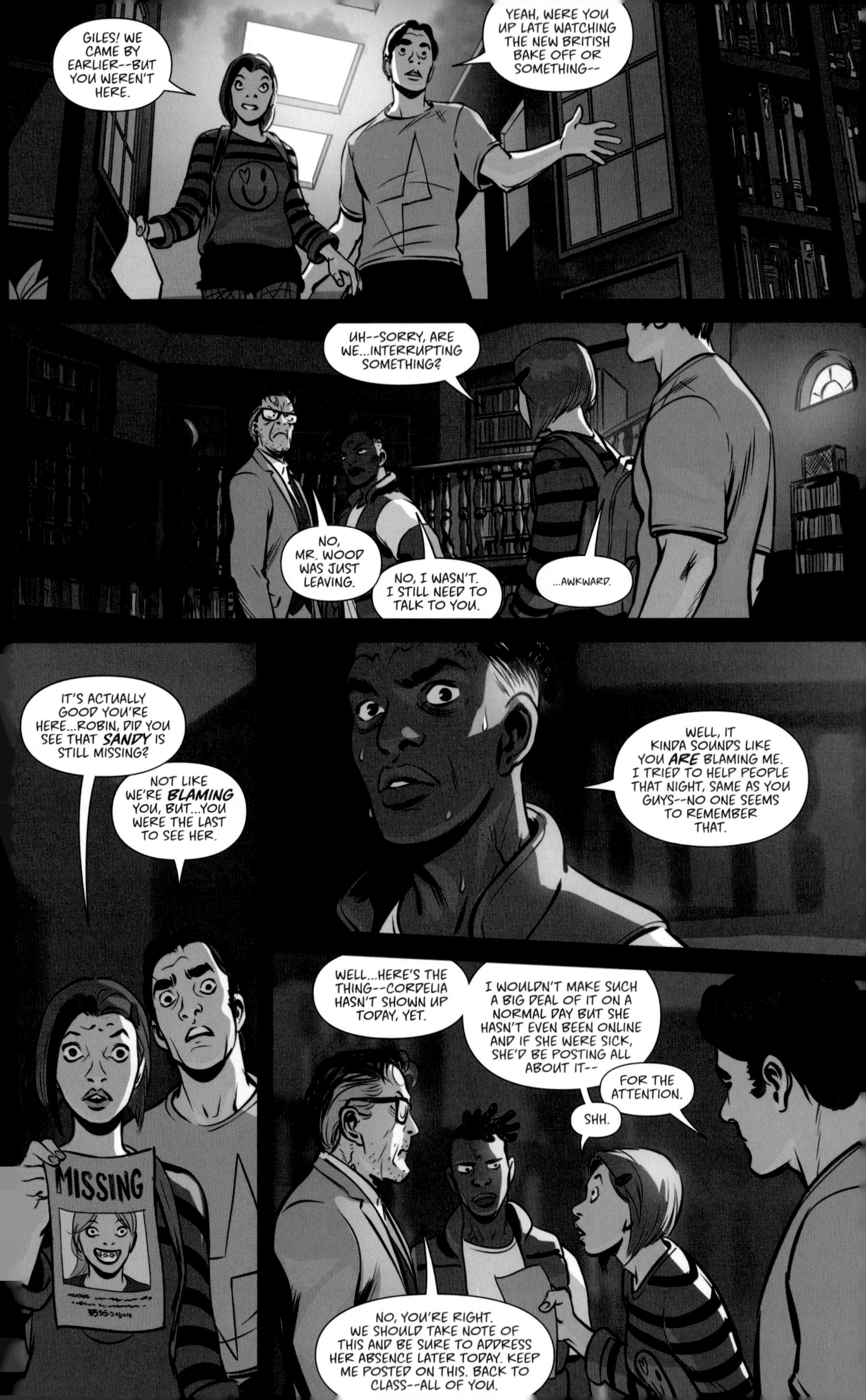
GILES! WE CAME BY EARLIER--BUT YOU WEREN'T HERE.
YEAH, WERE YOU UP LATE WATCHING THE NEW BRITISH BAKE OFF OR SOMETHING--
UH--SORRY, ARE WE...INTERRUPTING SOMETHING?
NO, MR. WOOD WAS JUST LEAVING.
NO, I WASN'T. I STILL NEED TO TALK TO YOU.
...AWKWARD.
IT'S ACTUALLY GOOD YOU'RE HERE...ROBIN, DID YOU SEE THAT SANDY IS STILL MISSING?
NOT LIKE WE'RE BLAMING YOU, BUT...YOU WERE THE LAST TO SEE HER.
WELL, IT KINDA SOUNDS LIKE YOU ARE BLAMING ME. I TRIED TO HELP PEOPLE THAT NIGHT, SAME AS YOU GUYS--NO ONE SEEMS TO REMEMBER THAT.
MISSING
WELL...HERE'S THE THING--CORDELIA HASN'T SHOWN UP TODAY, YET.
I WOULDN'T MAKE SUCH A BIG DEAL OF IT ON A NORMAL DAY BUT SHE HASN'T EVEN BEEN ONLINE AND IF SHE WERE SICK, SHE'D BE POSTING ALL ABOUT IT--
FOR THE ATTENTION.
SHH.
NO, YOU'RE RIGHT. WE SHOULD TAKE NOTE OF THIS AND BE SURE TO ADDRESS HER ABSENCE LATER TODAY. KEEP ME POSTED ON THIS. BACK TO CLASS--ALL OF YOU.

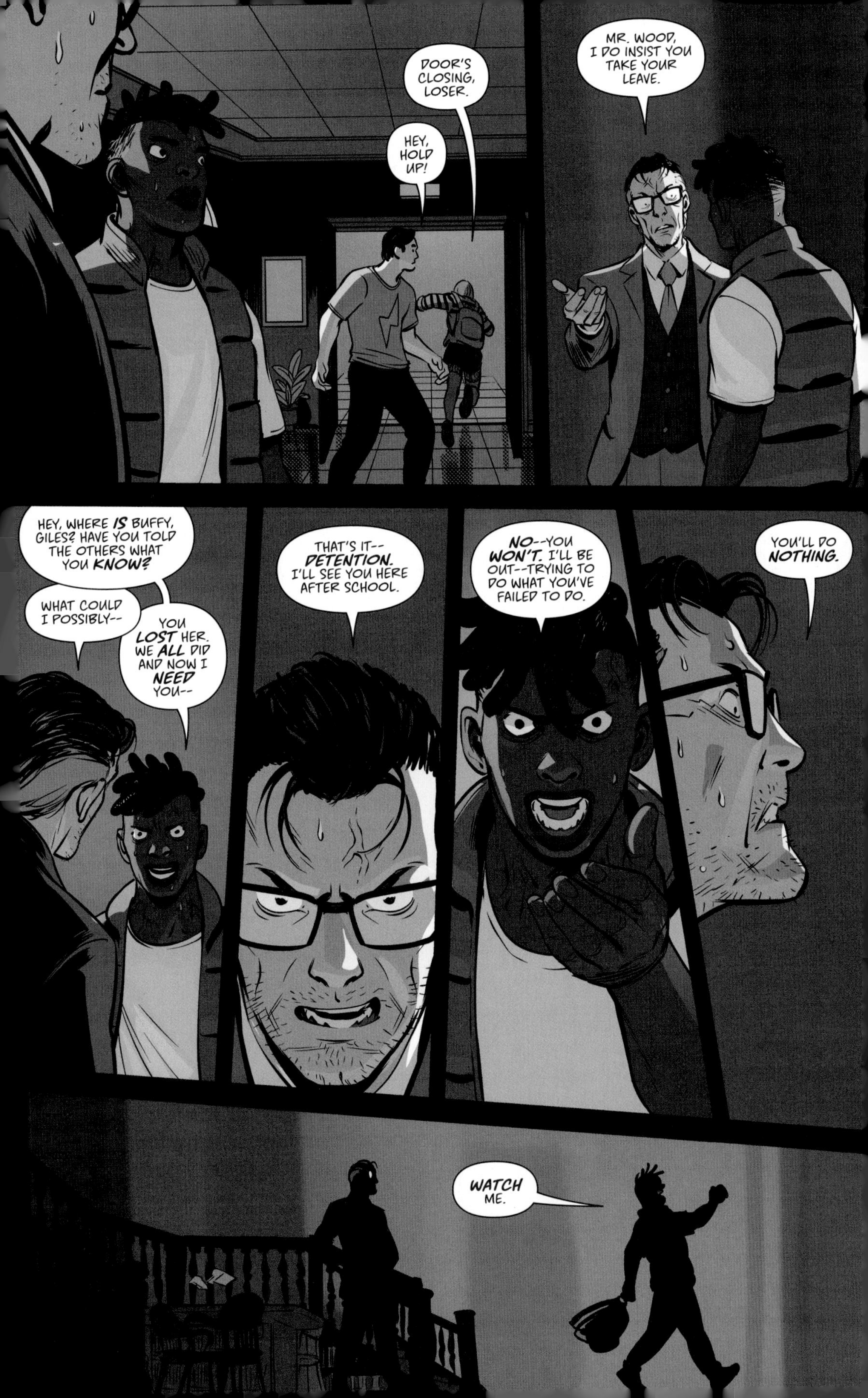
DOOR'S CLOSING, LOSER.
HEY, HOLD UP!
MR. WOOD, I DO INSIST YOU TAKE YOUR LEAVE.
HEY, WHERE IS BUFFY, GILES? HAVE YOU TOLD THE OTHERS WHAT YOU KNOW?
WHAT COULD I POSSIBLY--
YOU LOST HER. WE ALL DID AND NOW I NEED YOU--
THAT'S IT--DETENTION. I'LL SEE YOU HERE AFTER SCHOOL.
NO--YOU WON'T. I'LL BE OUT--TRYING TO DO WHAT YOU'VE FAILED TO DO.
YOU'LL DO NOTHING.
WATCH ME.

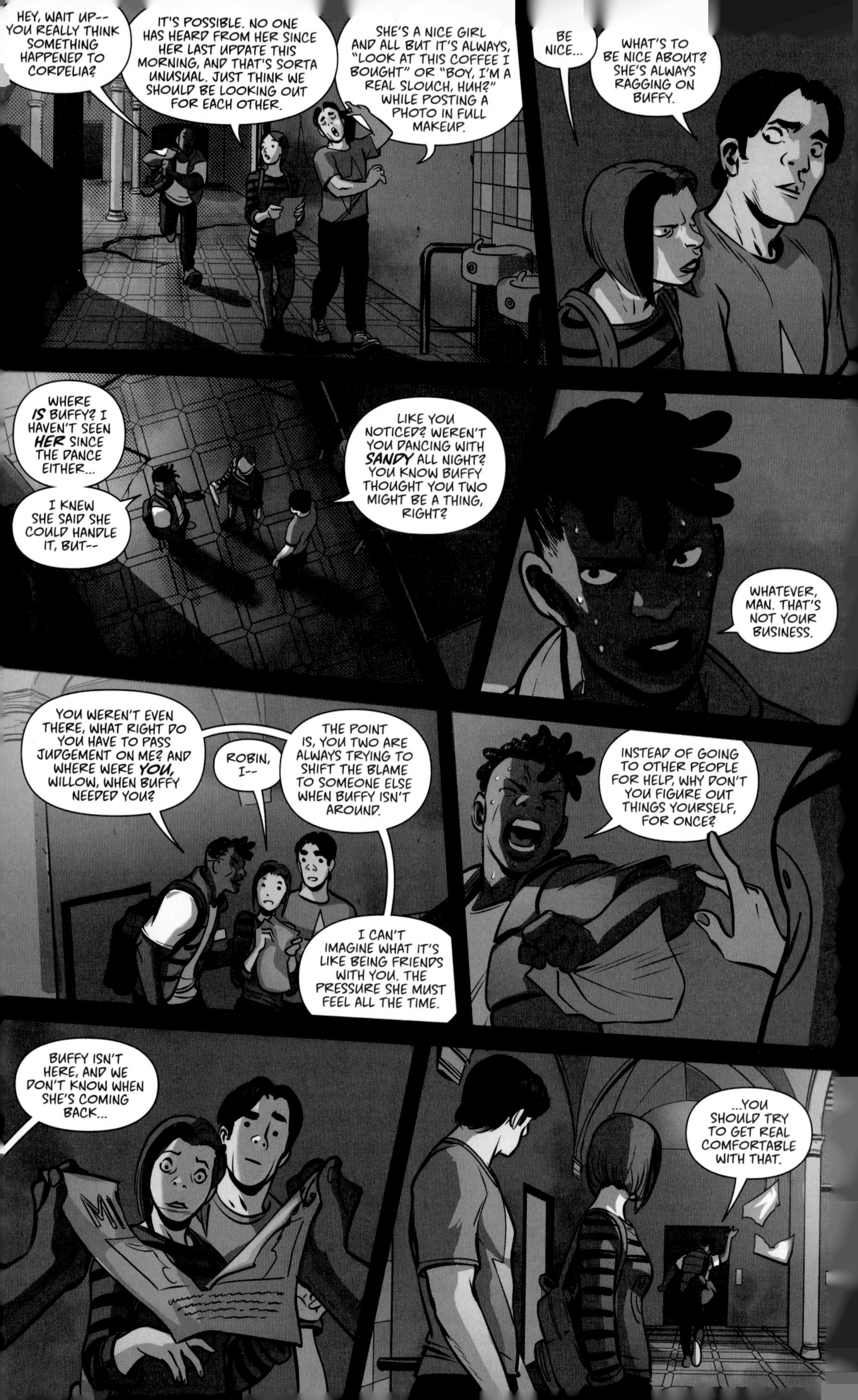
HEY, WAIT UP-- YOU REALLY THINK SOMETHING HAPPENED TO CORDELIA?
IT'S POSSIBLE. NO ONE HAS HEARD FROM HER SINCE HER LAST UPDATE THIS MORNING, AND THAT'S SORTA UNUSUAL. JUST THINK WE SHOULD BE LOOKING OUT FOR EACH OTHER.
SHE'S A NICE GIRL AND ALL BUT IT'S ALWAYS, "LOOK AT THIS COFFEE I BOUGHT" OR "BOY, I'M A REAL SLOUCH, HUH?" WHILE POSTING A PHOTO IN FULL MAKEUP.
BE NICE...
WHAT'S TO BE NICE ABOUT? SHE'S ALWAYS RAGGING ON BUFFY.
WHERE IS BUFFY? I HAVEN'T SEEN HER SINCE THE DANCE EITHER...
I KNEW SHE SAID SHE COULD HANDLE IT, BUT--
LIKE YOU NOTICED? WEREN'T YOU DANCING WITH SANDY ALL NIGHT? YOU KNOW BUFFY THOUGHT YOU TWO MIGHT BE A THING, RIGHT?
WHATEVER, MAN. THAT'S NOT YOUR BUSINESS.
YOU WEREN'T EVEN THERE, WHAT RIGHT DO YOU HAVE TO PASS JUDGEMENT ON ME? AND WHERE WERE YOU, WILLOW, WHEN BUFFY NEEDED YOU?
ROBIN, I--
THE POINT IS, YOU TWO ARE ALWAYS TRYING TO SHIFT THE BLAME TO SOMEONE ELSE WHEN BUFFY ISN'T AROUND.
I CAN'T IMAGINE WHAT IT'S LIKE BEING FRIENDS WITH YOU. THE PRESSURE SHE MUST FEEL ALL THE TIME.
INSTEAD OF GOING TO OTHER PEOPLE FOR HELP, WHY DON'T YOU FIGURE OUT THINGS YOURSELF, FOR ONCE?
BUFFY ISN'T HERE, AND WE DON'T KNOW WHEN SHE'S COMING BACK...
...YOU SHOULD TRY TO GET REAL COMFORTABLE WITH THAT.

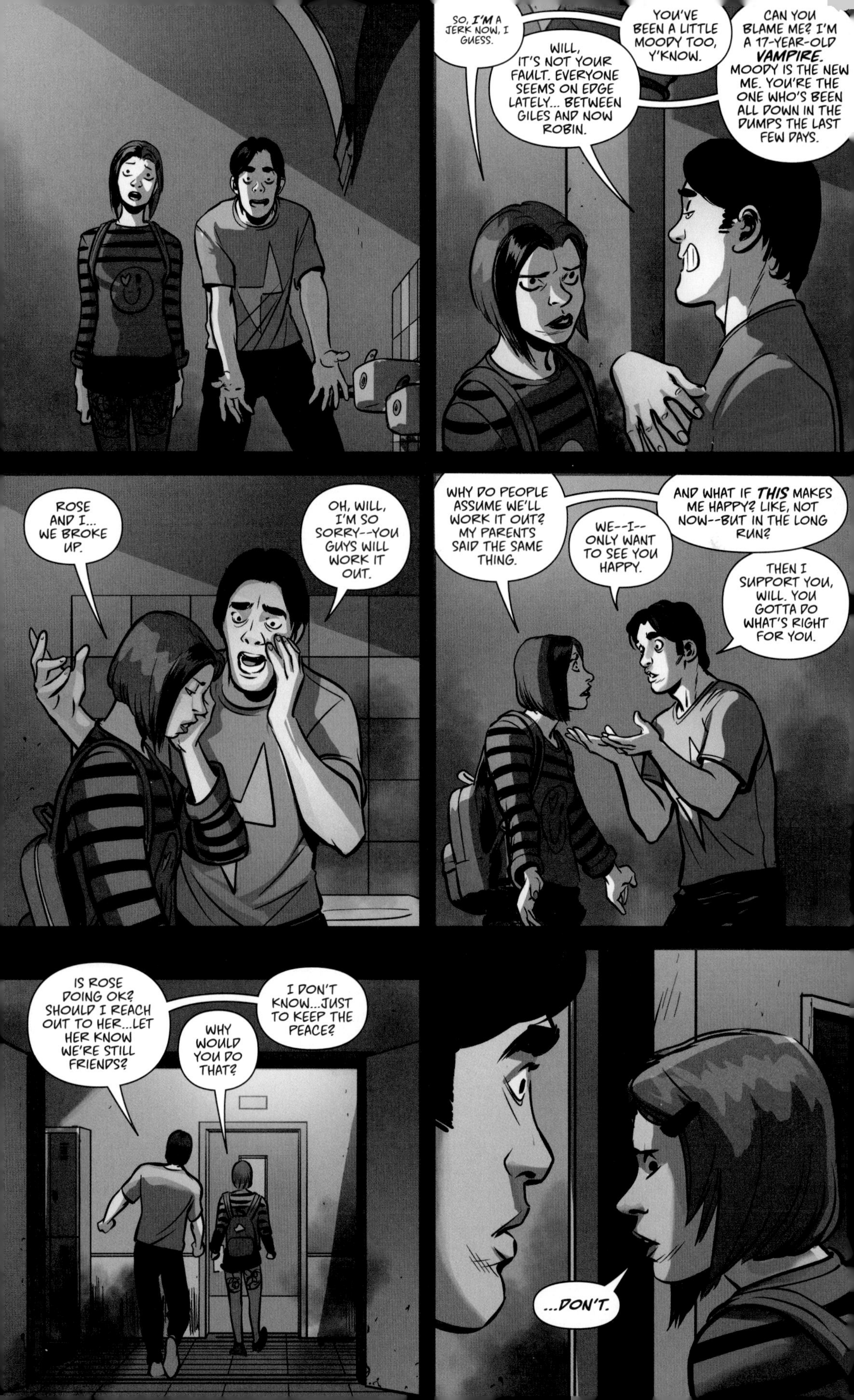
SO, I'M A JERK NOW, I GUESS.
WILL, IT'S NOT YOUR FAULT. EVERYONE SEEMS ON EDGE LATELY... BETWEEN GILES AND NOW ROBIN.
YOU'VE BEEN A LITTLE MOODY TOO, Y'KNOW.
CAN YOU BLAME ME? I'M A 17-YEAR-OLD VAMPIRE. MOODY IS THE NEW ME. YOU'RE THE ONE WHO'S BEEN ALL DOWN IN THE DUMPS THE LAST FEW DAYS.
ROSE AND I... WE BROKE UP.
OH, WILL, I'M SO SORRY--YOU GUYS WILL WORK IT OUT.
WHY DO PEOPLE ASSUME WE'LL WORK IT OUT? MY PARENTS SAID THE SAME THING.
WE--I--ONLY WANT TO SEE YOU HAPPY.
AND WHAT IF THIS MAKES ME HAPPY? LIKE, NOT NOW--BUT IN THE LONG RUN?
THEN I SUPPORT YOU, WILL. YOU GOTTA DO WHAT'S RIGHT FOR YOU.
IS ROSE DOING OK? SHOULD I REACH OUT TO HER...LET HER KNOW WE'RE STILL FRIENDS?
WHY WOULD YOU DO THAT?
I DON'T KNOW...JUST TO KEEP THE PEACE?
...DON'T.

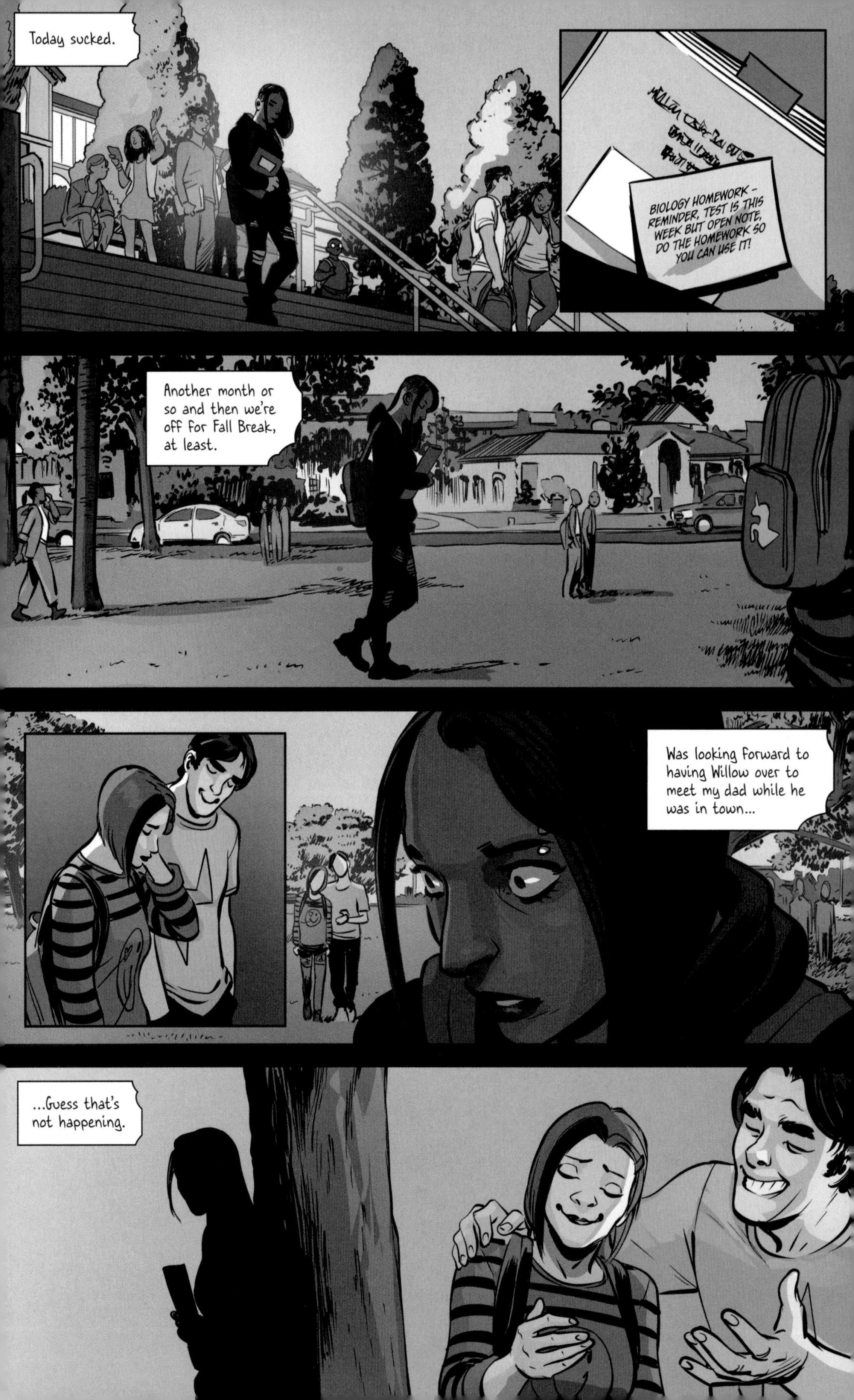
Today sucked.
BIOLOGY HOMEWORK - REMINDER, TEST IS THIS WEEK BUT OPEN NOTE, DO THE HOMEWORK SO YOU CAN USE IT!
Another month or so and then we're off for Fall Break, at least.
Was looking forward to having Willow over to meet my dad while he was in town...
...Guess that's not happening.

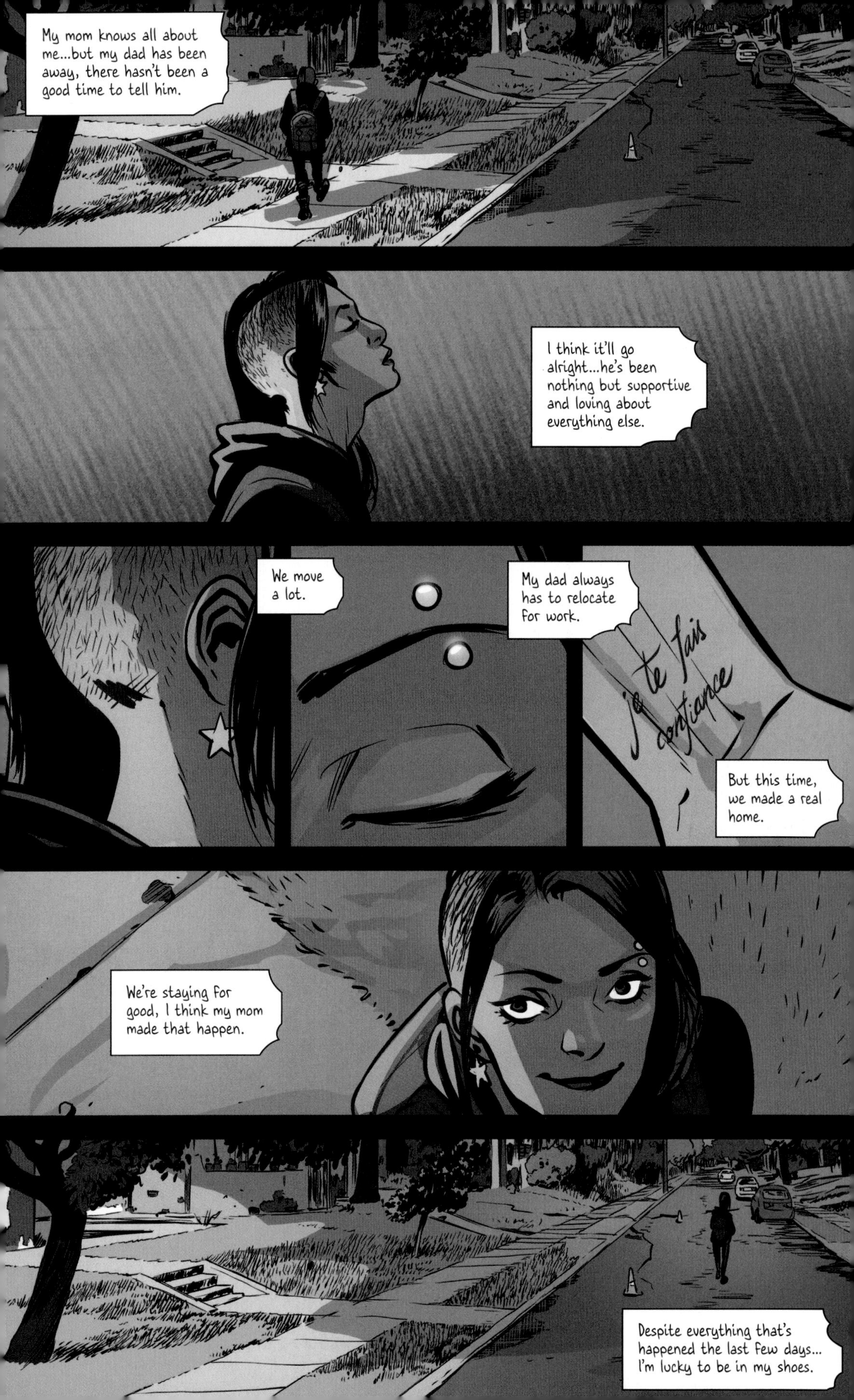
My mom knows all about me...but my dad has been away, there hasn't been a good time to tell him.
I think it'll go alright...he's been nothing but supportive and loving about everything else.
We move a lot.
My dad always has to relocate for work.
je te fais confiance
But this time, we made a real home.
We're staying for good, I think my mom made that happen.
Despite everything that's happened the last few days... I'm lucky to be in my shoes.

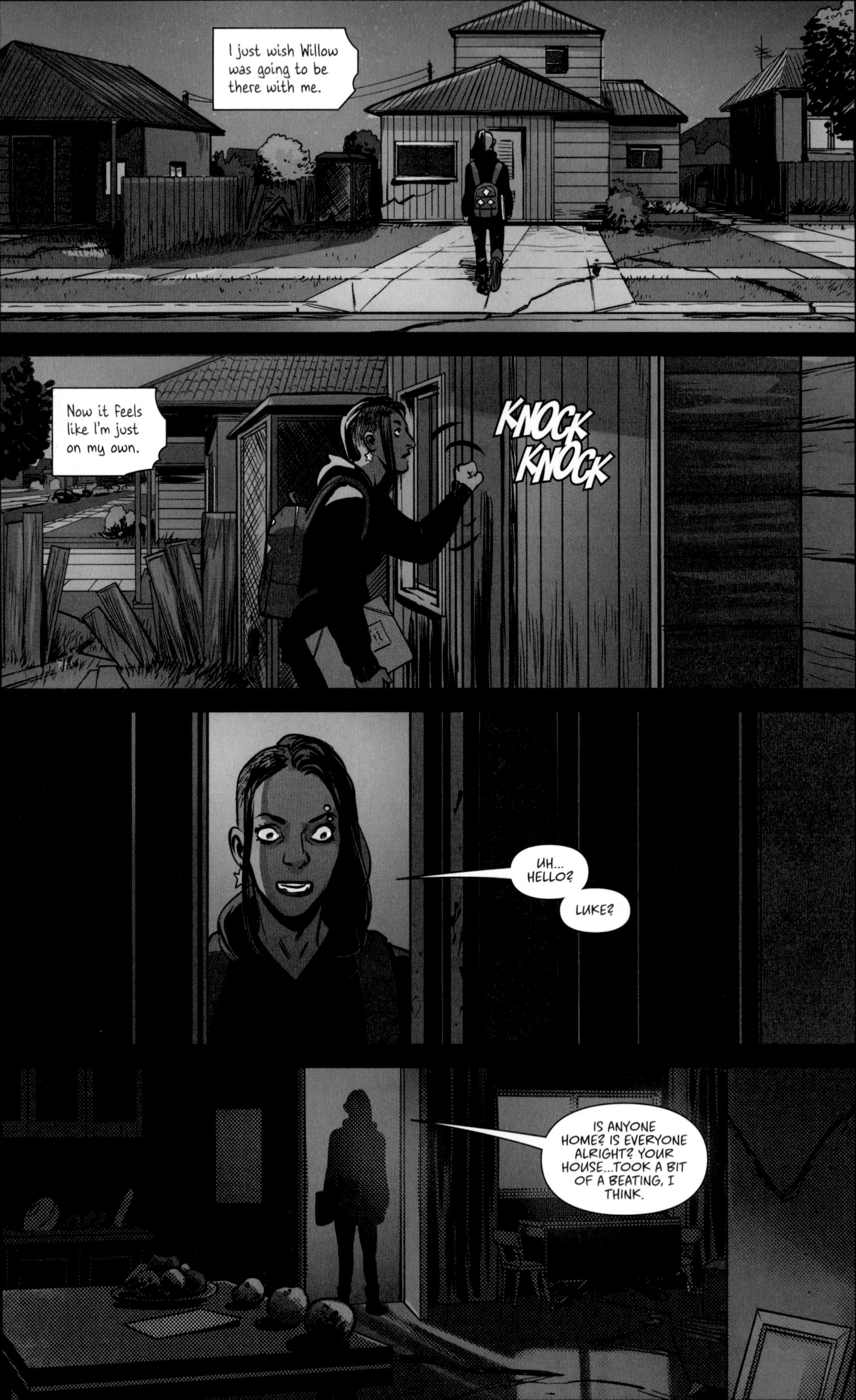
I just wish Willow was going to be there with me.
Now it feels like I'm just on my own.
KNOCK KNOCK
UH... HELLO?
LUKE?
IS ANYONE HOME? IS EVERYONE ALRIGHT? YOUR HOUSE...TOOK A BIT OF A BEATING, I THINK.

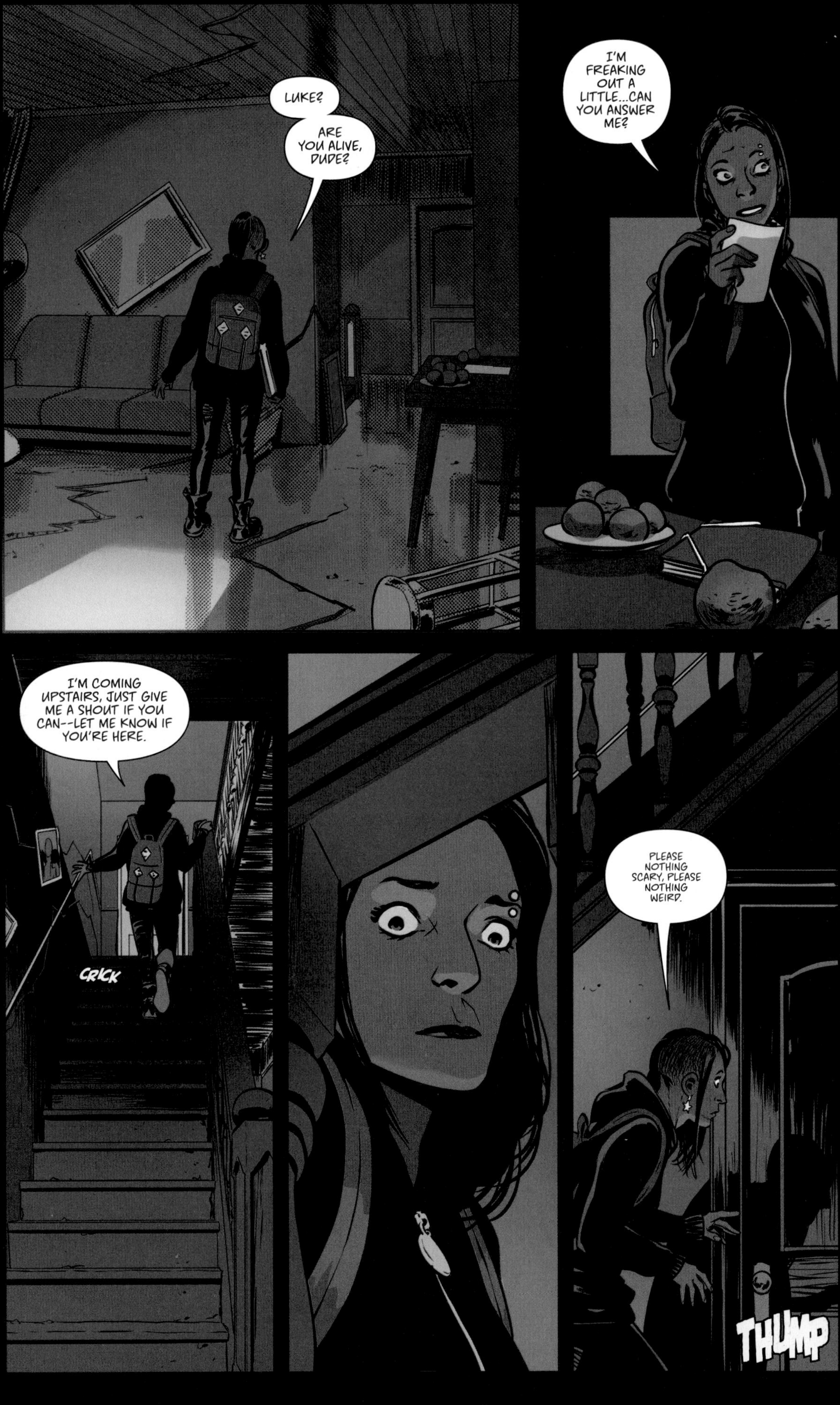
LUKE?
ARE YOU ALIVE, DUDE?
I'M FREAKING OUT A LITTLE...CAN YOU ANSWER ME?
I'M COMING UPSTAIRS, JUST GIVE ME A SHOUT IF YOU CAN--LET ME KNOW IF YOU'RE HERE.
CRICK
PLEASE NOTHING SCARY, PLEASE NOTHING WEIRD.
THUMP

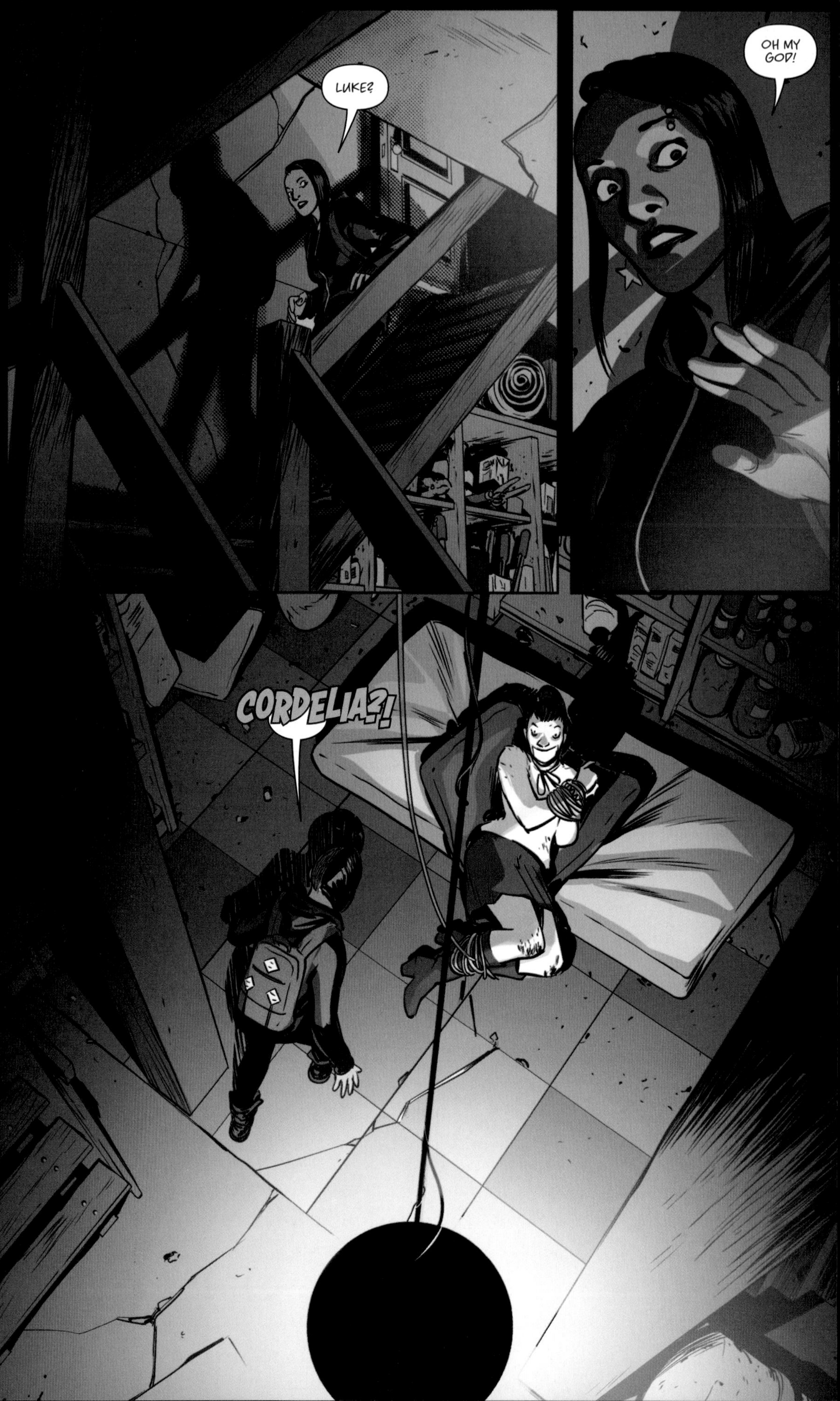
LUKE?
OH MY GOD!
CORDELIA?!

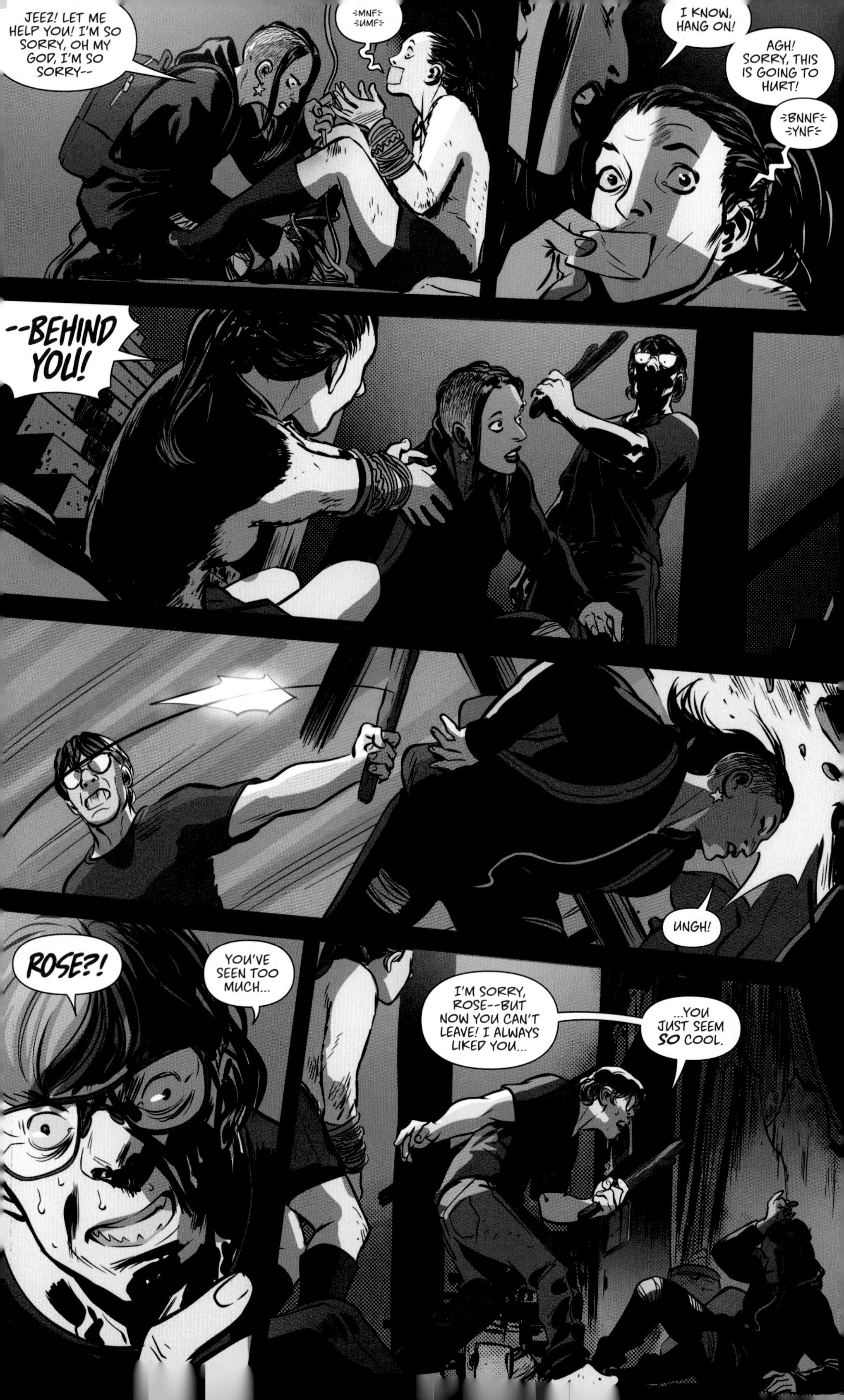
JEEZ! LET ME HELP YOU! I'M SO SORRY, OH MY GOD, I'M SO SORRY--
MNF UMF
I KNOW, HANG ON!
AGH! SORRY, THIS IS GOING TO HURT!
BNNF YNF
--BEHIND YOU!
UNGH!
ROSE?!
YOU'VE SEEN TOO MUCH...
I'M SORRY, ROSE--BUT NOW YOU CAN'T LEAVE! I ALWAYS LIKED YOU...
...YOU JUST SEEM SO COOL.

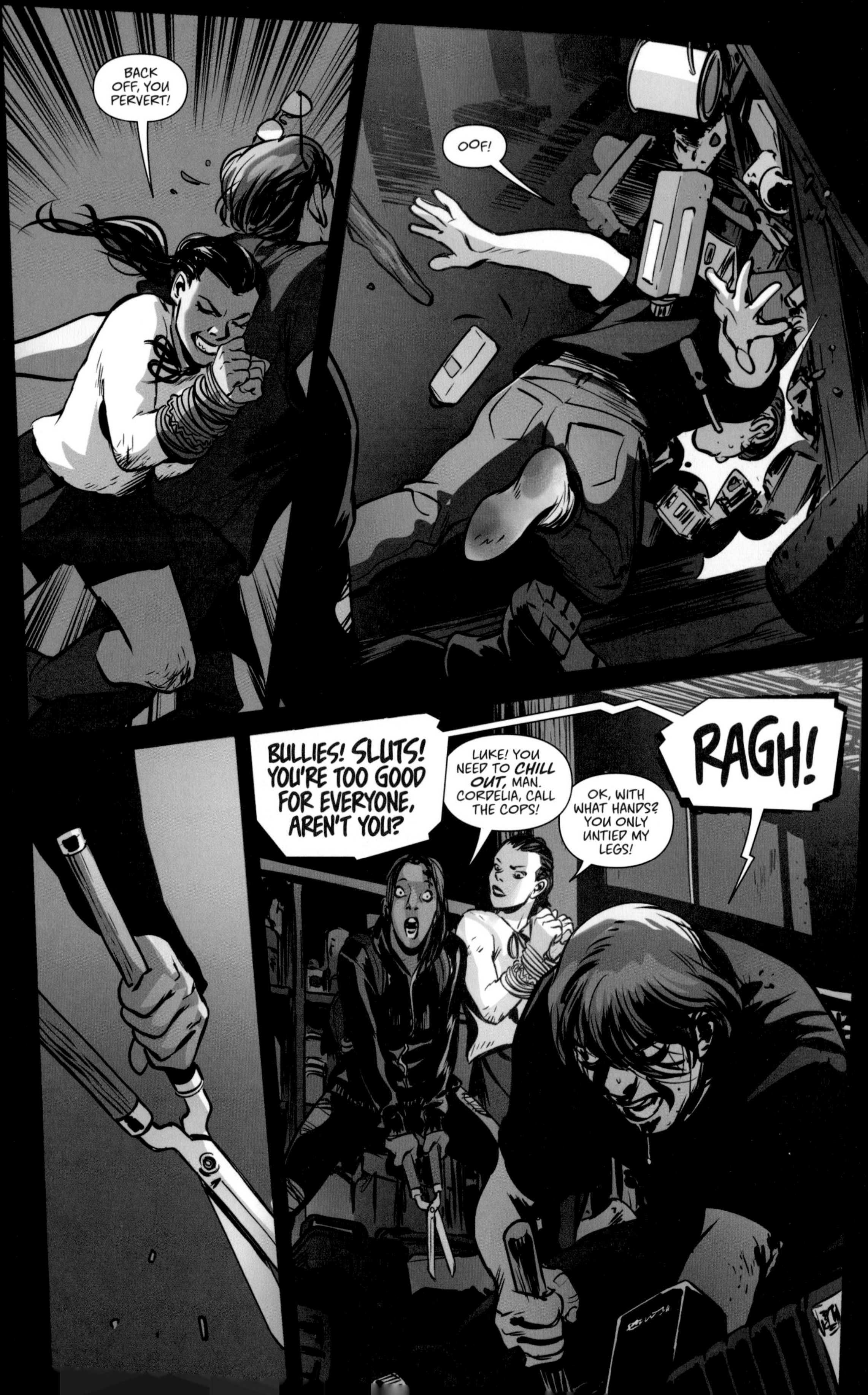
BACK OFF, YOU PERVERT!
OOF!
BULLIES! SLUTS! YOU'RE TOO GOOD FOR EVERYONE, AREN'T YOU?
RAGH!
LUKE! YOU NEED TO CHILL OUT, MAN. CORDELIA, CALL THE COPS!
OK, WITH WHAT HANDS? YOU ONLY UNTIED MY LEGS!

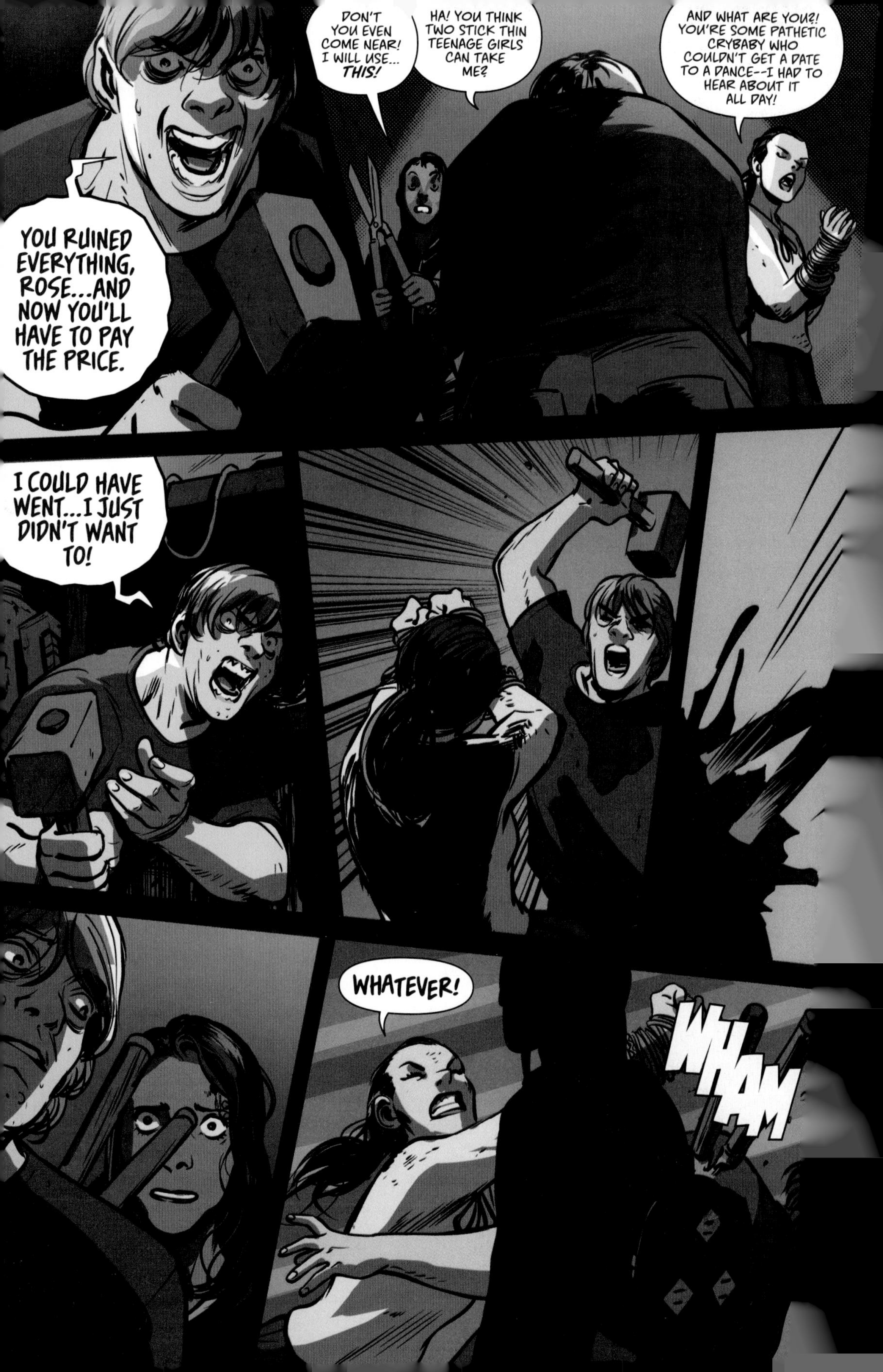
DON'T YOU EVEN COME NEAR! I WILL USE... THIS!
HA! YOU THINK TWO STICK THIN TEENAGE GIRLS CAN TAKE ME?
AND WHAT ARE YOU?! YOU'RE SOME PATHETIC CRYBABY WHO COULDN'T GET A DATE TO A DANCE--I HAD TO HEAR ABOUT IT ALL DAY!
YOU RUINED EVERYTHING, ROSE...AND NOW YOU'LL HAVE TO PAY THE PRICE.
I COULD HAVE WENT...I JUST DIDN'T WANT TO!
WHATEVER!
WHAM

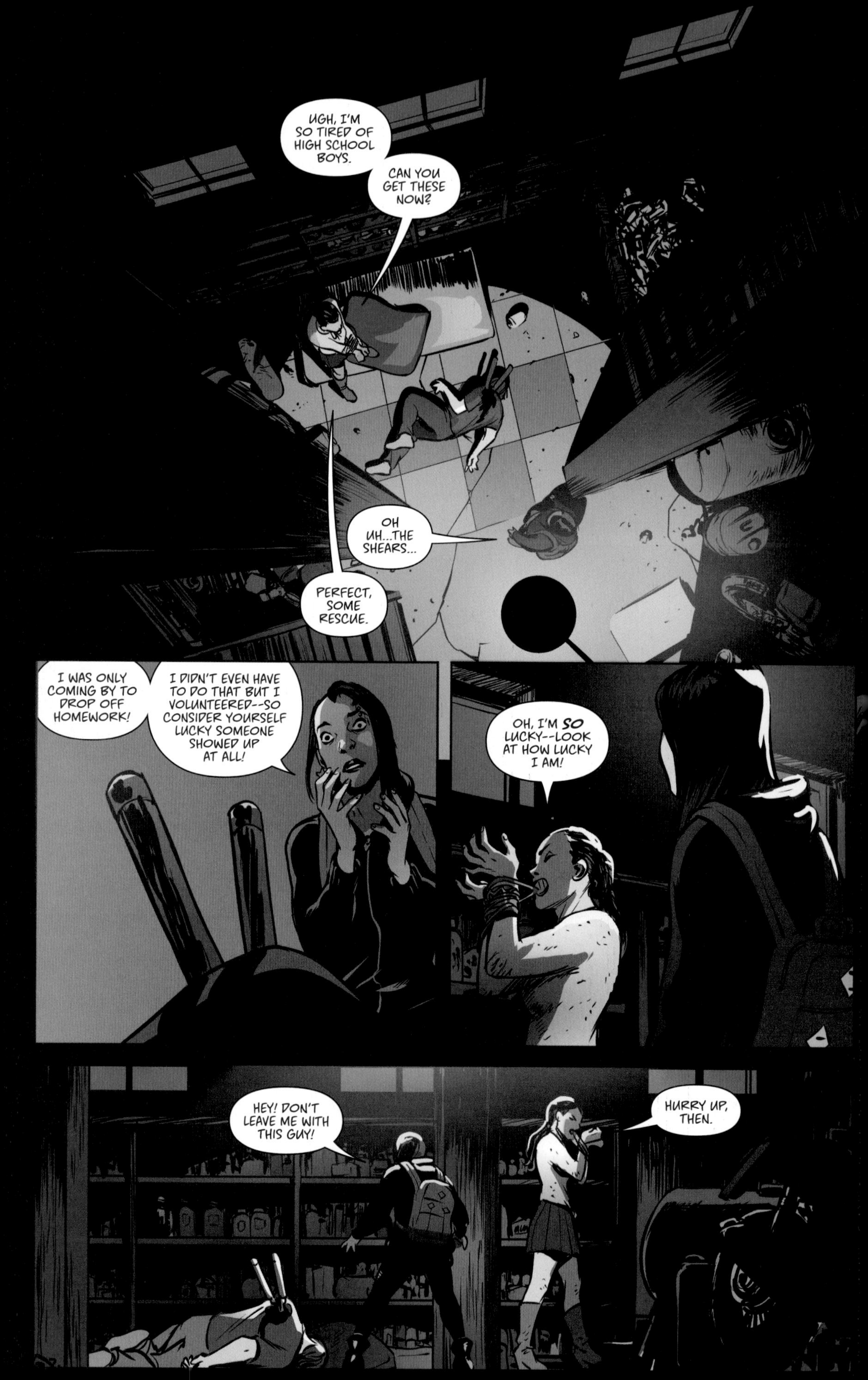
UGH, I'M SO TIRED OF HIGH SCHOOL BOYS.
CAN YOU GET THESE NOW?
OH UH...THE SHEARS...
PERFECT, SOME RESCUE.
I WAS ONLY COMING BY TO DROP OFF HOMEWORK!
I DIDN'T EVEN HAVE TO DO THAT BUT I VOLUNTEERED--SO CONSIDER YOURSELF LUCKY SOMEONE SHOWED UP AT ALL!
OH, I'M SO LUCKY--LOOK AT HOW LUCKY I AM!
HEY! DON'T LEAVE ME WITH THIS GUY!
HURRY UP, THEN.

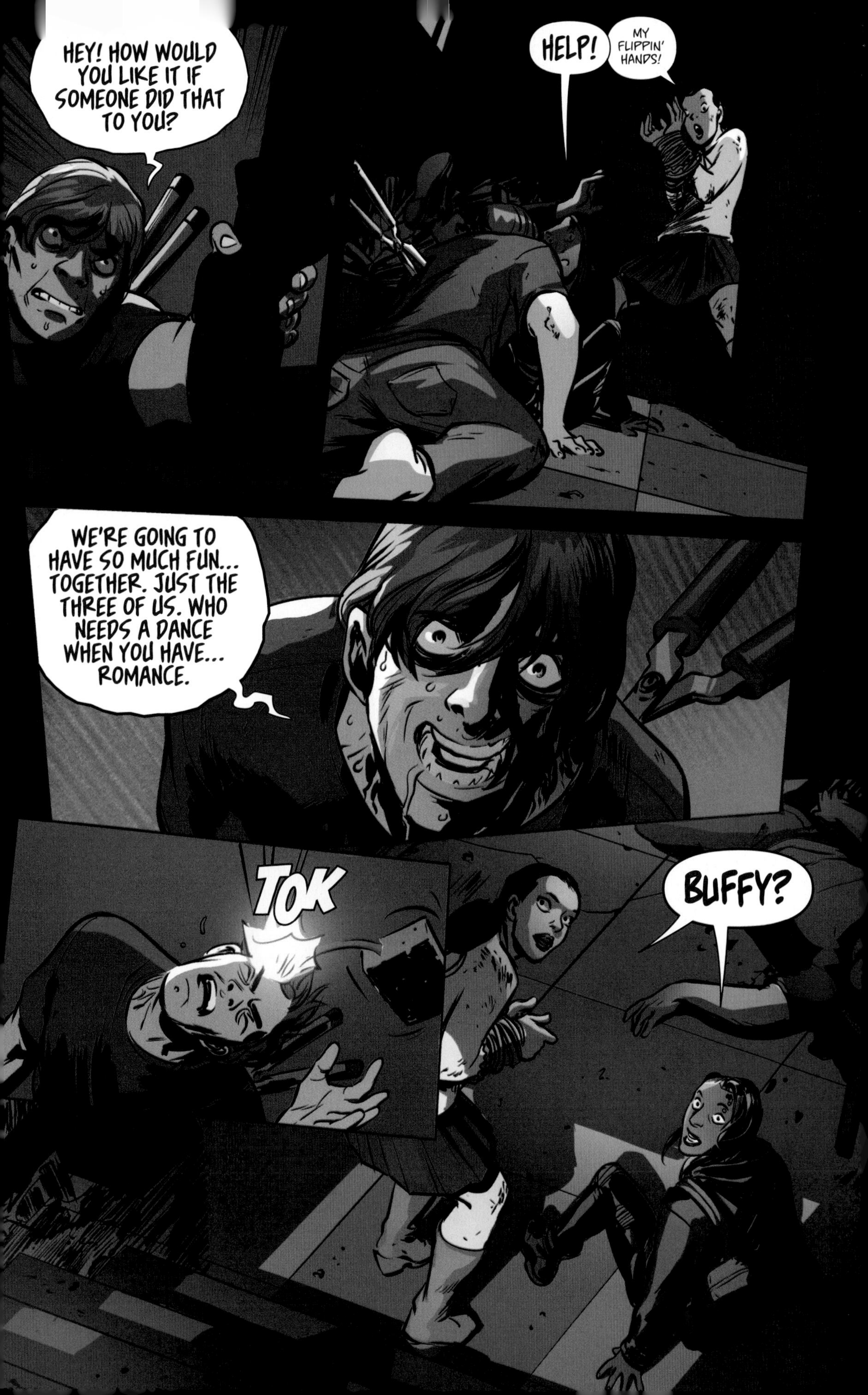
HEY! HOW WOULD YOU LIKE IT IF SOMEONE DID THAT TO YOU?
HELP!
MY FLIPPIN' HANDS!
WE'RE GOING TO HAVE SO MUCH FUN... TOGETHER. JUST THE THREE OF US. WHO NEEDS A DANCE WHEN YOU HAVE... ROMANCE.
TOK
BUFFY?

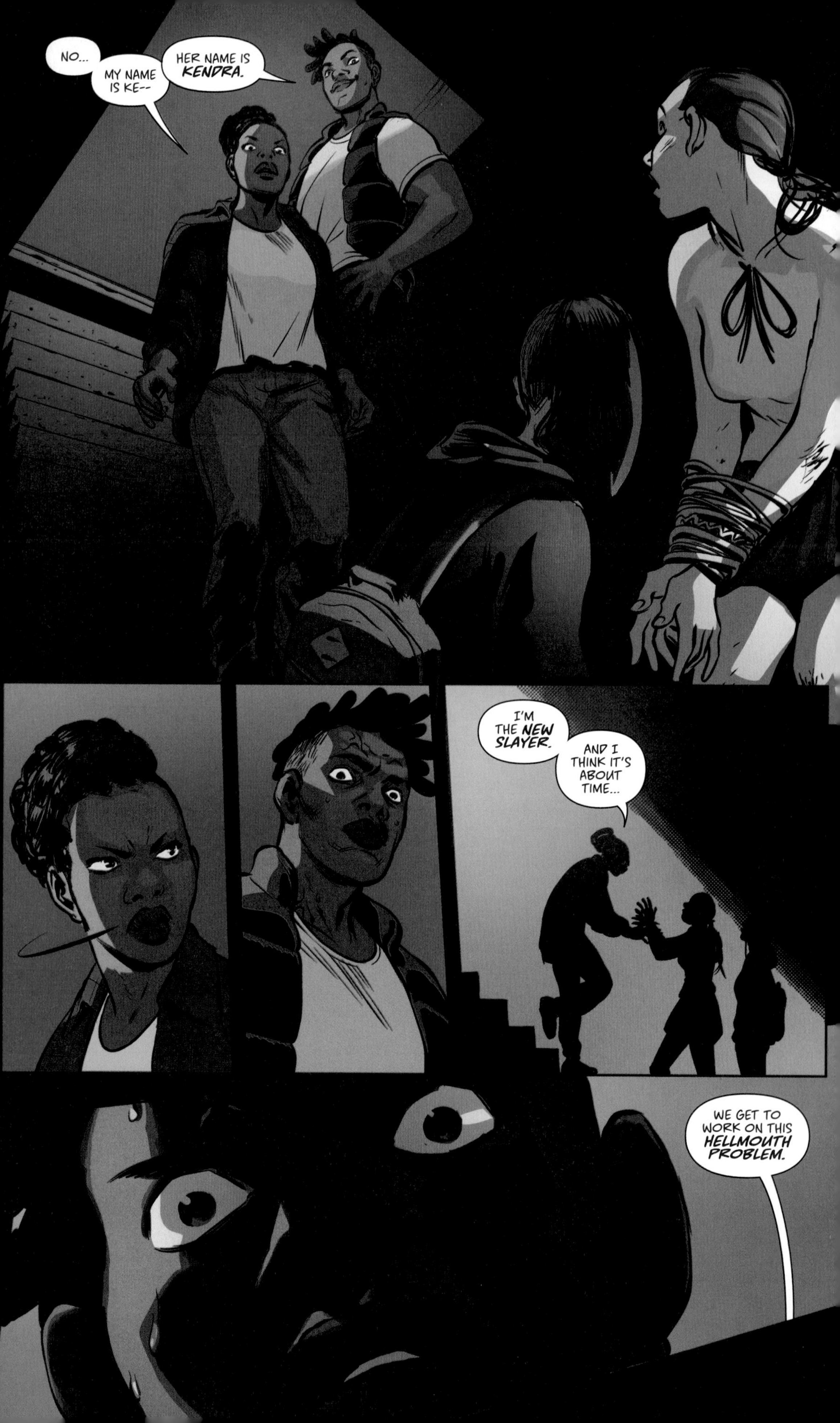
NO...
MY NAME IS KE--
HER NAME IS *KENDRA.*
I'M THE *NEW SLAYER.*
AND I THINK IT'S ABOUT TIME...
WE GET TO WORK ON THIS *HELLMOUTH PROBLEM.*

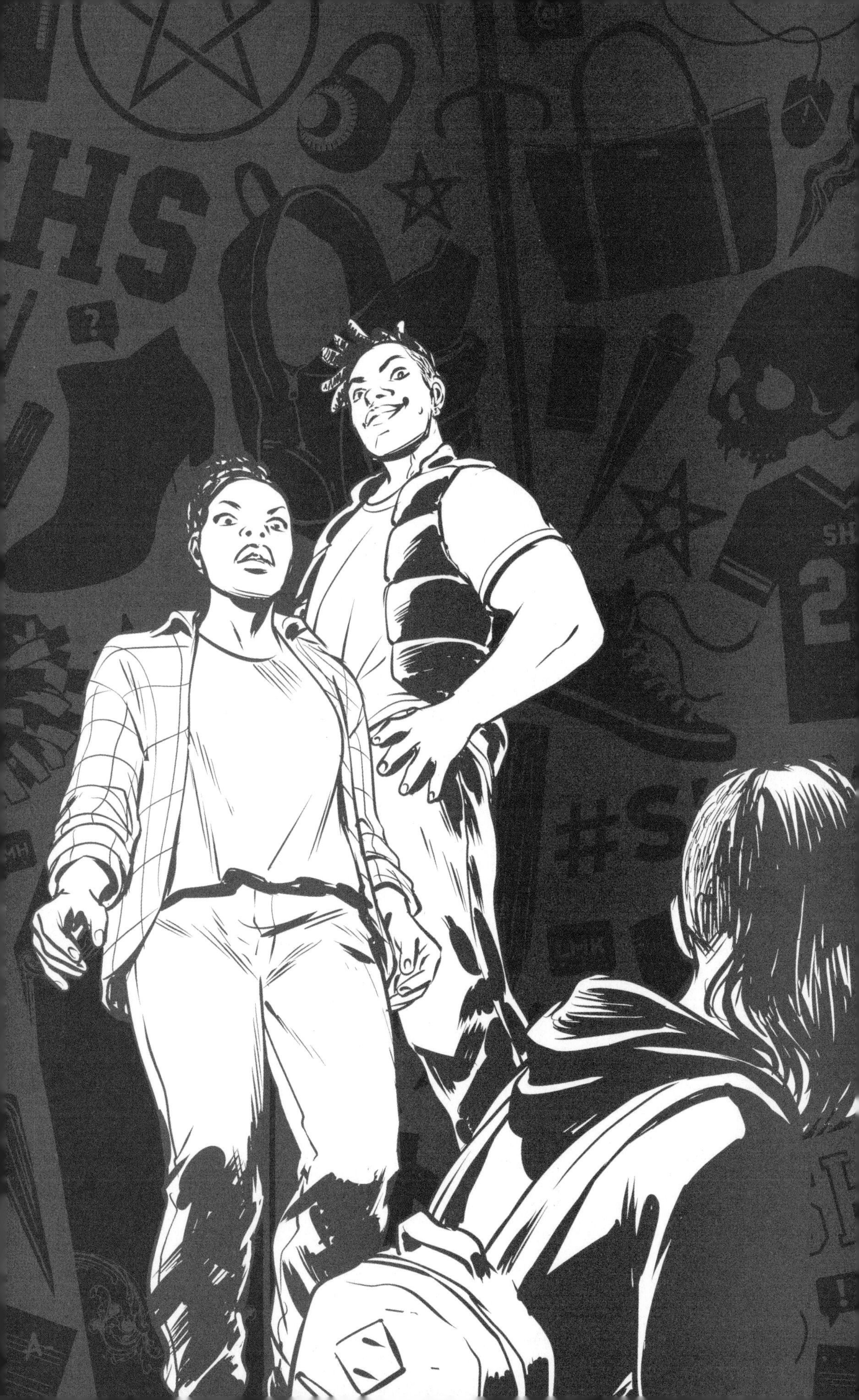

CHAPTER
ELEVEN

Issue Eleven Cover by **Marc Aspinall**

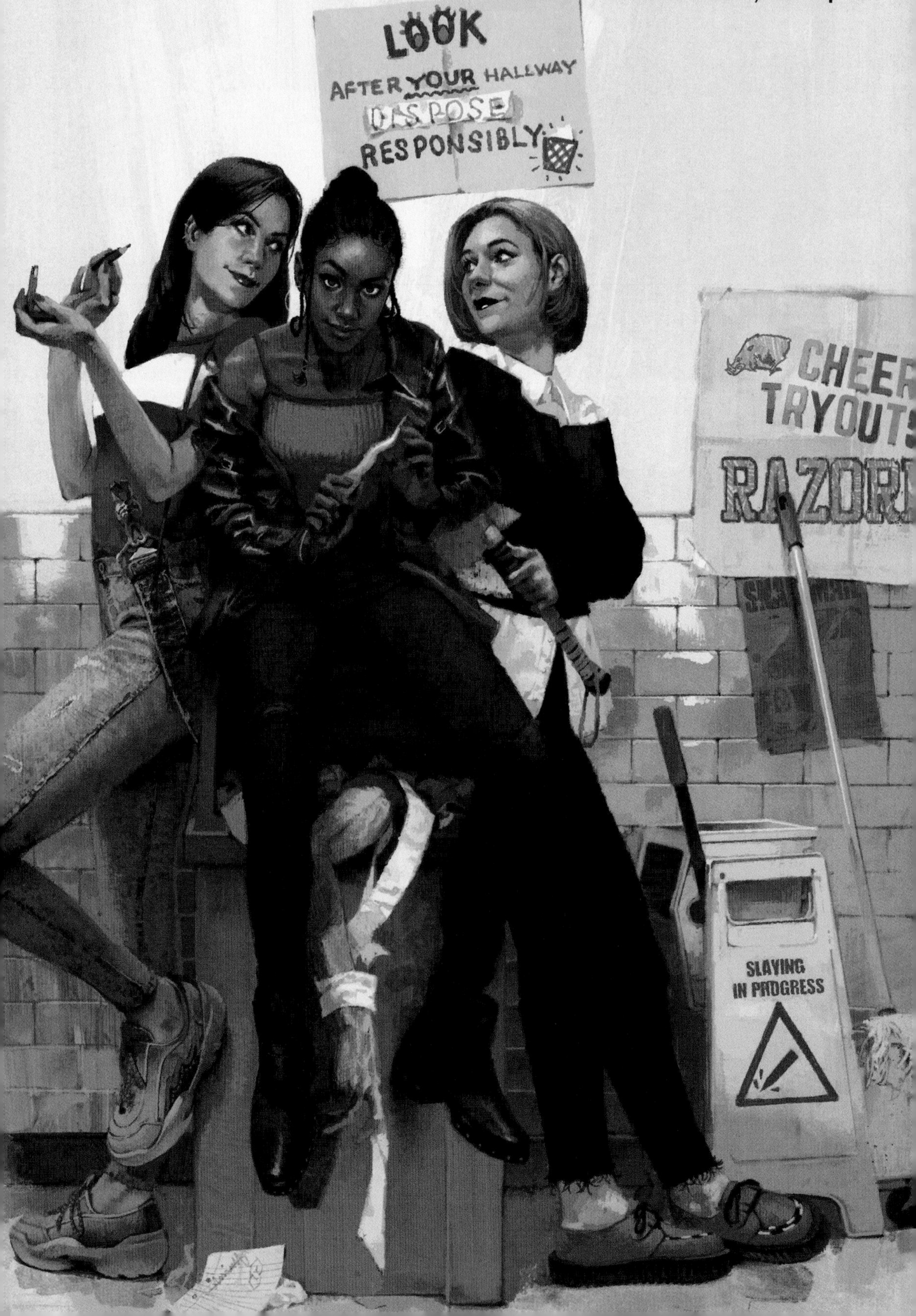
LOOK
AFTER YOUR HALLWAY
DISPOSE
RESPONSIBLY
SLAYING
IN PROGRESS

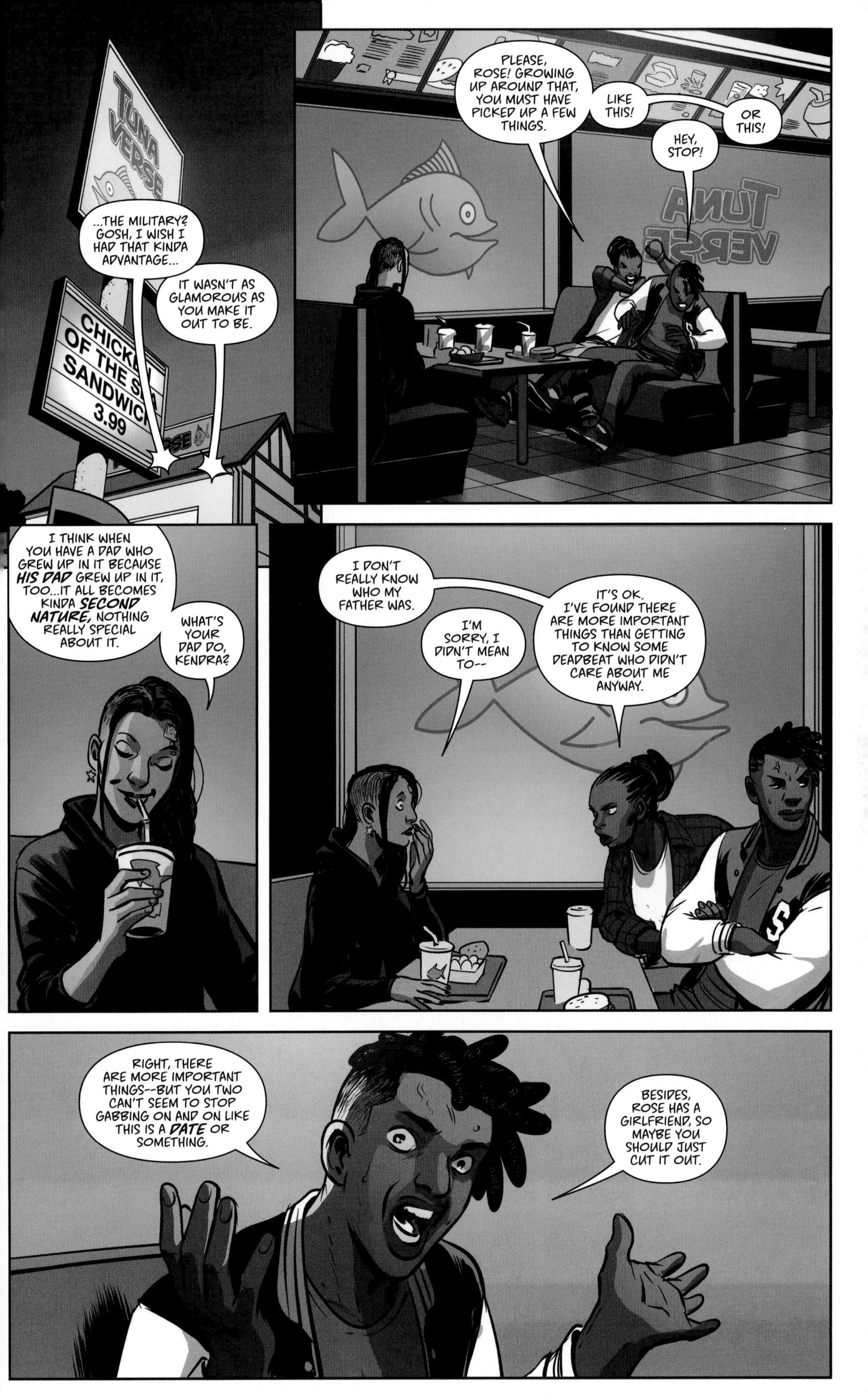
TUNA VERSE
...THE MILITARY? GOSH, I WISH I HAD THAT KINDA ADVANTAGE...
IT WASN'T AS GLAMOROUS AS YOU MAKE IT OUT TO BE.
PLEASE, ROSE! GROWING UP AROUND THAT, YOU MUST HAVE PICKED UP A FEW THINGS.
LIKE THIS!
OR THIS!
HEY, STOP!
I THINK WHEN YOU HAVE A DAD WHO GREW UP IN IT BECAUSE HIS DAD GREW UP IN IT, TOO...IT ALL BECOMES KINDA SECOND NATURE, NOTHING REALLY SPECIAL ABOUT IT.
WHAT'S YOUR DAD DO, KENDRA?
I DON'T REALLY KNOW WHO MY FATHER WAS.
I'M SORRY, I DIDN'T MEAN TO--
IT'S OK. I'VE FOUND THERE ARE MORE IMPORTANT THINGS THAN GETTING TO KNOW SOME DEADBEAT WHO DIDN'T CARE ABOUT ME ANYWAY.
RIGHT, THERE ARE MORE IMPORTANT THINGS--BUT YOU TWO CAN'T SEEM TO STOP GABBING ON AND ON LIKE THIS IS A DATE OR SOMETHING.
BESIDES, ROSE HAS A GIRLFRIEND, SO MAYBE YOU SHOULD JUST CUT IT OUT.

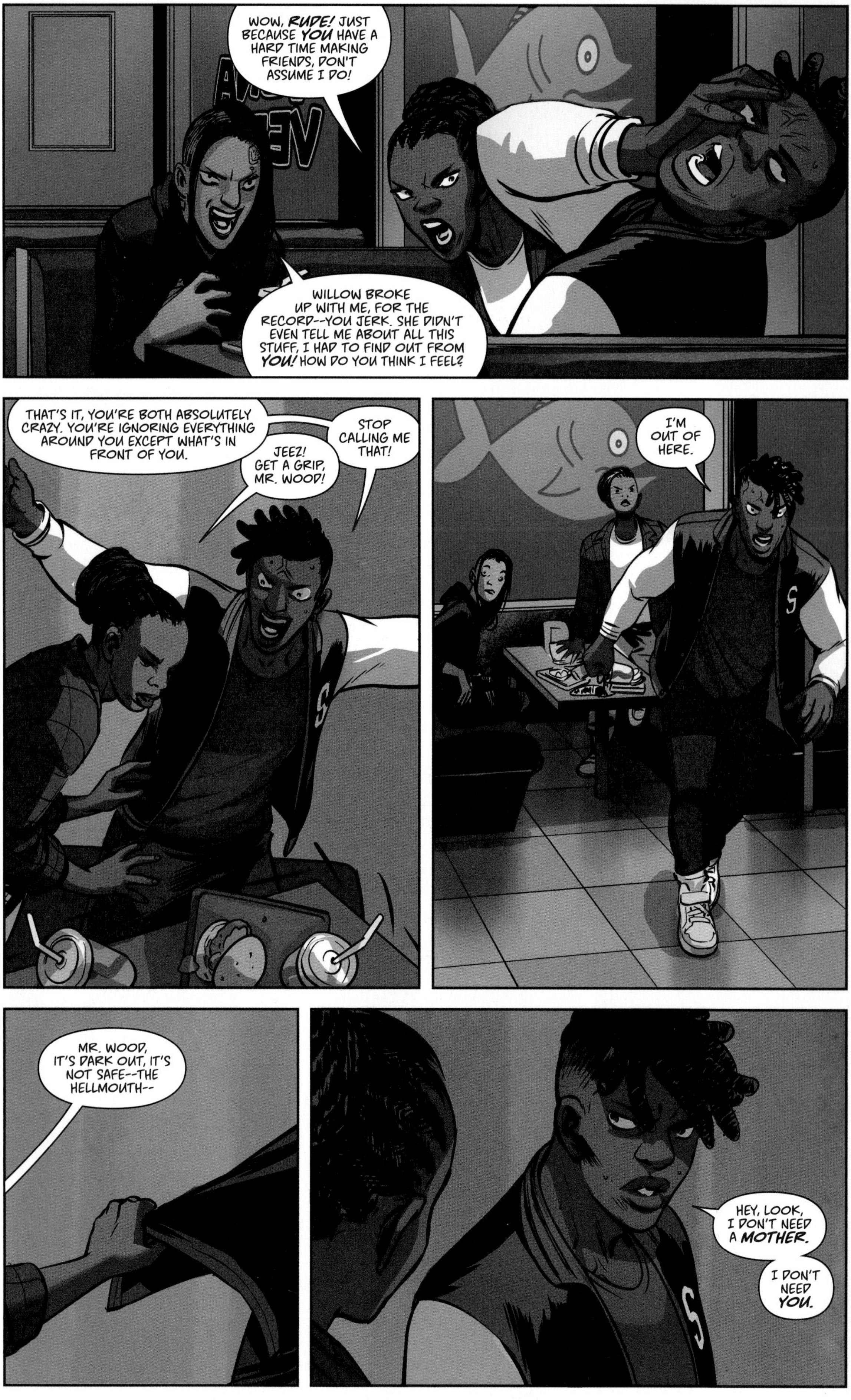
WOW, RUDE! JUST BECAUSE YOU HAVE A HARD TIME MAKING FRIENDS, DON'T ASSUME I DO!
WILLOW BROKE UP WITH ME, FOR THE RECORD--YOU JERK. SHE DIDN'T EVEN TELL ME ABOUT ALL THIS STUFF, I HAD TO FIND OUT FROM YOU! HOW DO YOU THINK I FEEL?
THAT'S IT, YOU'RE BOTH ABSOLUTELY CRAZY. YOU'RE IGNORING EVERYTHING AROUND YOU EXCEPT WHAT'S IN FRONT OF YOU.
STOP CALLING ME THAT!
JEEZ! GET A GRIP, MR. WOOD!
I'M OUT OF HERE.
MR. WOOD, IT'S DARK OUT, IT'S NOT SAFE--THE HELLMOUTH--
HEY, LOOK, I DON'T NEED A MOTHER.
I DON'T NEED YOU.

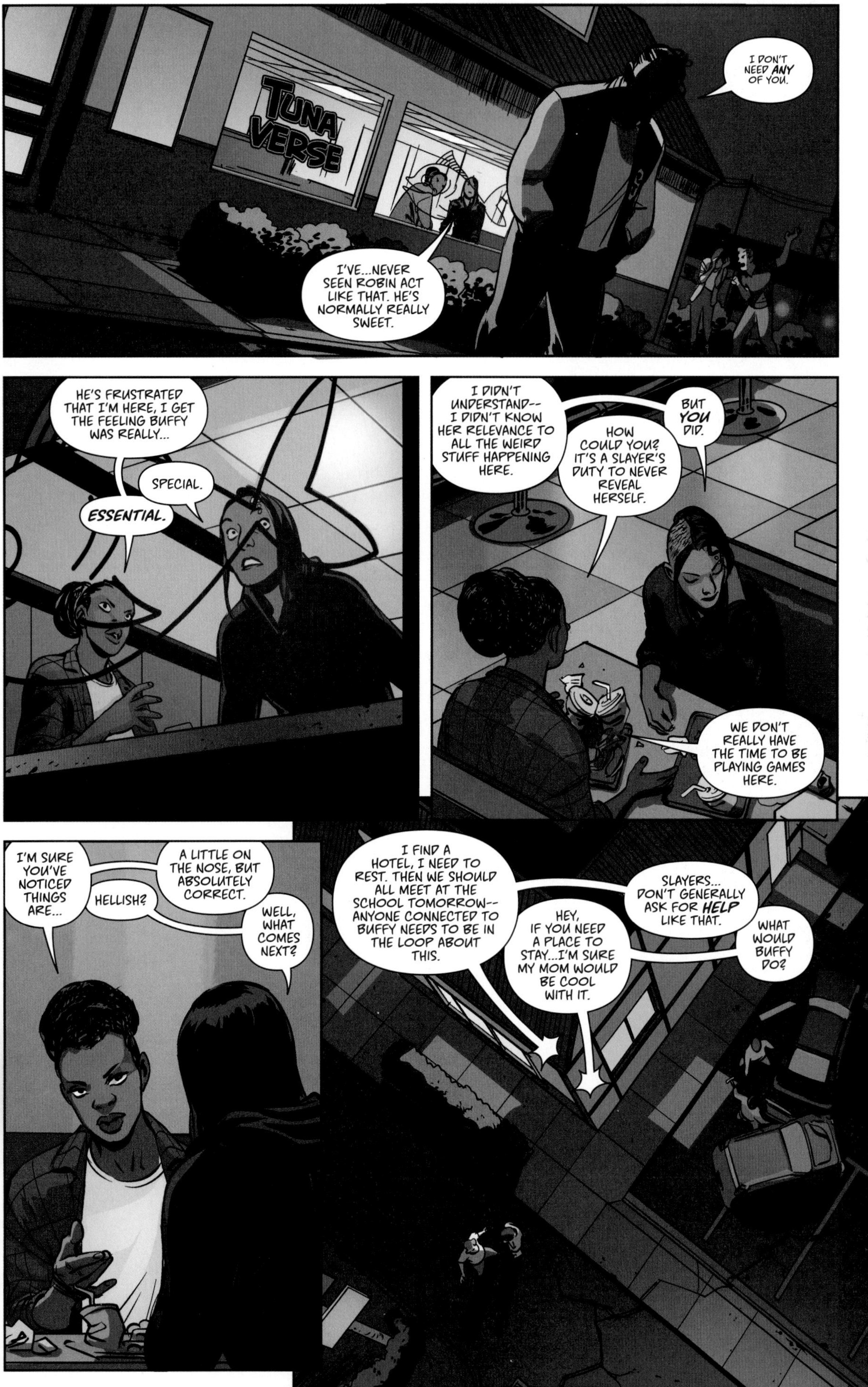
I DON'T NEED ANY OF YOU.
TUNA VERSE
I'VE...NEVER SEEN ROBIN ACT LIKE THAT. HE'S NORMALLY REALLY SWEET.
HE'S FRUSTRATED THAT I'M HERE, I GET THE FEELING BUFFY WAS REALLY...
SPECIAL.
ESSENTIAL.
I DIDN'T UNDERSTAND-- I DIDN'T KNOW HER RELEVANCE TO ALL THE WEIRD STUFF HAPPENING HERE.
BUT YOU DID.
HOW COULD YOU? IT'S A SLAYER'S DUTY TO NEVER REVEAL HERSELF.
WE DON'T REALLY HAVE THE TIME TO BE PLAYING GAMES HERE.
I'M SURE YOU'VE NOTICED THINGS ARE...
HELLISH?
A LITTLE ON THE NOSE, BUT ABSOLUTELY CORRECT.
WELL, WHAT COMES NEXT?
I FIND A HOTEL, I NEED TO REST. THEN WE SHOULD ALL MEET AT THE SCHOOL TOMORROW-- ANYONE CONNECTED TO BUFFY NEEDS TO BE IN THE LOOP ABOUT THIS.
SLAYERS... DON'T GENERALLY ASK FOR HELP LIKE THAT.
HEY, IF YOU NEED A PLACE TO STAY...I'M SURE MY MOM WOULD BE COOL WITH IT.
WHAT WOULD BUFFY DO?

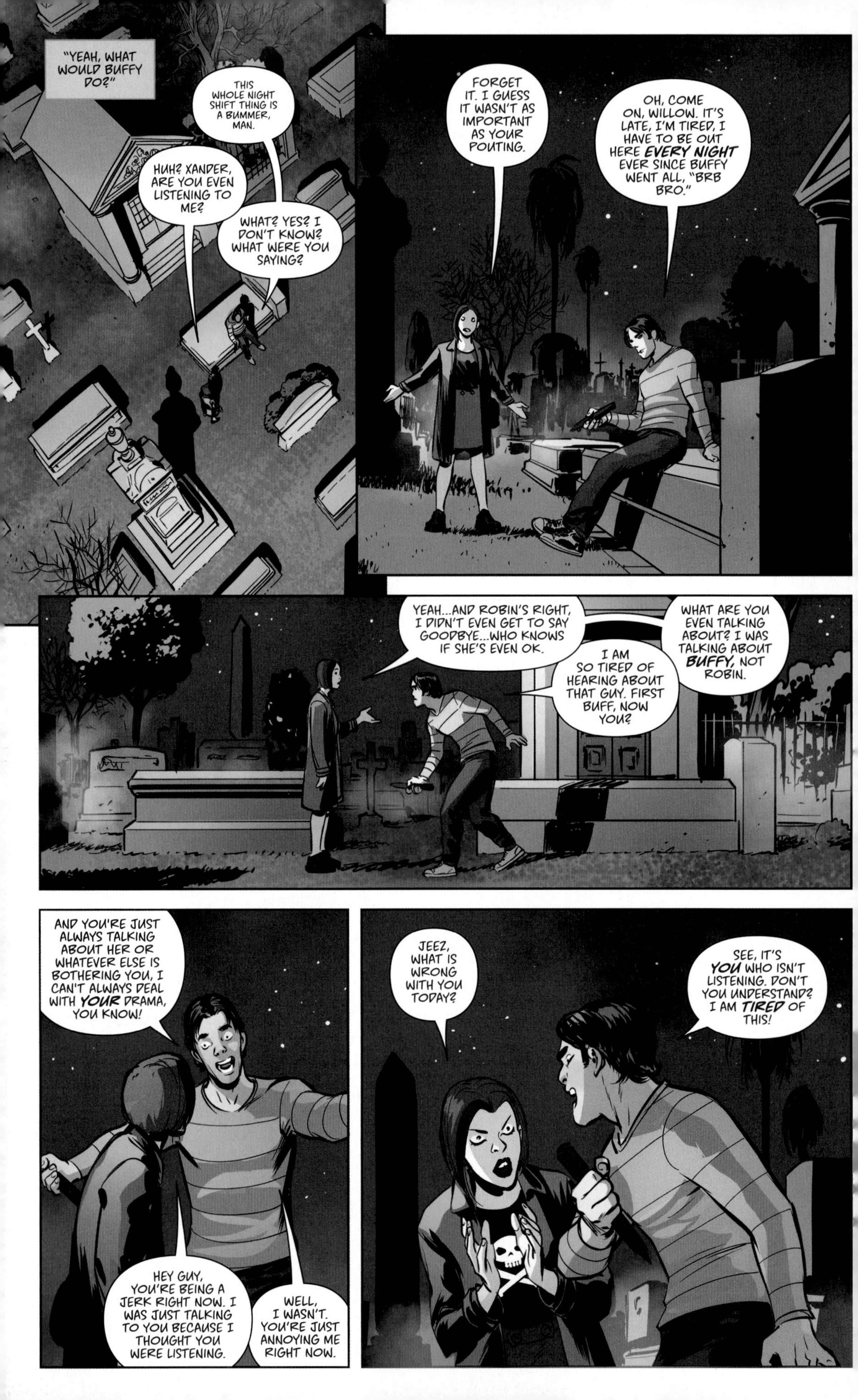
"YEAH, WHAT WOULD BUFFY DO?"
THIS WHOLE NIGHT SHIFT THING IS A BUMMER, MAN.
HUH? XANDER, ARE YOU EVEN LISTENING TO ME?
WHAT? YES? I DON'T KNOW? WHAT WERE YOU SAYING?
FORGET IT. I GUESS IT WASN'T AS IMPORTANT AS YOUR POUTING.
OH, COME ON, WILLOW. IT'S LATE, I'M TIRED, I HAVE TO BE OUT HERE **EVERY NIGHT** EVER SINCE BUFFY WENT ALL, "BRB BRO."
YEAH...AND ROBIN'S RIGHT, I DIDN'T EVEN GET TO SAY GOODBYE...WHO KNOWS IF SHE'S EVEN OK.
I AM SO TIRED OF HEARING ABOUT THAT GUY. FIRST BUFF, NOW YOU?
WHAT ARE YOU EVEN TALKING ABOUT? I WAS TALKING ABOUT **BUFFY,** NOT ROBIN.
AND YOU'RE JUST ALWAYS TALKING ABOUT HER OR WHATEVER ELSE IS BOTHERING YOU, I CAN'T ALWAYS DEAL WITH **YOUR** DRAMA, YOU KNOW!
HEY GUY, YOU'RE BEING A JERK RIGHT NOW. I WAS JUST TALKING TO YOU BECAUSE I THOUGHT YOU WERE LISTENING.
WELL, I WASN'T. YOU'RE JUST ANNOYING ME RIGHT NOW.
JEEZ, WHAT IS WRONG WITH YOU TODAY?
SEE, IT'S **YOU** WHO ISN'T LISTENING. DON'T YOU UNDERSTAND? I AM **TIRED** OF THIS!

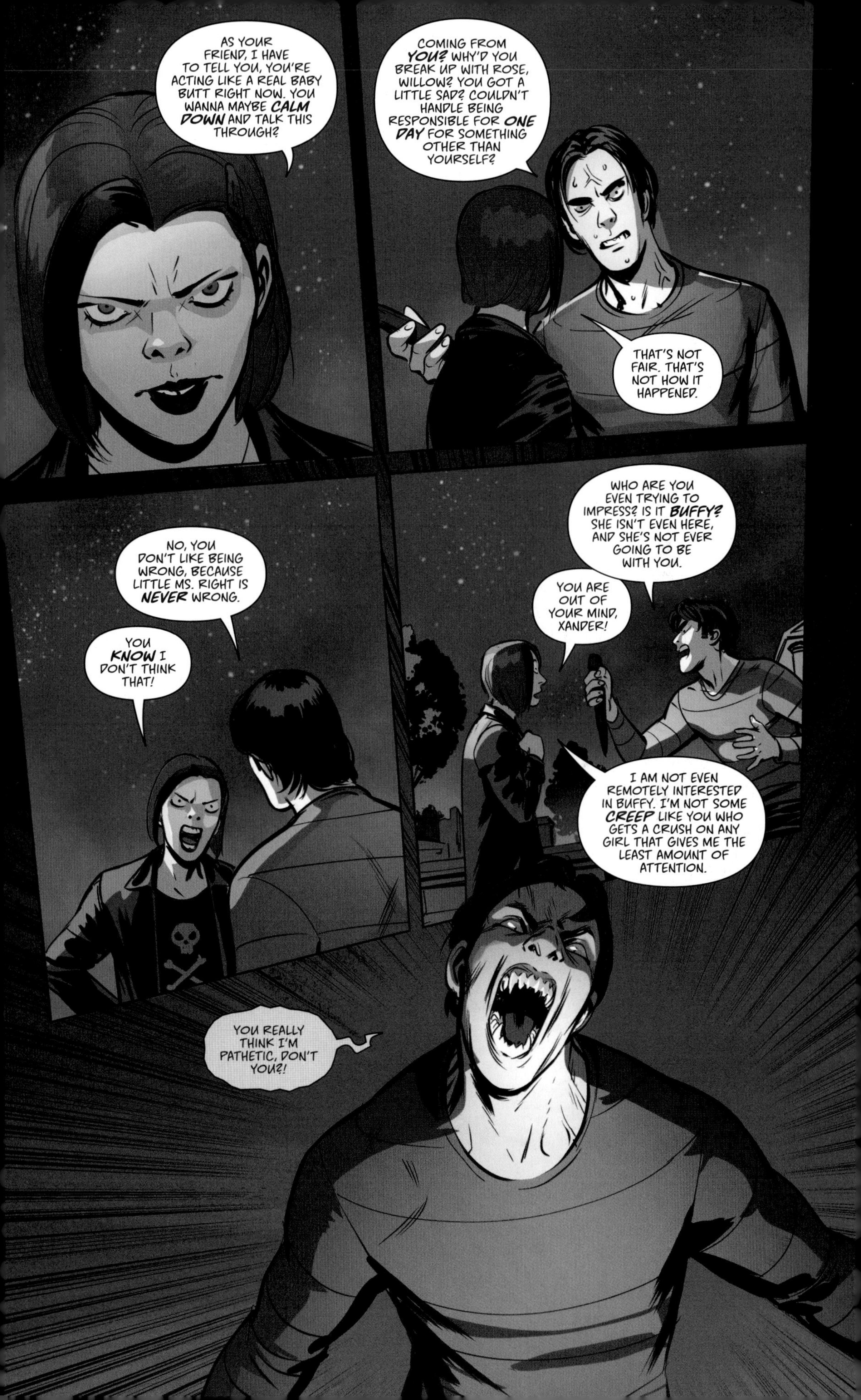
AS YOUR FRIEND, I HAVE TO TELL YOU, YOU'RE ACTING LIKE A REAL BABY BUTT RIGHT NOW. YOU WANNA MAYBE CALM DOWN AND TALK THIS THROUGH?
COMING FROM YOU? WHY'D YOU BREAK UP WITH ROSE, WILLOW? YOU GOT A LITTLE SAD? COULDN'T HANDLE BEING RESPONSIBLE FOR ONE DAY FOR SOMETHING OTHER THAN YOURSELF?
THAT'S NOT FAIR. THAT'S NOT HOW IT HAPPENED.
NO, YOU DON'T LIKE BEING WRONG, BECAUSE LITTLE MS. RIGHT IS NEVER WRONG.
YOU KNOW I DON'T THINK THAT!
WHO ARE YOU EVEN TRYING TO IMPRESS? IS IT BUFFY? SHE ISN'T EVEN HERE, AND SHE'S NOT EVER GOING TO BE WITH YOU.
YOU ARE OUT OF YOUR MIND, XANDER!
I AM NOT EVEN REMOTELY INTERESTED IN BUFFY. I'M NOT SOME CREEP LIKE YOU WHO GETS A CRUSH ON ANY GIRL THAT GIVES ME THE LEAST AMOUNT OF ATTENTION.
YOU REALLY THINK I'M PATHETIC, DON'T YOU?!

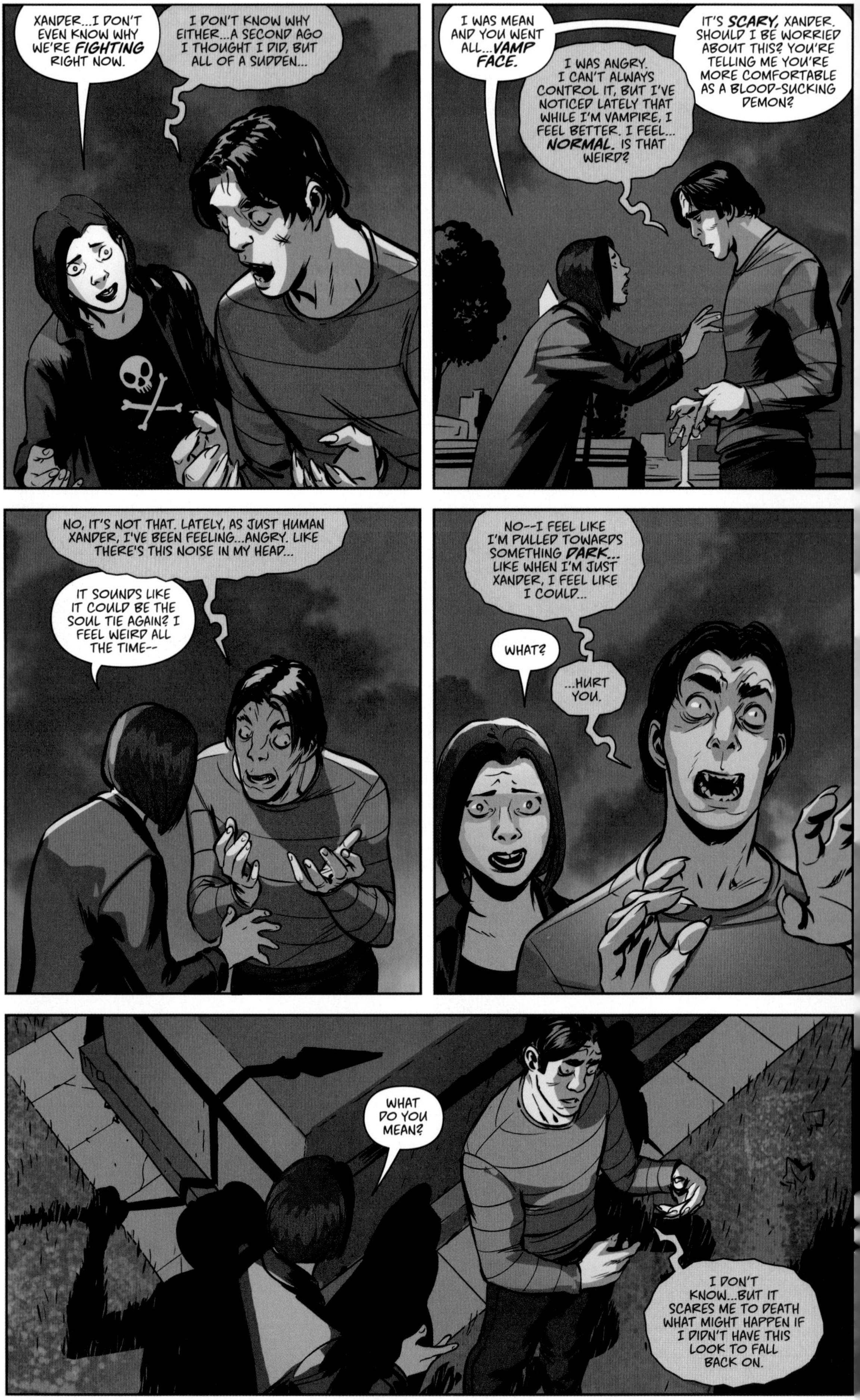
XANDER...I DON'T EVEN KNOW WHY WE'RE FIGHTING RIGHT NOW.
I DON'T KNOW WHY EITHER...A SECOND AGO I THOUGHT I DID, BUT ALL OF A SUDDEN...
I WAS MEAN AND YOU WENT ALL...VAMP FACE.
I WAS ANGRY. I CAN'T ALWAYS CONTROL IT, BUT I'VE NOTICED LATELY THAT WHILE I'M VAMPIRE, I FEEL BETTER. I FEEL... NORMAL. IS THAT WEIRD?
IT'S SCARY, XANDER. SHOULD I BE WORRIED ABOUT THIS? YOU'RE TELLING ME YOU'RE MORE COMFORTABLE AS A BLOOD-SUCKING DEMON?
NO, IT'S NOT THAT. LATELY, AS JUST HUMAN XANDER, I'VE BEEN FEELING...ANGRY. LIKE THERE'S THIS NOISE IN MY HEAD...
IT SOUNDS LIKE IT COULD BE THE SOUL TIE AGAIN? I FEEL WEIRD ALL THE TIME--
NO--I FEEL LIKE I'M PULLED TOWARDS SOMETHING DARK... LIKE WHEN I'M JUST XANDER, I FEEL LIKE I COULD...
WHAT?
...HURT YOU.
WHAT DO YOU MEAN?
I DON'T KNOW...BUT IT SCARES ME TO DEATH WHAT MIGHT HAPPEN IF I DIDN'T HAVE THIS LOOK TO FALL BACK ON.

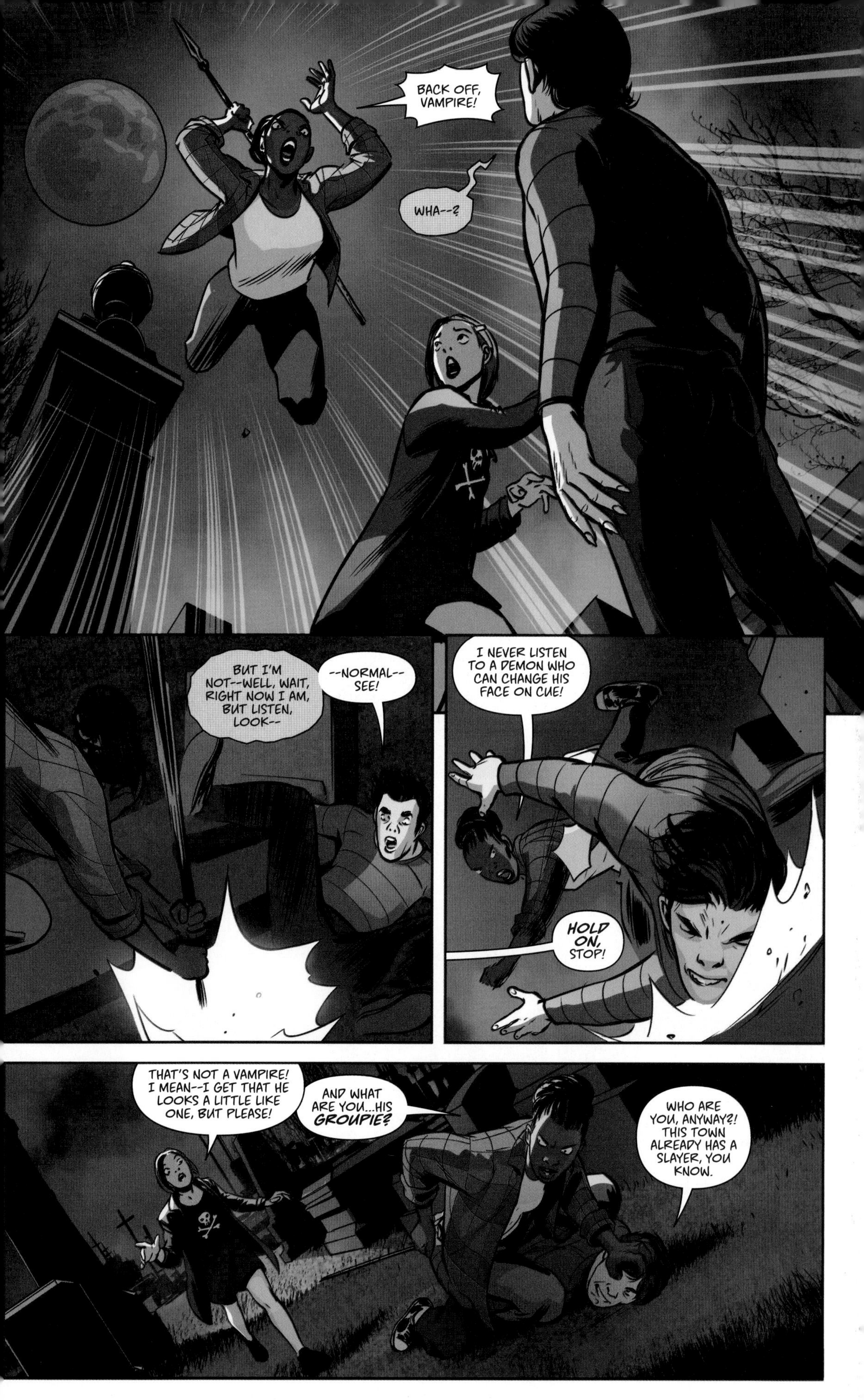
BACK OFF, VAMPIRE!
WHA--?
BUT I'M NOT--WELL, WAIT, RIGHT NOW I AM, BUT LISTEN, LOOK--
--NORMAL-- SEE!
I NEVER LISTEN TO A DEMON WHO CAN CHANGE HIS FACE ON CUE!
HOLD ON, STOP!
THAT'S NOT A VAMPIRE! I MEAN--I GET THAT HE LOOKS A LITTLE LIKE ONE, BUT PLEASE!
AND WHAT ARE YOU...HIS GROUPIE?
WHO ARE YOU, ANYWAY?! THIS TOWN ALREADY HAS A SLAYER, YOU KNOW.

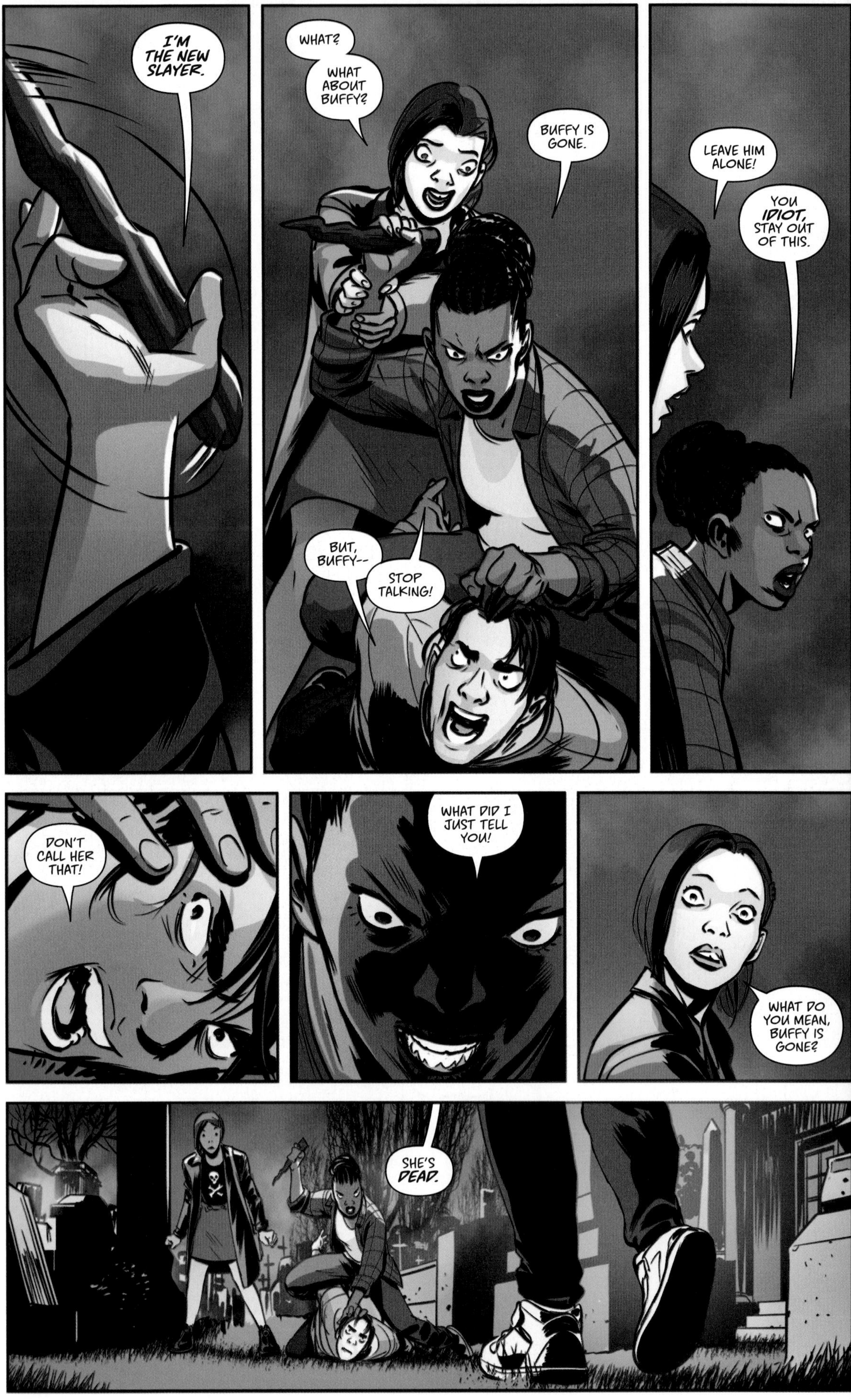
I'M THE NEW SLAYER.
WHAT?
WHAT ABOUT BUFFY?
BUFFY IS GONE.
BUT, BUFFY--
STOP TALKING!
LEAVE HIM ALONE!
YOU IDIOT, STAY OUT OF THIS.
DON'T CALL HER THAT!
WHAT DID I JUST TELL YOU!
WHAT DO YOU MEAN, BUFFY IS GONE?
SHE'S DEAD.

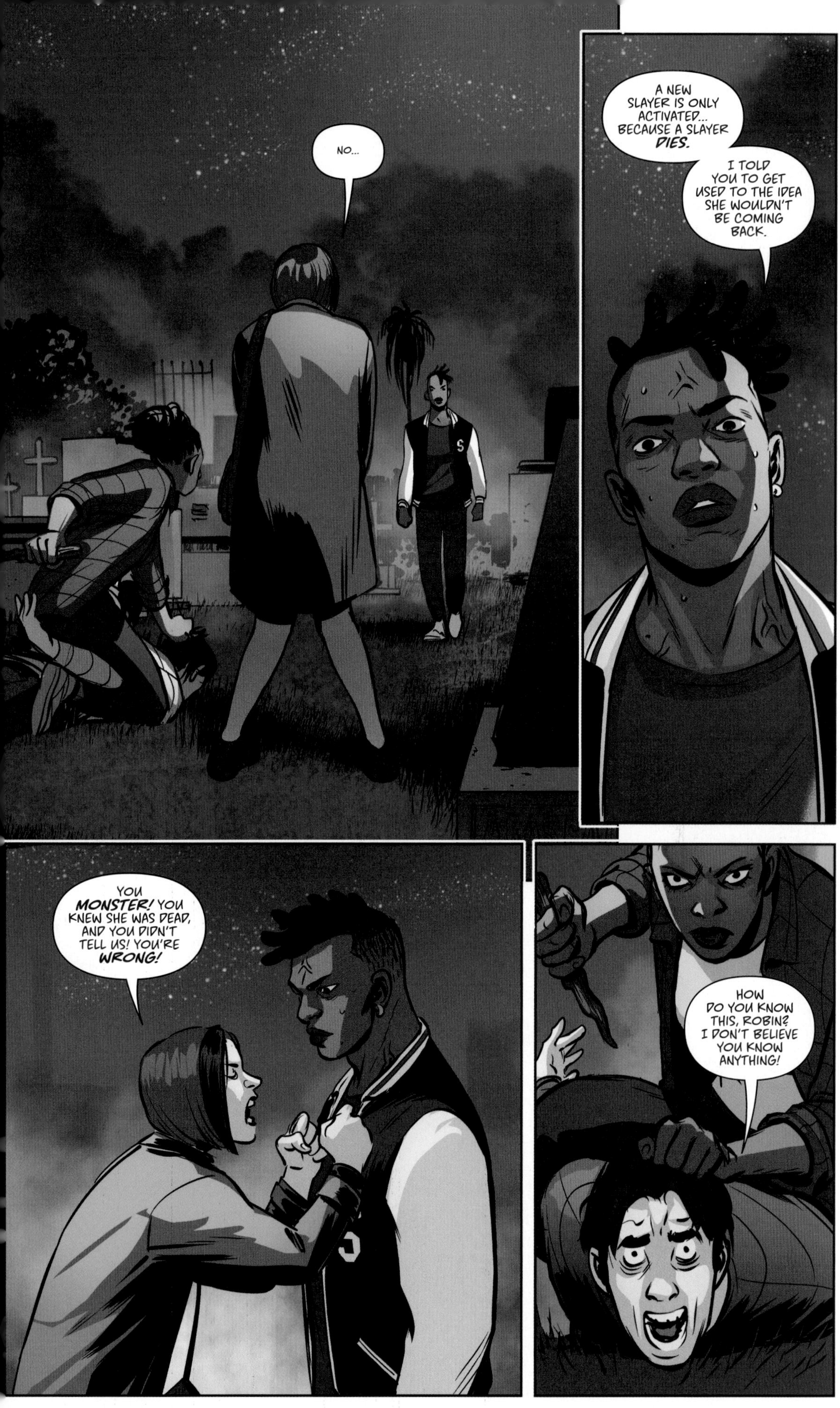
NO...
A NEW SLAYER IS ONLY ACTIVATED... BECAUSE A SLAYER DIES.
I TOLD YOU TO GET USED TO THE IDEA SHE WOULDN'T BE COMING BACK.
YOU MONSTER! YOU KNEW SHE WAS DEAD, AND YOU DIDN'T TELL US! YOU'RE WRONG!
HOW DO YOU KNOW THIS, ROBIN? I DON'T BELIEVE YOU KNOW ANYTHING!

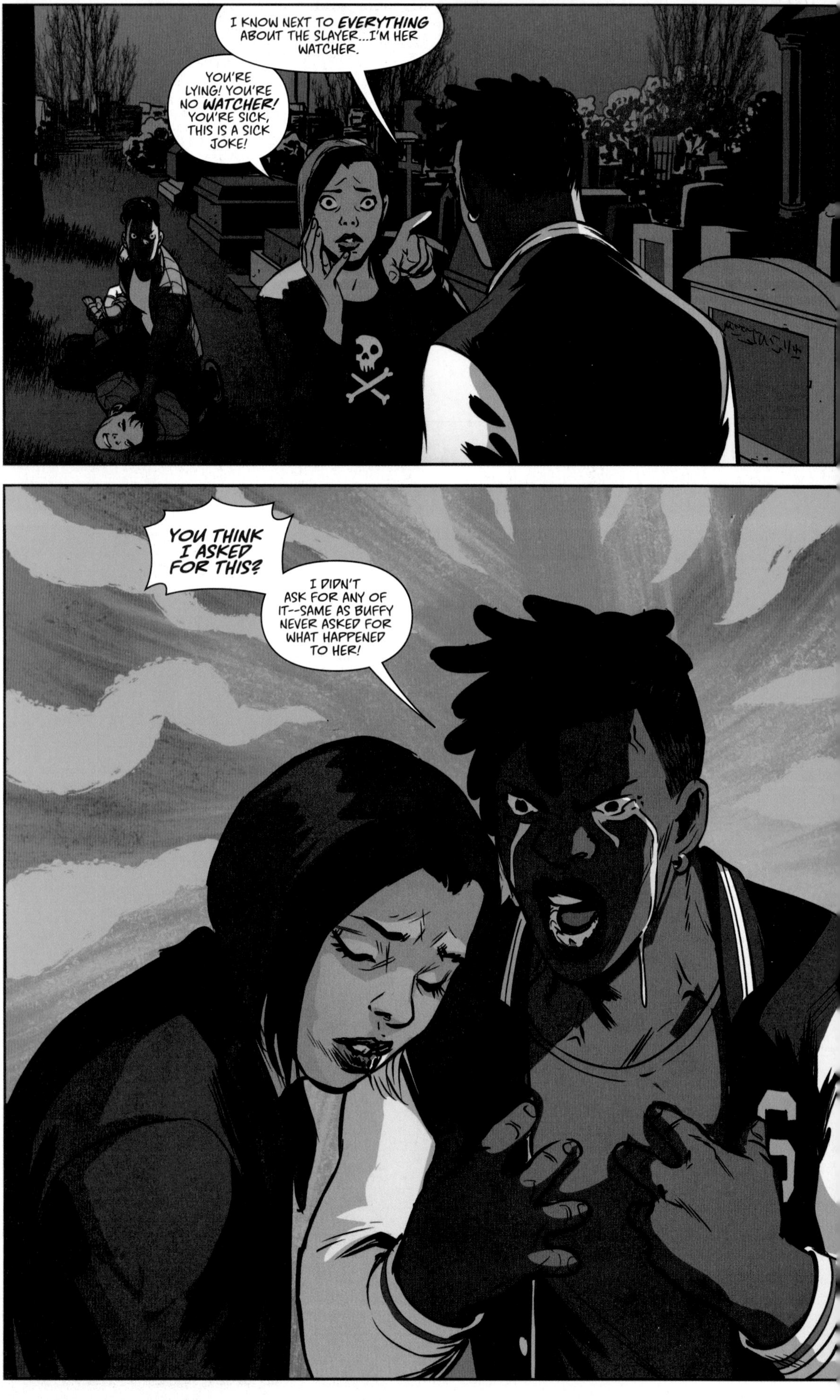
I KNOW NEXT TO EVERYTHING ABOUT THE SLAYER...I'M HER WATCHER.
YOU'RE LYING! YOU'RE NO WATCHER! YOU'RE SICK, THIS IS A SICK JOKE!
YOU THINK I ASKED FOR THIS?
I DIDN'T ASK FOR ANY OF IT--SAME AS BUFFY NEVER ASKED FOR WHAT HAPPENED TO HER!

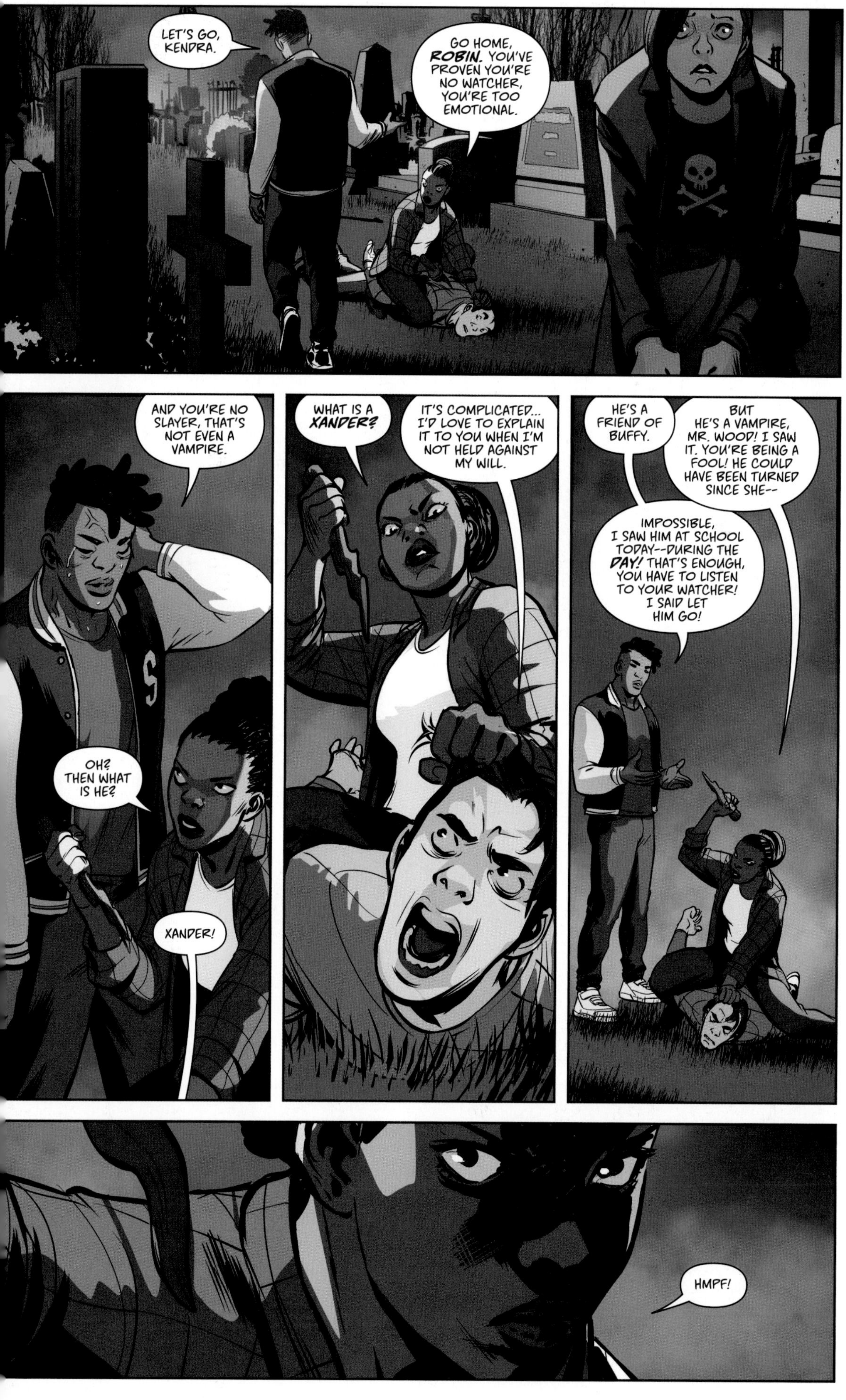
LET'S GO, KENDRA.
GO HOME, ROBIN. YOU'VE PROVEN YOU'RE NO WATCHER, YOU'RE TOO EMOTIONAL.
AND YOU'RE NO SLAYER, THAT'S NOT EVEN A VAMPIRE.
OH? THEN WHAT IS HE?
XANDER!
WHAT IS A XANDER?
IT'S COMPLICATED... I'D LOVE TO EXPLAIN IT TO YOU WHEN I'M NOT HELD AGAINST MY WILL.
HE'S A FRIEND OF BUFFY.
BUT HE'S A VAMPIRE, MR. WOOD! I SAW IT. YOU'RE BEING A FOOL! HE COULD HAVE BEEN TURNED SINCE SHE--
IMPOSSIBLE, I SAW HIM AT SCHOOL TODAY--DURING THE DAY! THAT'S ENOUGH, YOU HAVE TO LISTEN TO YOUR WATCHER! I SAID LET HIM GO!
HMPF!

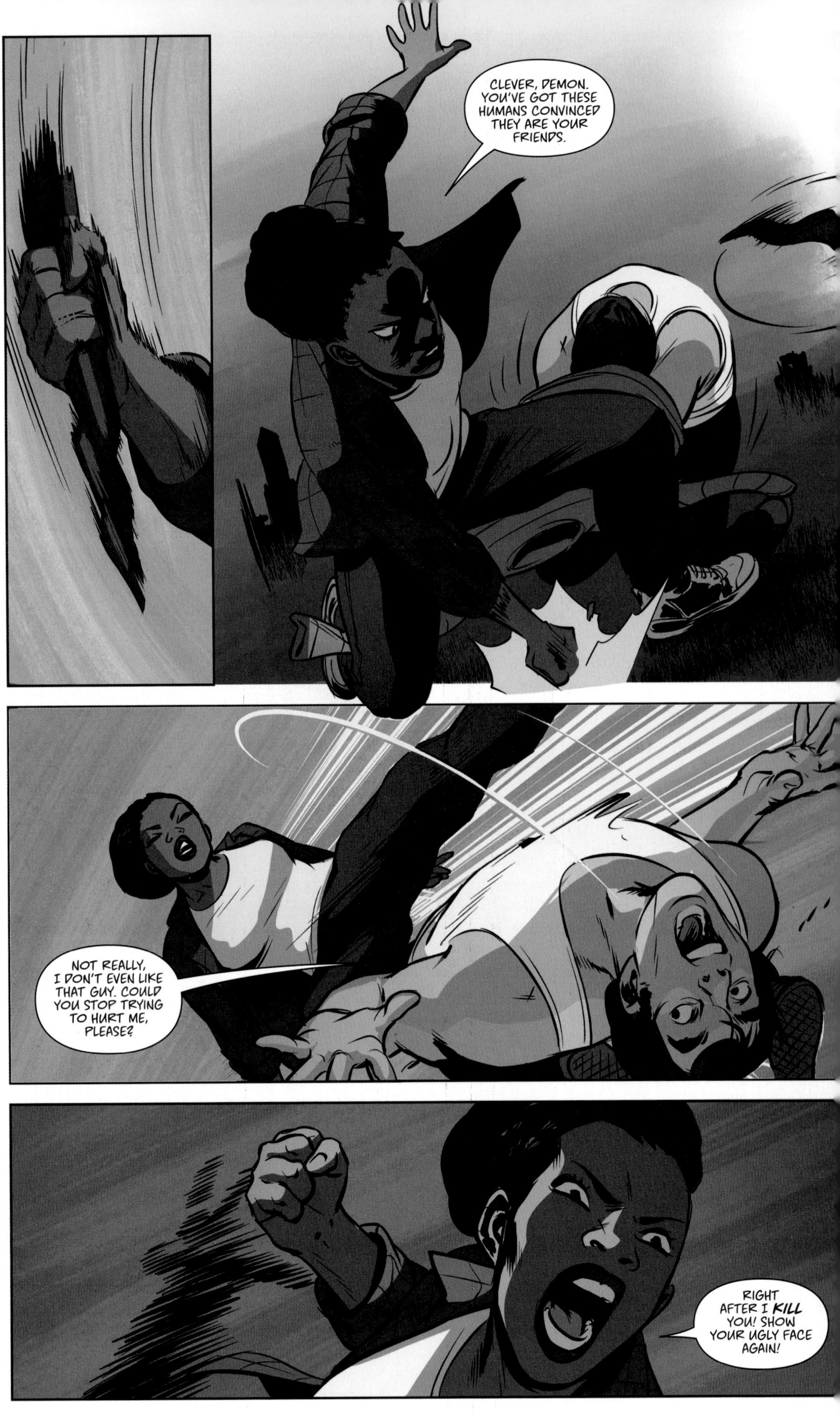
CLEVER, DEMON. YOU'VE GOT THESE HUMANS CONVINCED THEY ARE YOUR FRIENDS.
NOT REALLY, I DON'T EVEN LIKE THAT GUY. COULD YOU STOP TRYING TO HURT ME, PLEASE?
RIGHT AFTER I KILL YOU! SHOW YOUR UGLY FACE AGAIN!

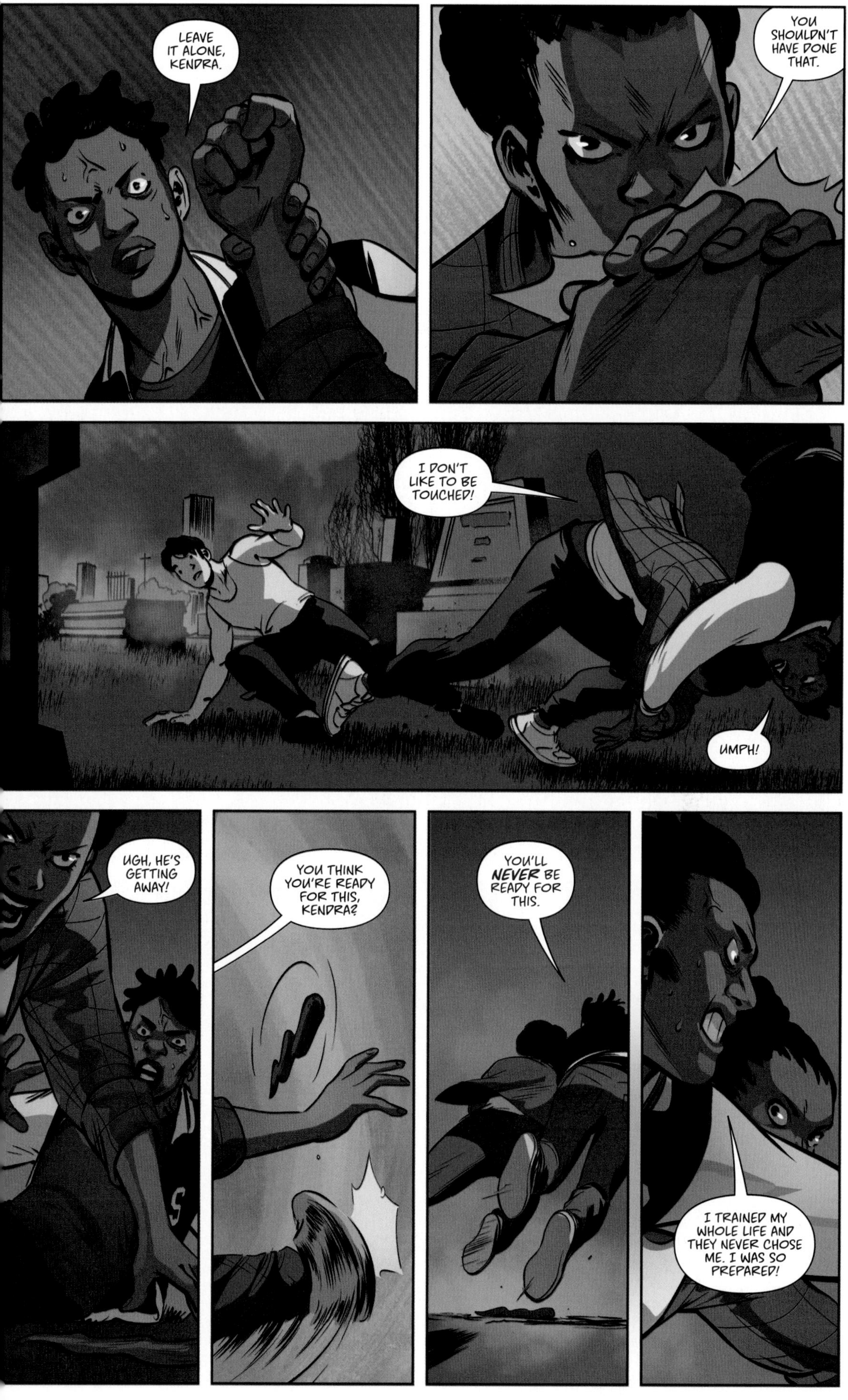
LEAVE IT ALONE, KENDRA.
YOU SHOULDN'T HAVE DONE THAT.
I DON'T LIKE TO BE TOUCHED!
UMPH!
UGH, HE'S GETTING AWAY!
YOU THINK YOU'RE READY FOR THIS, KENDRA?
YOU'LL NEVER BE READY FOR THIS.
I TRAINED MY WHOLE LIFE AND THEY NEVER CHOSE ME. I WAS SO PREPARED!

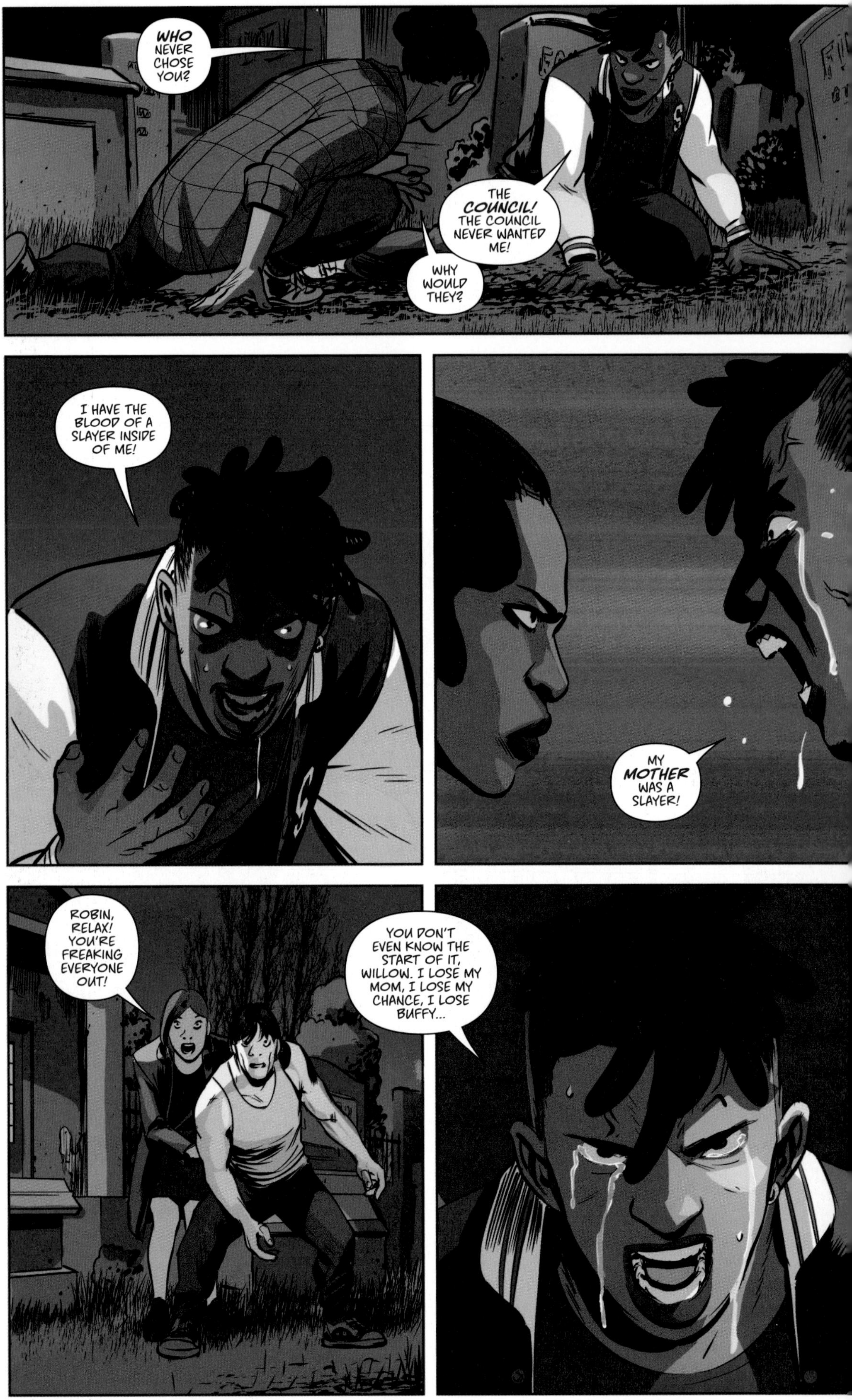
WHO NEVER CHOSE YOU?
THE COUNCIL! THE COUNCIL NEVER WANTED ME!
WHY WOULD THEY?
I HAVE THE BLOOD OF A SLAYER INSIDE OF ME!
MY MOTHER WAS A SLAYER!
ROBIN, RELAX! YOU'RE FREAKING EVERYONE OUT!
YOU DON'T EVEN KNOW THE START OF IT, WILLOW. I LOSE MY MOM, I LOSE MY CHANCE, I LOSE BUFFY...

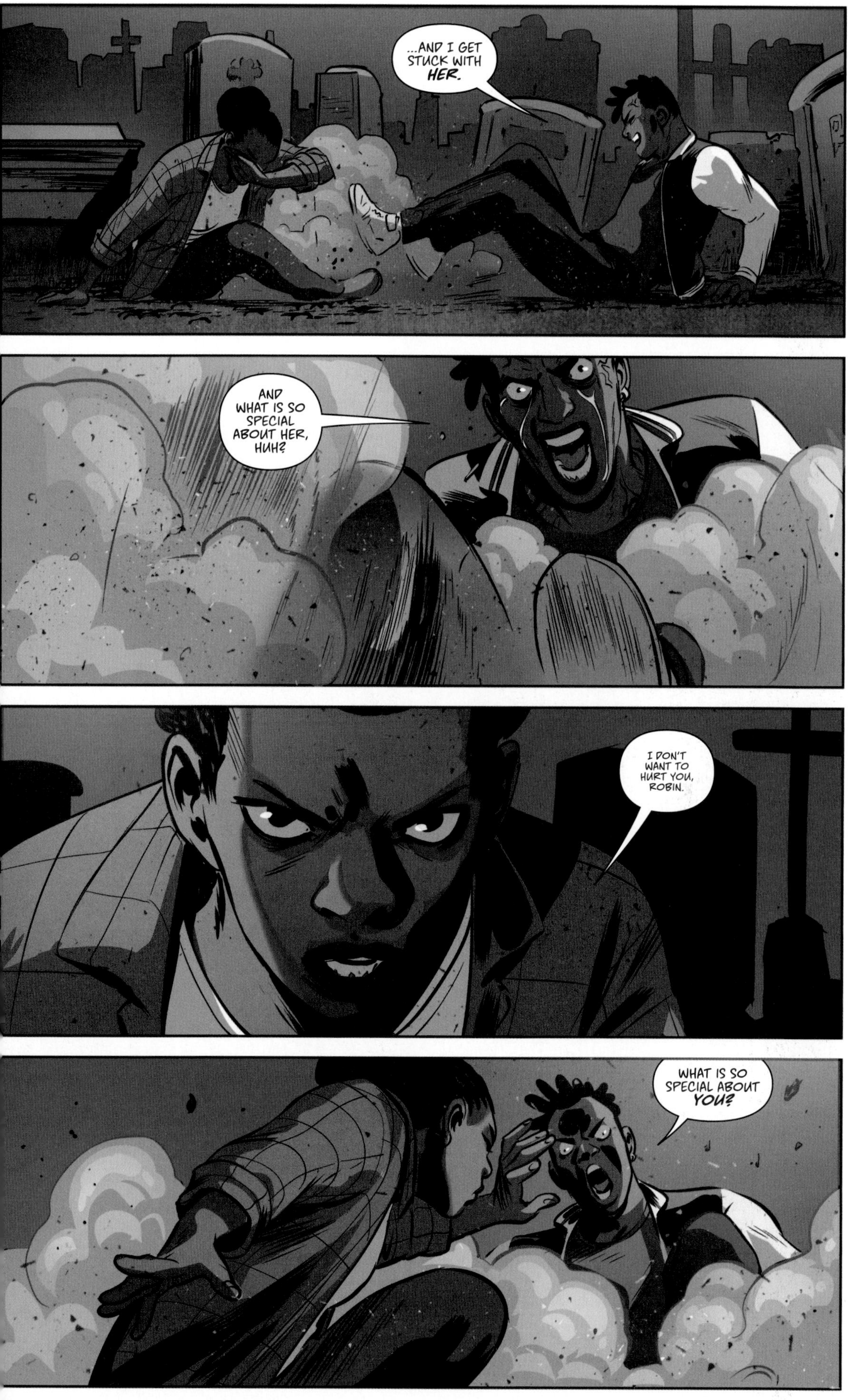
...AND I GET STUCK WITH HER.
AND WHAT IS SO SPECIAL ABOUT HER, HUH?
I DON'T WANT TO HURT YOU, ROBIN.
WHAT IS SO SPECIAL ABOUT YOU?

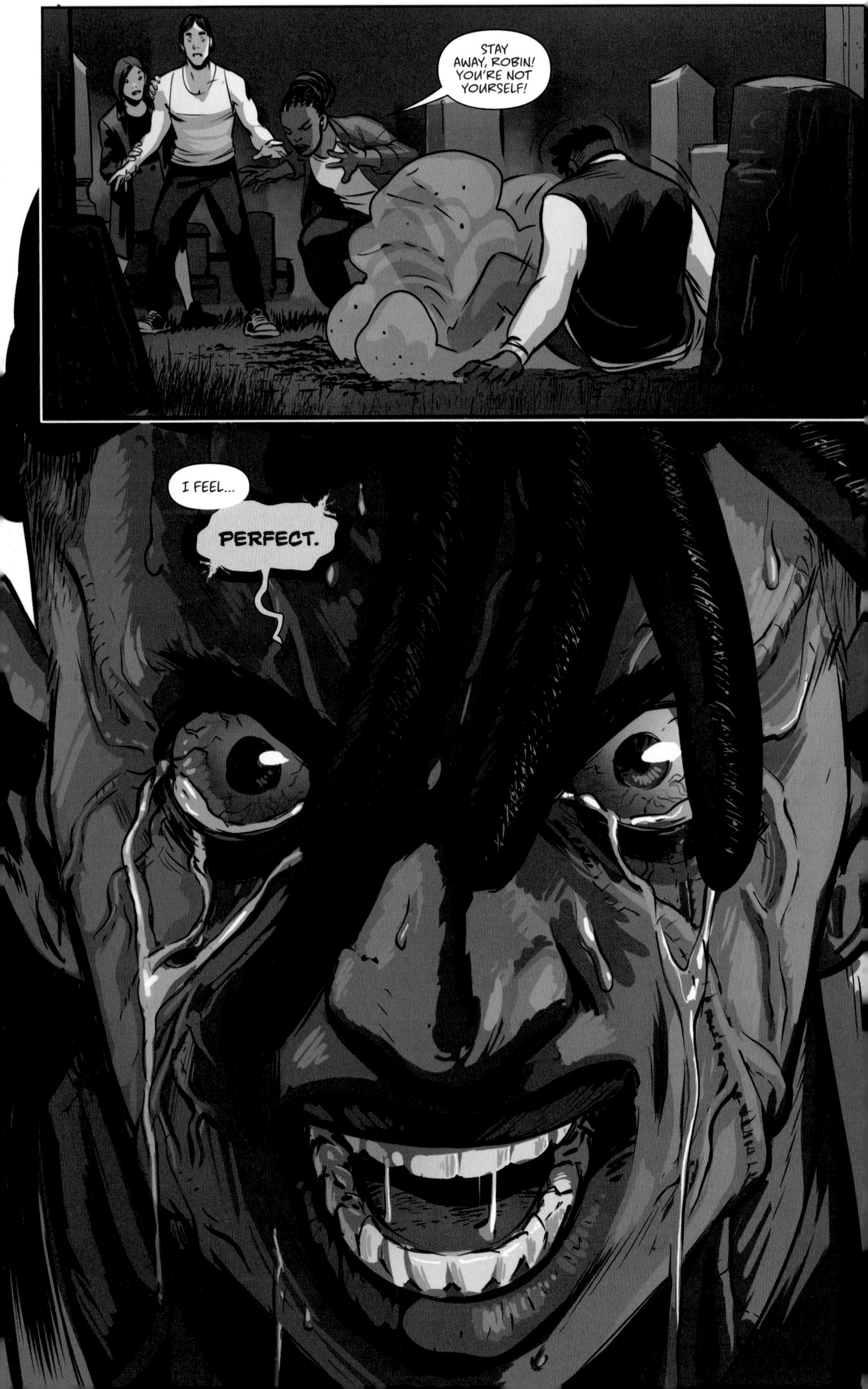
STAY AWAY, ROBIN! YOU'RE NOT YOURSELF!
I FEEL...
PERFECT.

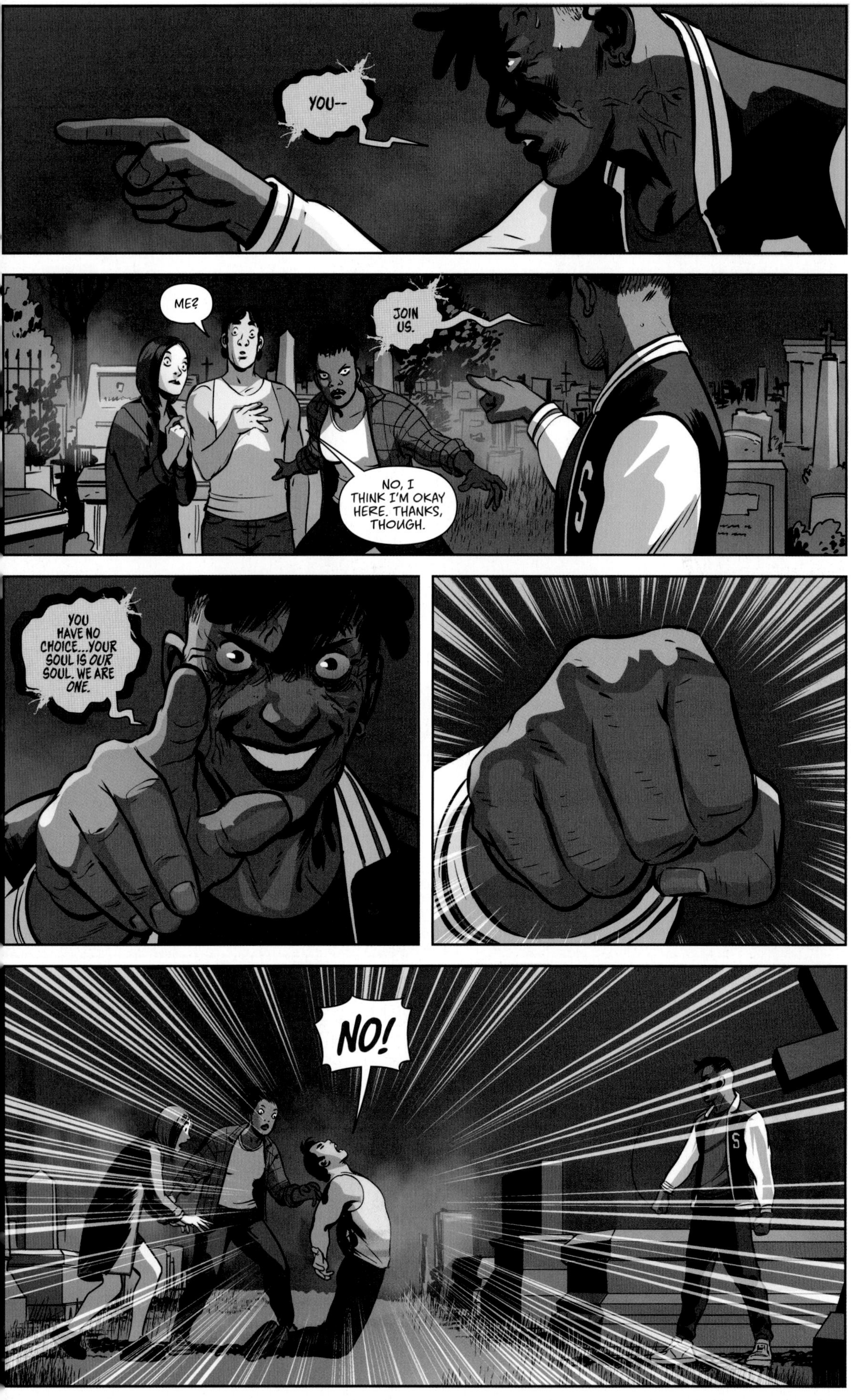
YOU--
ME?
JOIN US.
NO, I THINK I'M OKAY HERE. THANKS, THOUGH.
YOU HAVE NO CHOICE...YOUR SOUL IS OUR SOUL. WE ARE ONE.
NO!

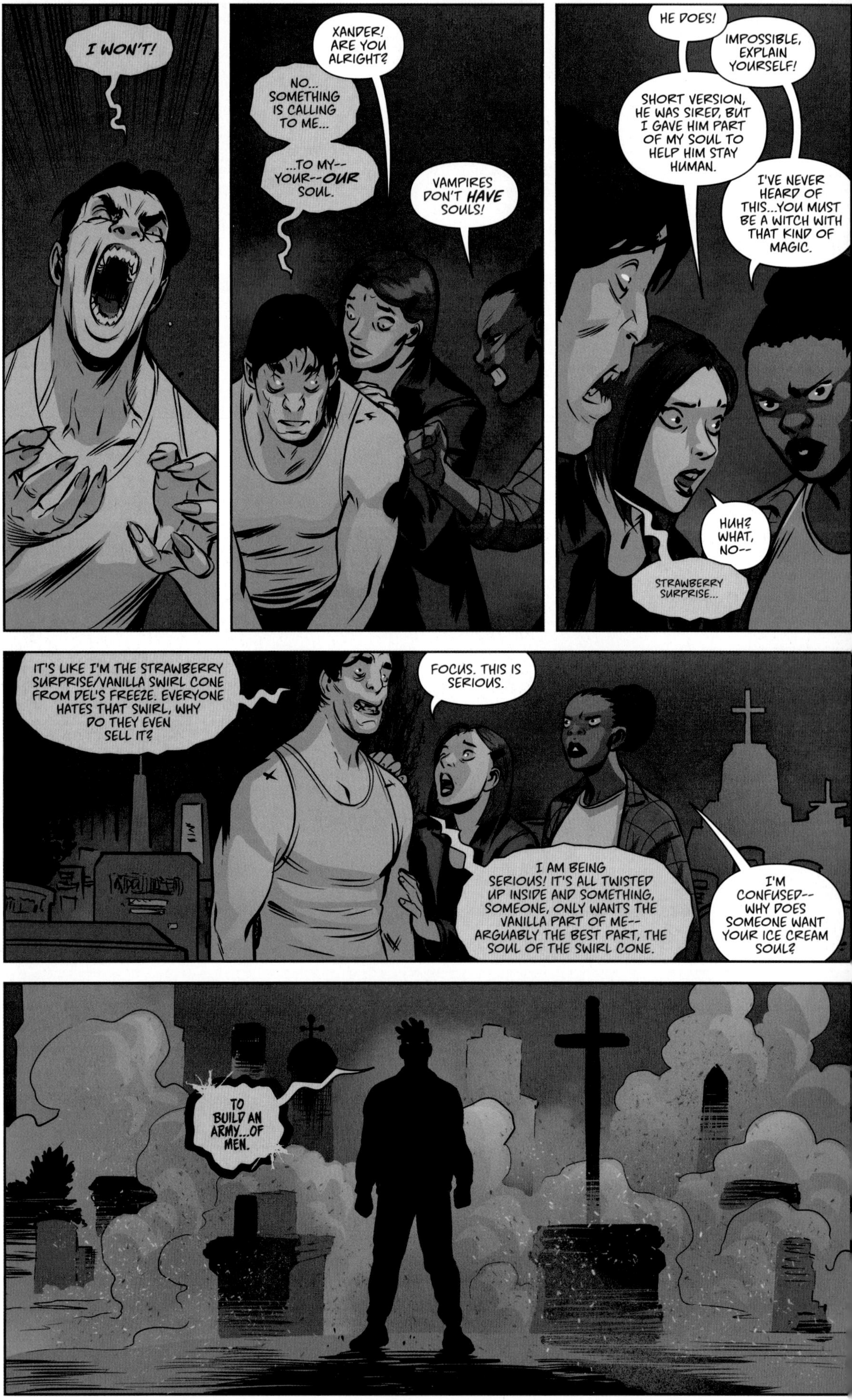
I WON'T!
XANDER! ARE YOU ALRIGHT?
NO... SOMETHING IS CALLING TO ME...
...TO MY--YOUR--OUR SOUL.
VAMPIRES DON'T HAVE SOULS!
HE DOES!
IMPOSSIBLE, EXPLAIN YOURSELF!
SHORT VERSION, HE WAS SIRED, BUT I GAVE HIM PART OF MY SOUL TO HELP HIM STAY HUMAN.
I'VE NEVER HEARD OF THIS...YOU MUST BE A WITCH WITH THAT KIND OF MAGIC.
HUH? WHAT, NO--
STRAWBERRY SURPRISE...
IT'S LIKE I'M THE STRAWBERRY SURPRISE/VANILLA SWIRL CONE FROM DEL'S FREEZE. EVERYONE HATES THAT SWIRL, WHY DO THEY EVEN SELL IT?
FOCUS. THIS IS SERIOUS.
I AM BEING SERIOUS! IT'S ALL TWISTED UP INSIDE AND SOMETHING, SOMEONE, ONLY WANTS THE VANILLA PART OF ME--ARGUABLY THE BEST PART, THE SOUL OF THE SWIRL CONE.
I'M CONFUSED--WHY DOES SOMEONE WANT YOUR ICE CREAM SOUL?
TO BUILD AN ARMY...OF MEN.

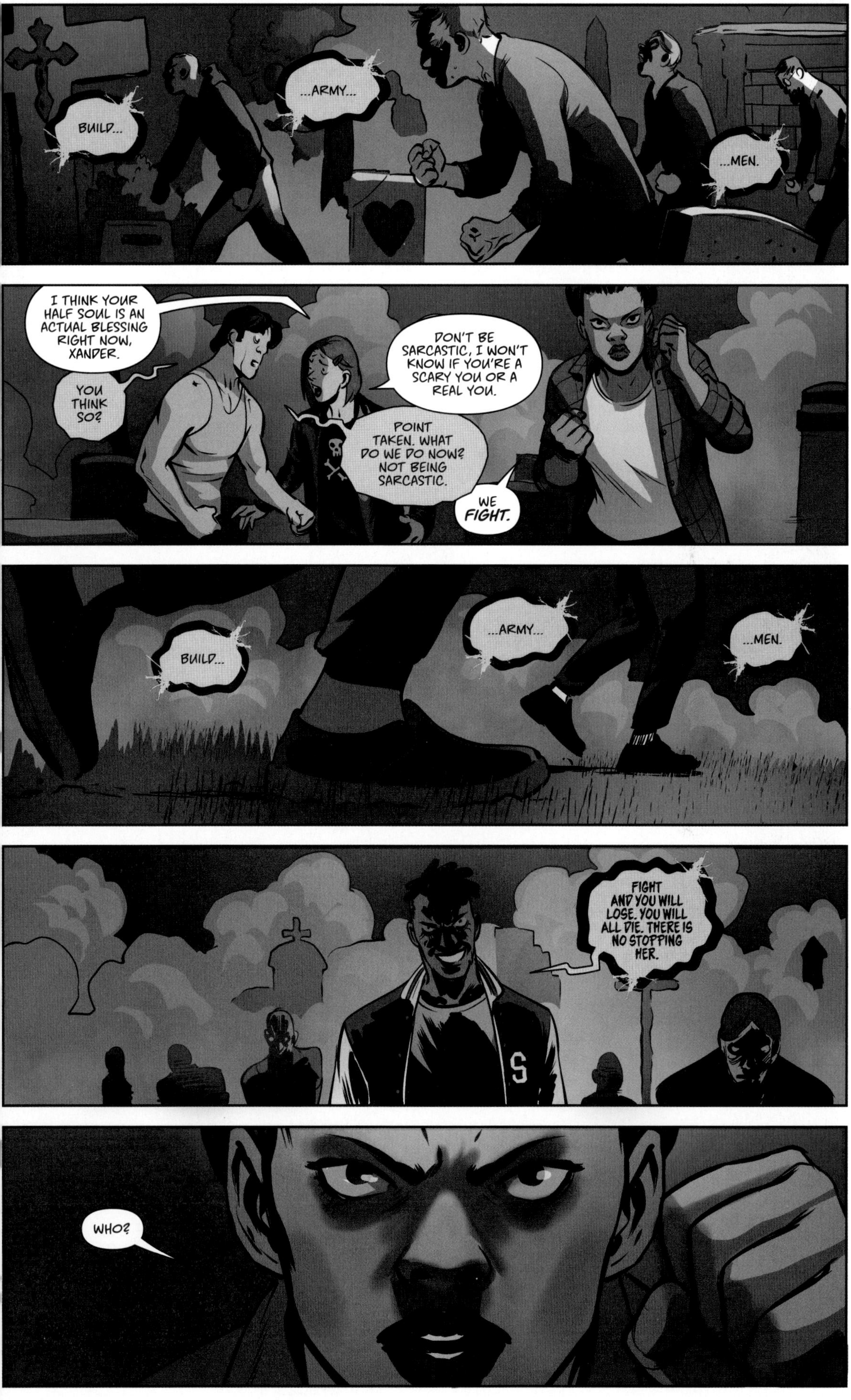
BUILD...
...ARMY...
...MEN.
I THINK YOUR HALF SOUL IS AN ACTUAL BLESSING RIGHT NOW, XANDER.
YOU THINK SO?
DON'T BE SARCASTIC, I WON'T KNOW IF YOU'RE A SCARY YOU OR A REAL YOU.
POINT TAKEN. WHAT DO WE DO NOW? NOT BEING SARCASTIC.
WE FIGHT.
BUILD...
...ARMY...
...MEN.
FIGHT AND YOU WILL LOSE. YOU WILL ALL DIE. THERE IS NO STOPPING HER.
WHO?

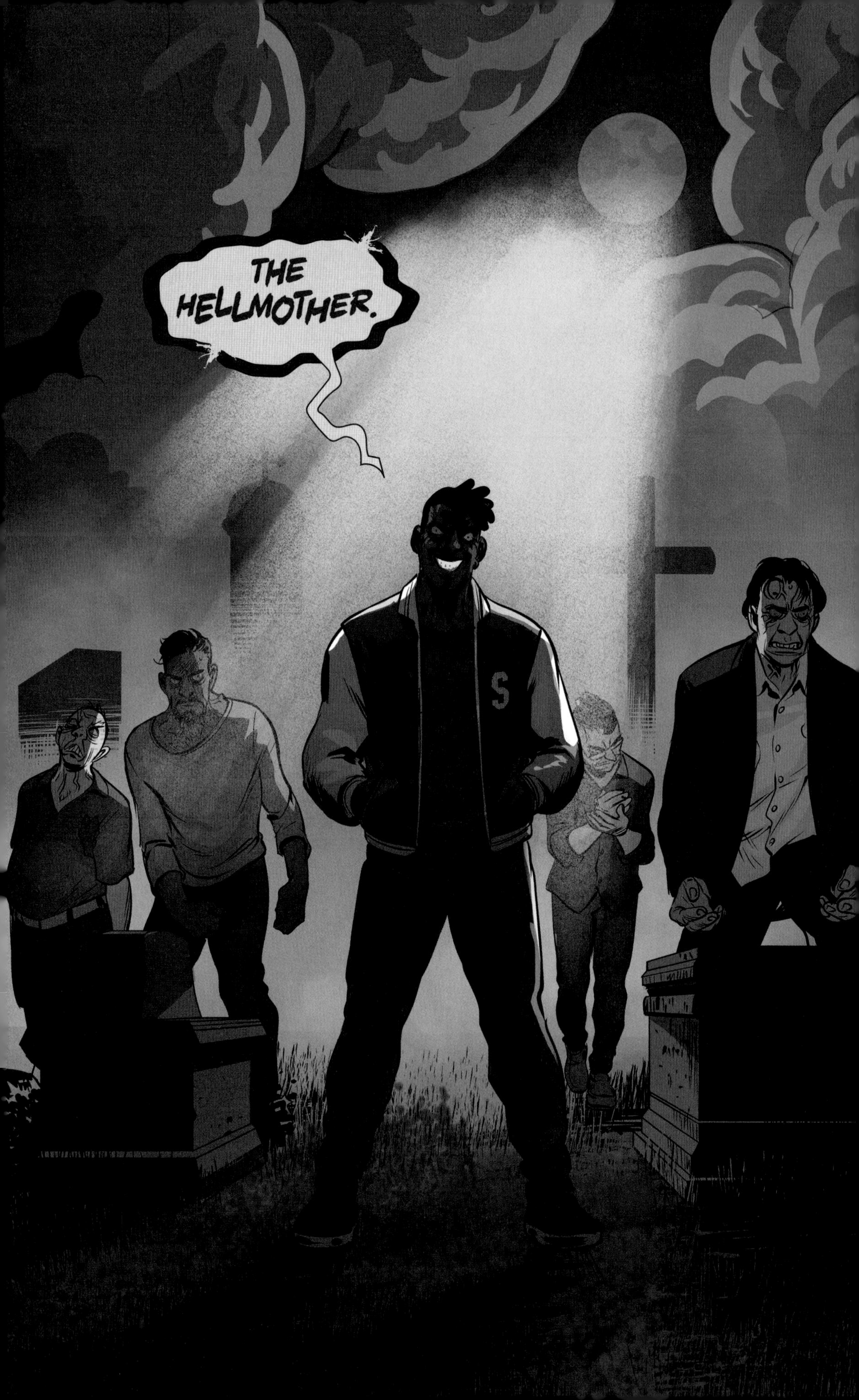
THE HELLMOTHER.

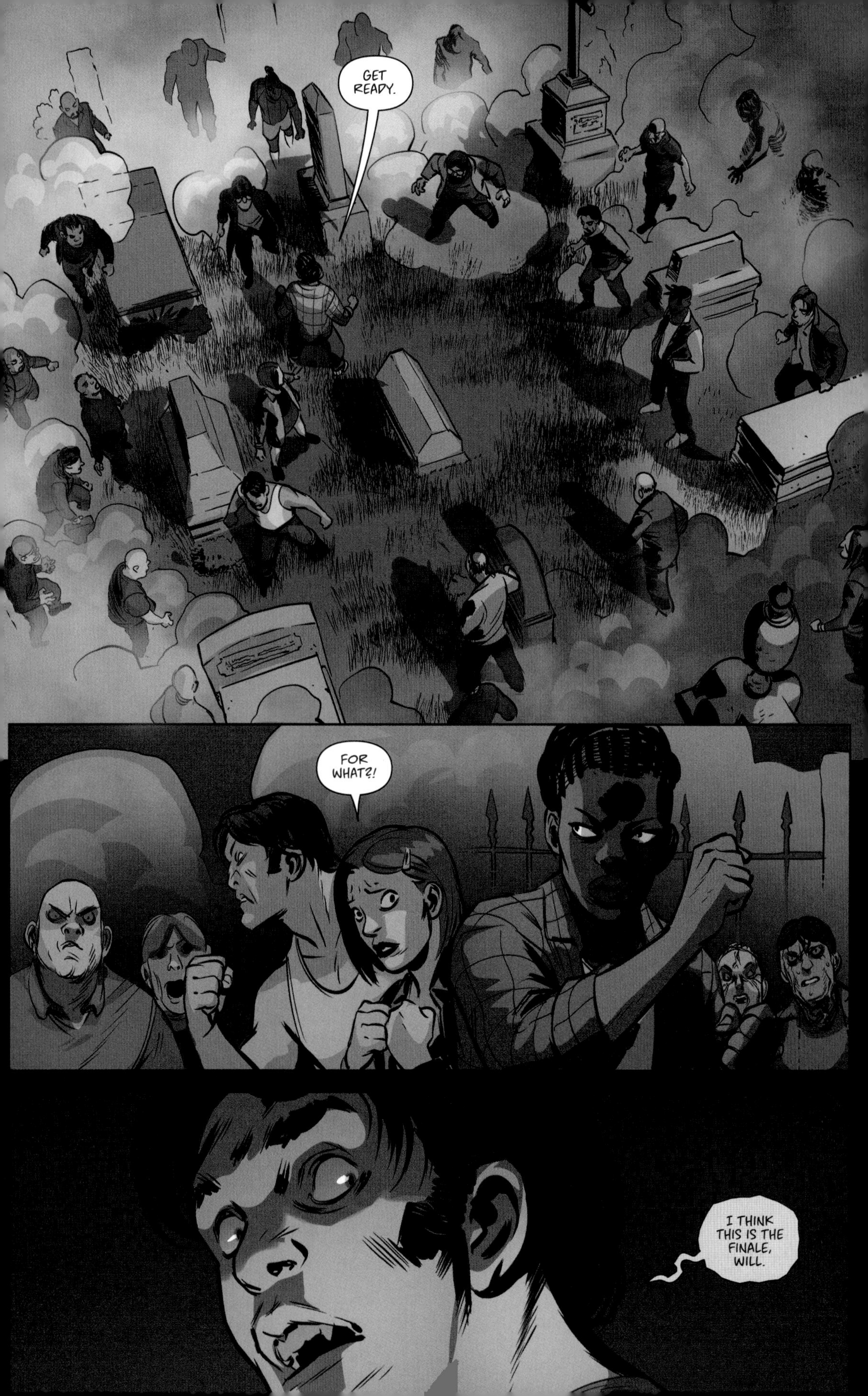
GET READY.
FOR WHAT?!
I THINK THIS IS THE FINALE, WILL.

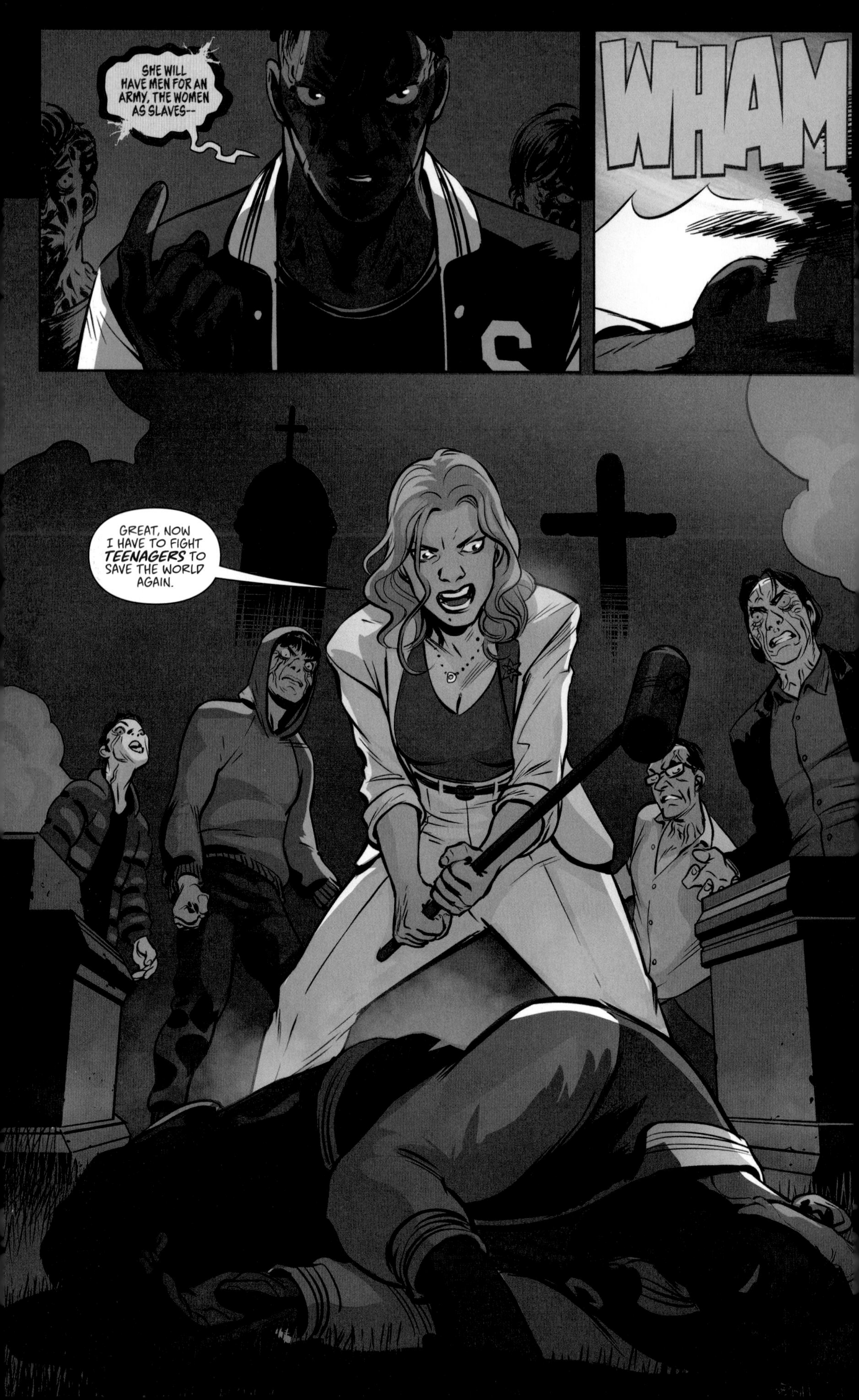
SHE WILL HAVE MEN FOR AN ARMY, THE WOMEN AS SLAVES--
WHAM
GREAT, NOW I HAVE TO FIGHT TEENAGERS TO SAVE THE WORLD AGAIN.

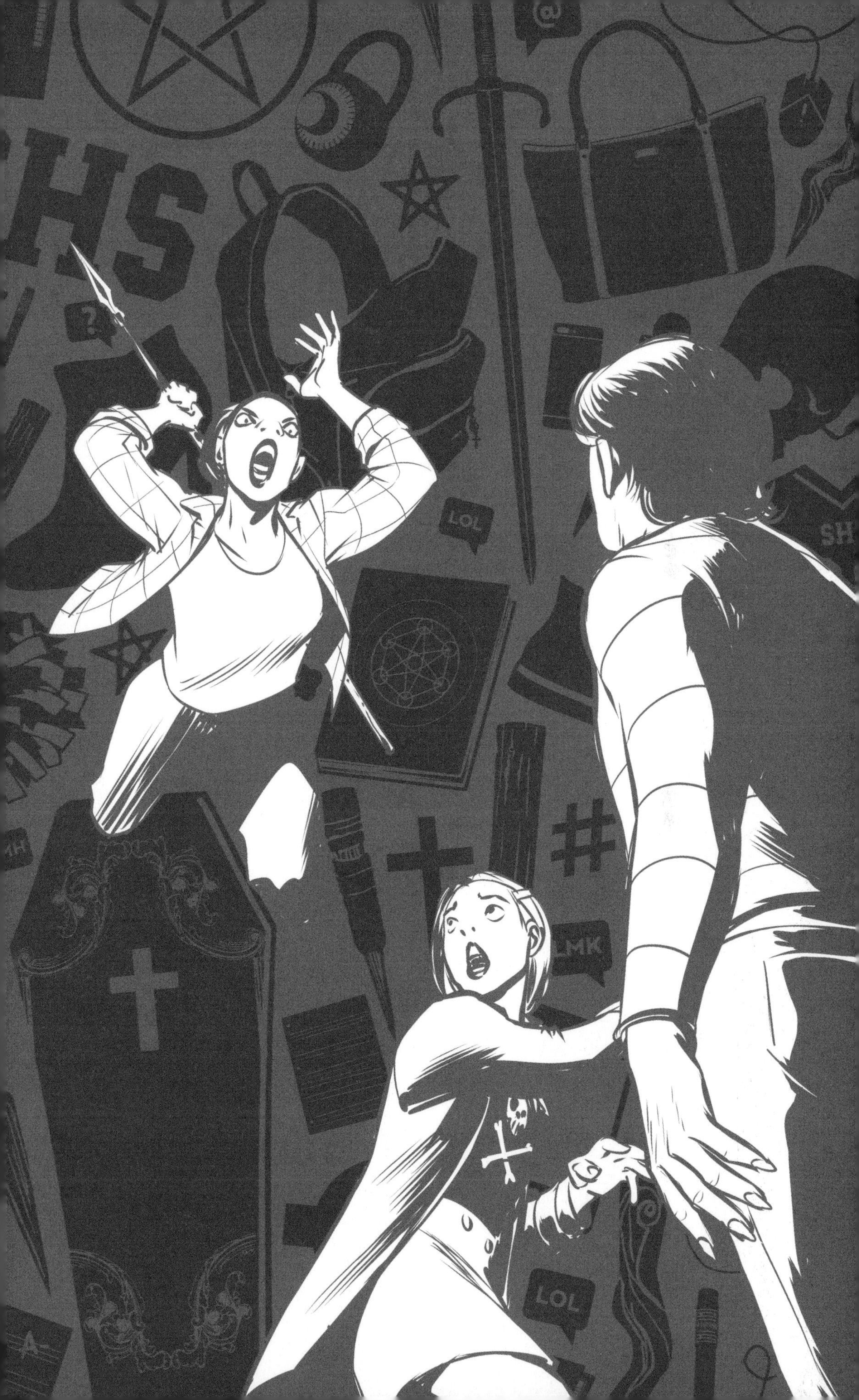
HS
LOL
LMK
LOL
SH

CHAPTER
TWELVE

Issue Twelve Cover by **Marc Aspinall**

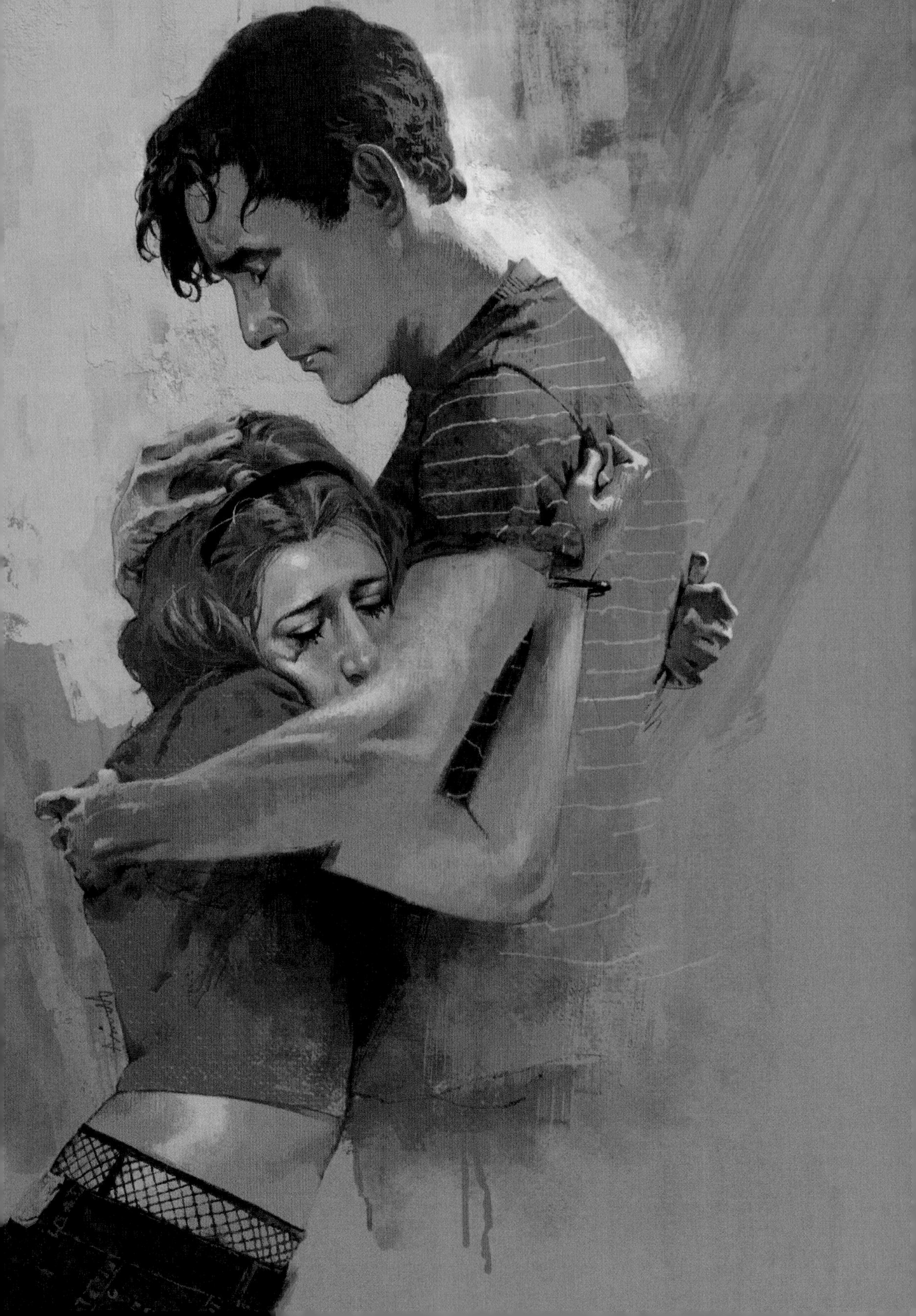

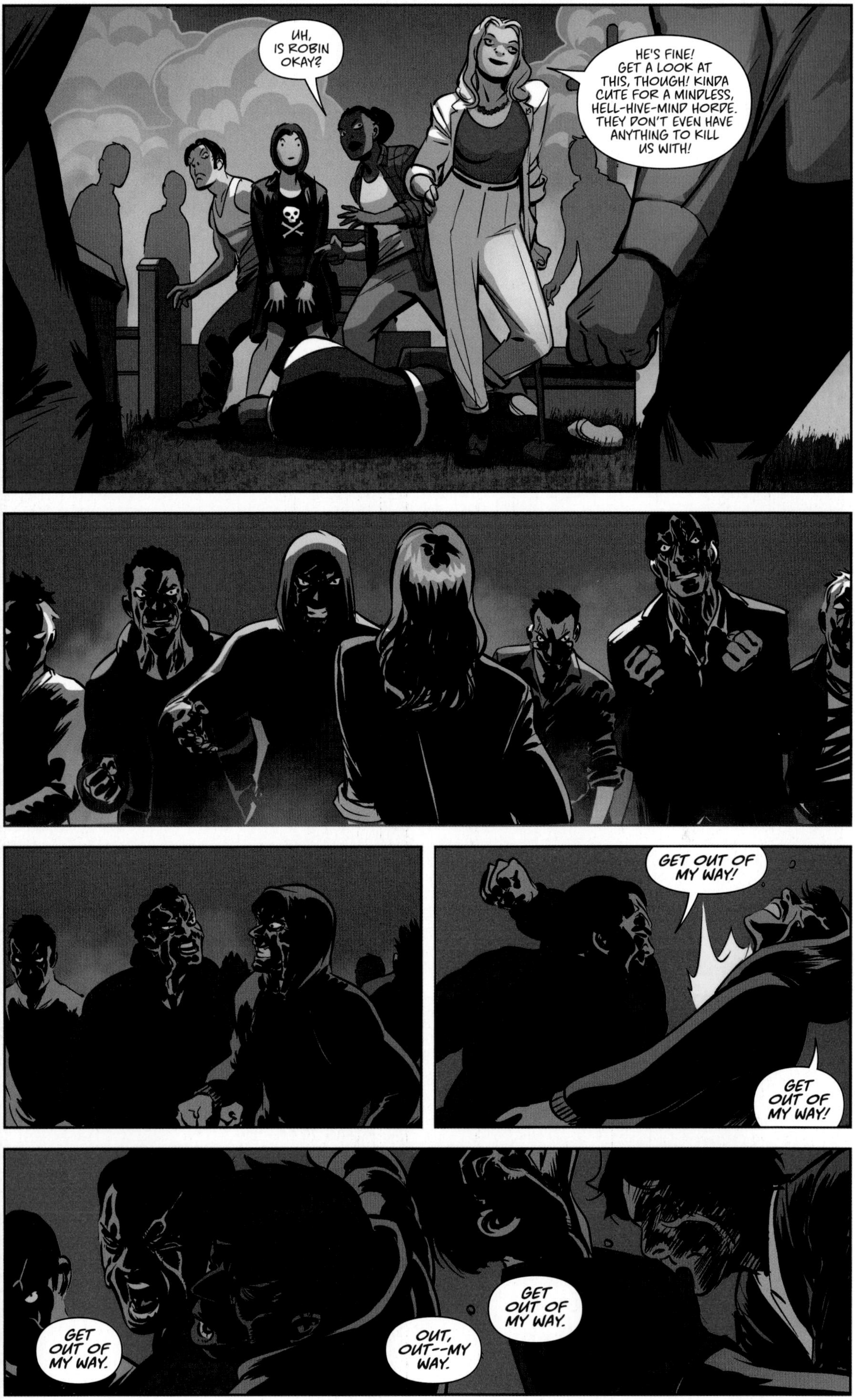
UH, IS ROBIN OKAY?
HE'S FINE! GET A LOOK AT THIS, THOUGH! KINDA CUTE FOR A MINDLESS, HELL-HIVE-MIND HORDE. THEY DON'T EVEN HAVE ANYTHING TO KILL US WITH!
GET OUT OF MY WAY!
GET OUT OF MY WAY!
GET OUT OF MY WAY.
OUT, OUT--MY WAY.
GET OUT OF MY WAY.

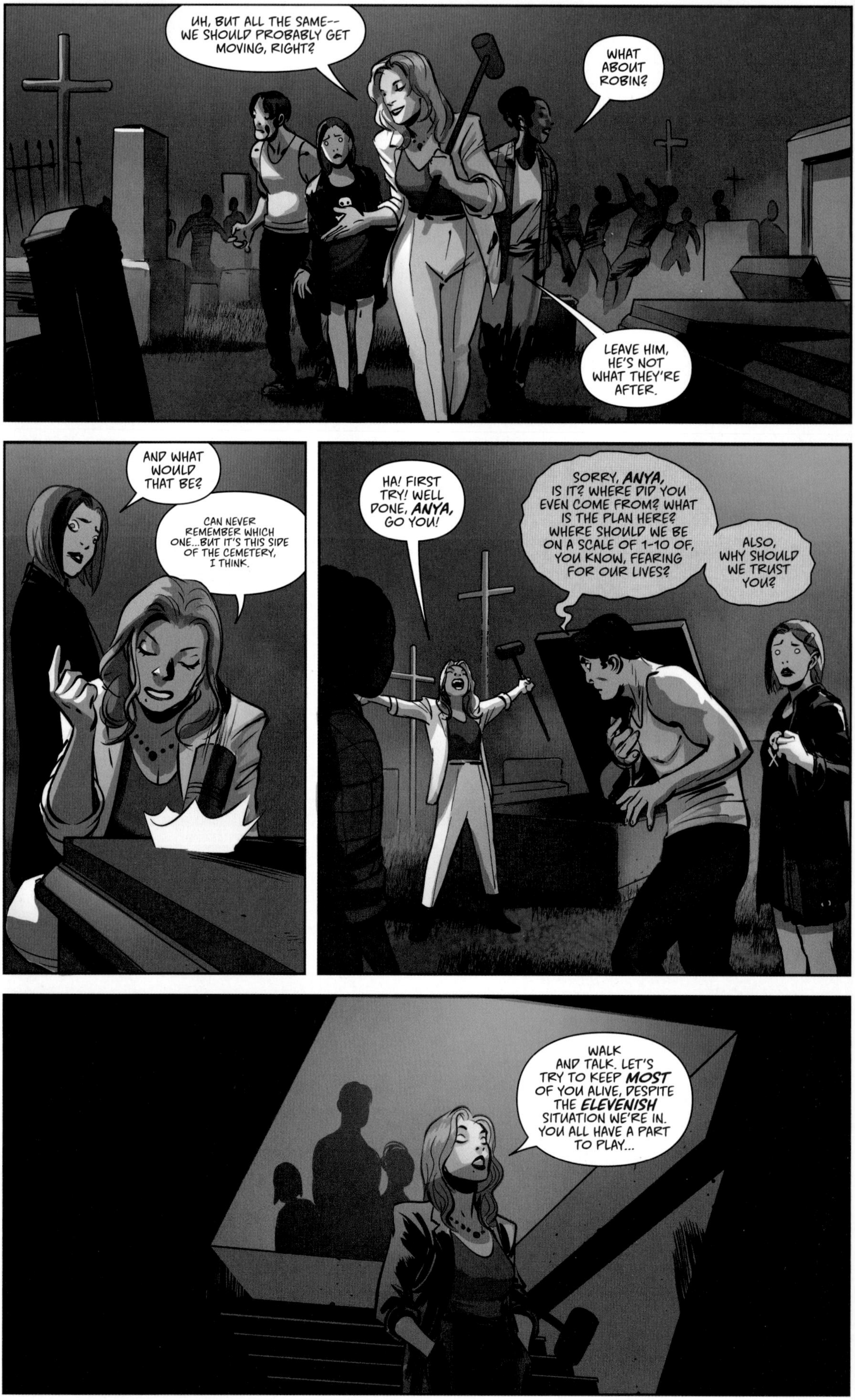
UH, BUT ALL THE SAME--
WE SHOULD PROBABLY GET MOVING, RIGHT?
WHAT ABOUT ROBIN?
LEAVE HIM, HE'S NOT WHAT THEY'RE AFTER.
AND WHAT WOULD THAT BE?
CAN NEVER REMEMBER WHICH ONE...BUT IT'S THIS SIDE OF THE CEMETERY, I THINK.
HA! FIRST TRY! WELL DONE, ANYA, GO YOU!
SORRY, ANYA, IS IT? WHERE DID YOU EVEN COME FROM? WHAT IS THE PLAN HERE? WHERE SHOULD WE BE ON A SCALE OF 1-10 OF, YOU KNOW, FEARING FOR OUR LIVES?
ALSO, WHY SHOULD WE TRUST YOU?
WALK AND TALK. LET'S TRY TO KEEP MOST OF YOU ALIVE, DESPITE THE ELEVENISH SITUATION WE'RE IN. YOU ALL HAVE A PART TO PLAY...

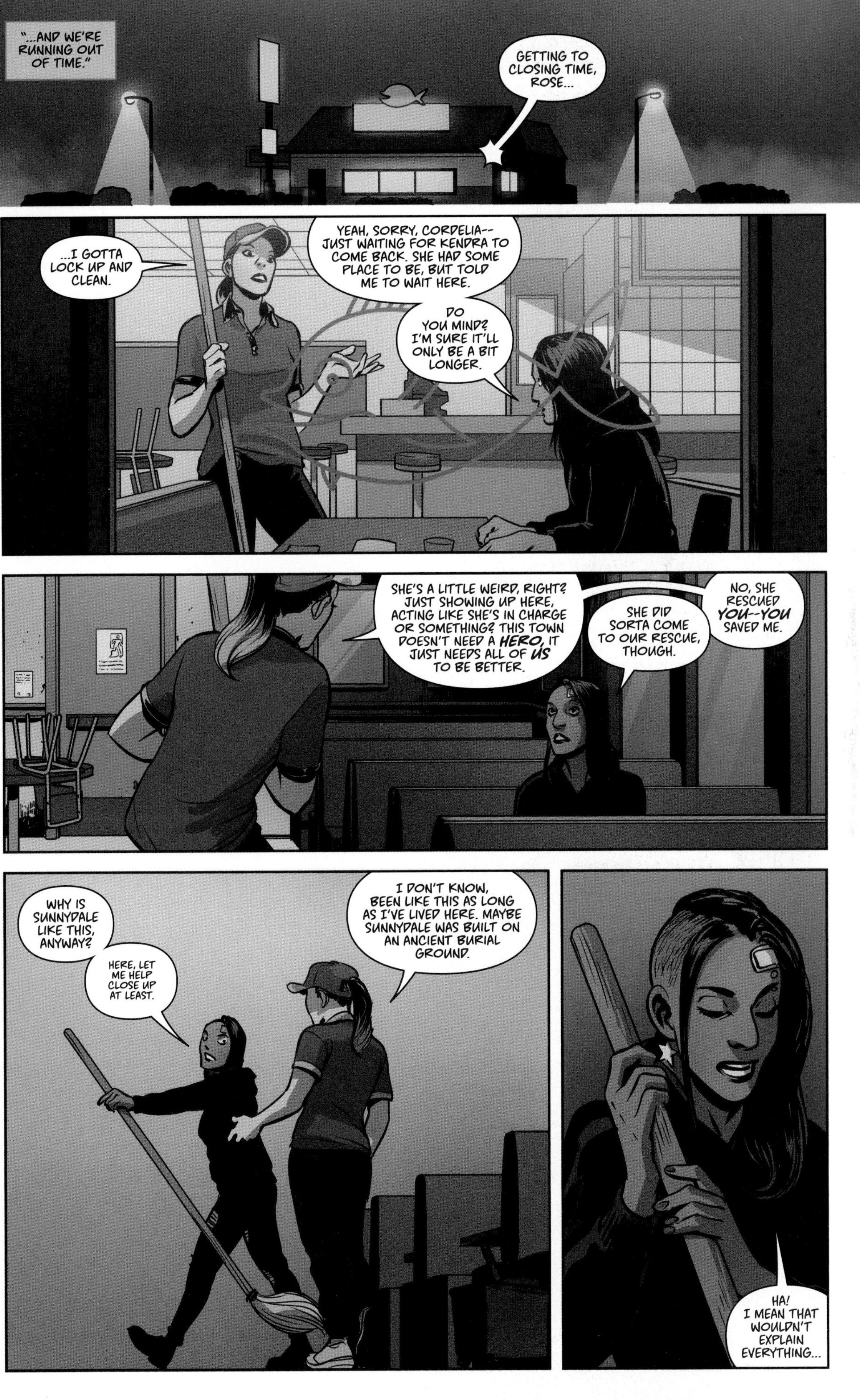
"...AND WE'RE RUNNING OUT OF TIME."
GETTING TO CLOSING TIME, ROSE...
...I GOTTA LOCK UP AND CLEAN.
YEAH, SORRY, CORDELIA-- JUST WAITING FOR KENDRA TO COME BACK. SHE HAD SOME PLACE TO BE, BUT TOLD ME TO WAIT HERE.
DO YOU MIND? I'M SURE IT'LL ONLY BE A BIT LONGER.
SHE'S A LITTLE WEIRD, RIGHT? JUST SHOWING UP HERE, ACTING LIKE SHE'S IN CHARGE OR SOMETHING? THIS TOWN DOESN'T NEED A HERO, IT JUST NEEDS ALL OF US TO BE BETTER.
SHE DID SORTA COME TO OUR RESCUE, THOUGH.
NO, SHE RESCUED YOU--YOU SAVED ME.
WHY IS SUNNYDALE LIKE THIS, ANYWAY?
HERE, LET ME HELP CLOSE UP AT LEAST.
I DON'T KNOW, BEEN LIKE THIS AS LONG AS I'VE LIVED HERE. MAYBE SUNNYDALE WAS BUILT ON AN ANCIENT BURIAL GROUND.
HA! I MEAN THAT WOULDN'T EXPLAIN EVERYTHING...

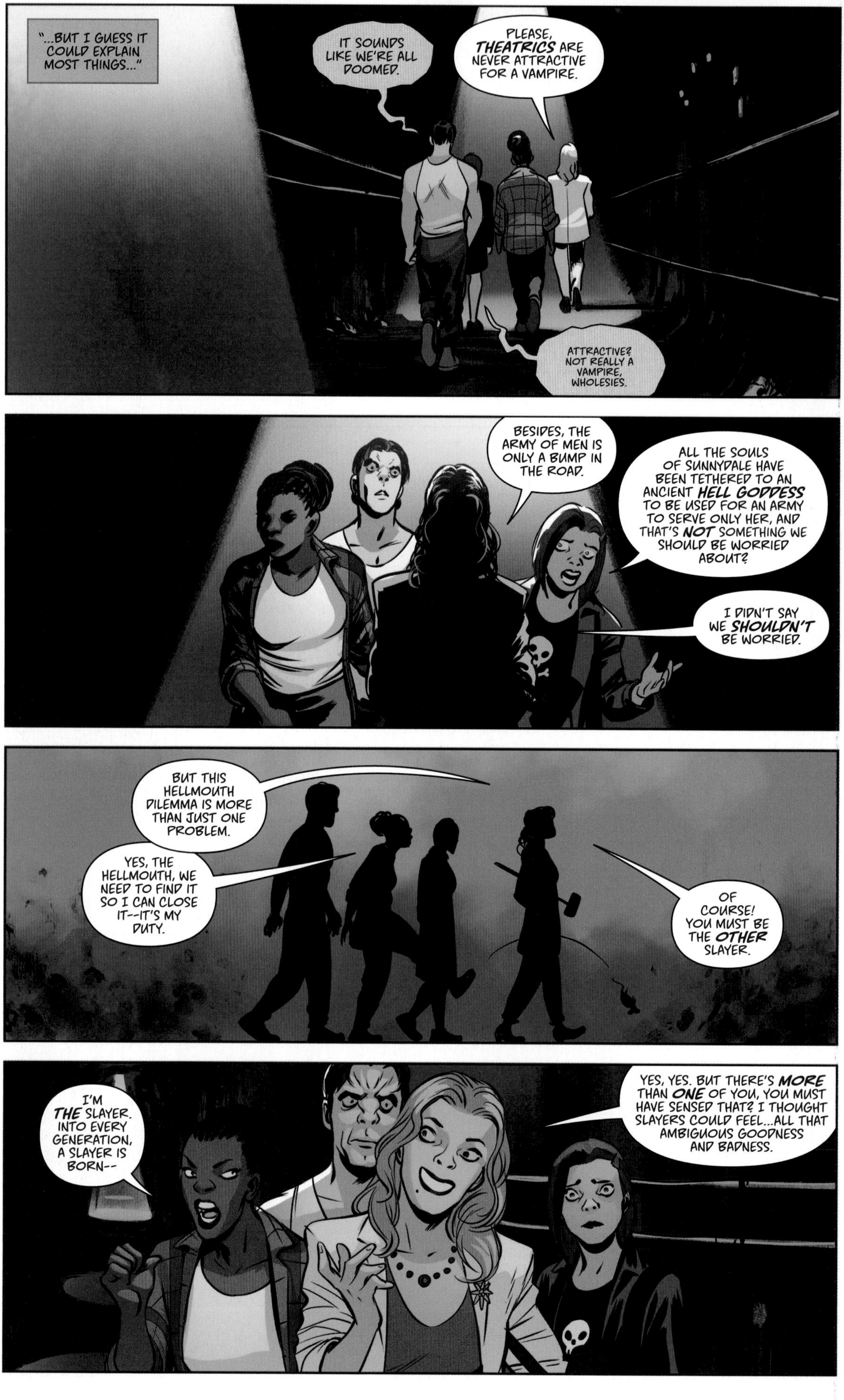
"...BUT I GUESS IT COULD EXPLAIN MOST THINGS..."
IT SOUNDS LIKE WE'RE ALL DOOMED.
PLEASE, THEATRICS ARE NEVER ATTRACTIVE FOR A VAMPIRE.
ATTRACTIVE? NOT REALLY A VAMPIRE, WHOLESIES.
BESIDES, THE ARMY OF MEN IS ONLY A BUMP IN THE ROAD.
ALL THE SOULS OF SUNNYDALE HAVE BEEN TETHERED TO AN ANCIENT HELL GODDESS TO BE USED FOR AN ARMY TO SERVE ONLY HER, AND THAT'S NOT SOMETHING WE SHOULD BE WORRIED ABOUT?
I DIDN'T SAY WE SHOULDN'T BE WORRIED.
BUT THIS HELLMOUTH DILEMMA IS MORE THAN JUST ONE PROBLEM.
YES, THE HELLMOUTH, WE NEED TO FIND IT SO I CAN CLOSE IT--IT'S MY DUTY.
OF COURSE! YOU MUST BE THE OTHER SLAYER.
I'M THE SLAYER. INTO EVERY GENERATION, A SLAYER IS BORN--
YES, YES. BUT THERE'S MORE THAN ONE OF YOU, YOU MUST HAVE SENSED THAT? I THOUGHT SLAYERS COULD FEEL...ALL THAT AMBIGUOUS GOODNESS AND BADNESS.

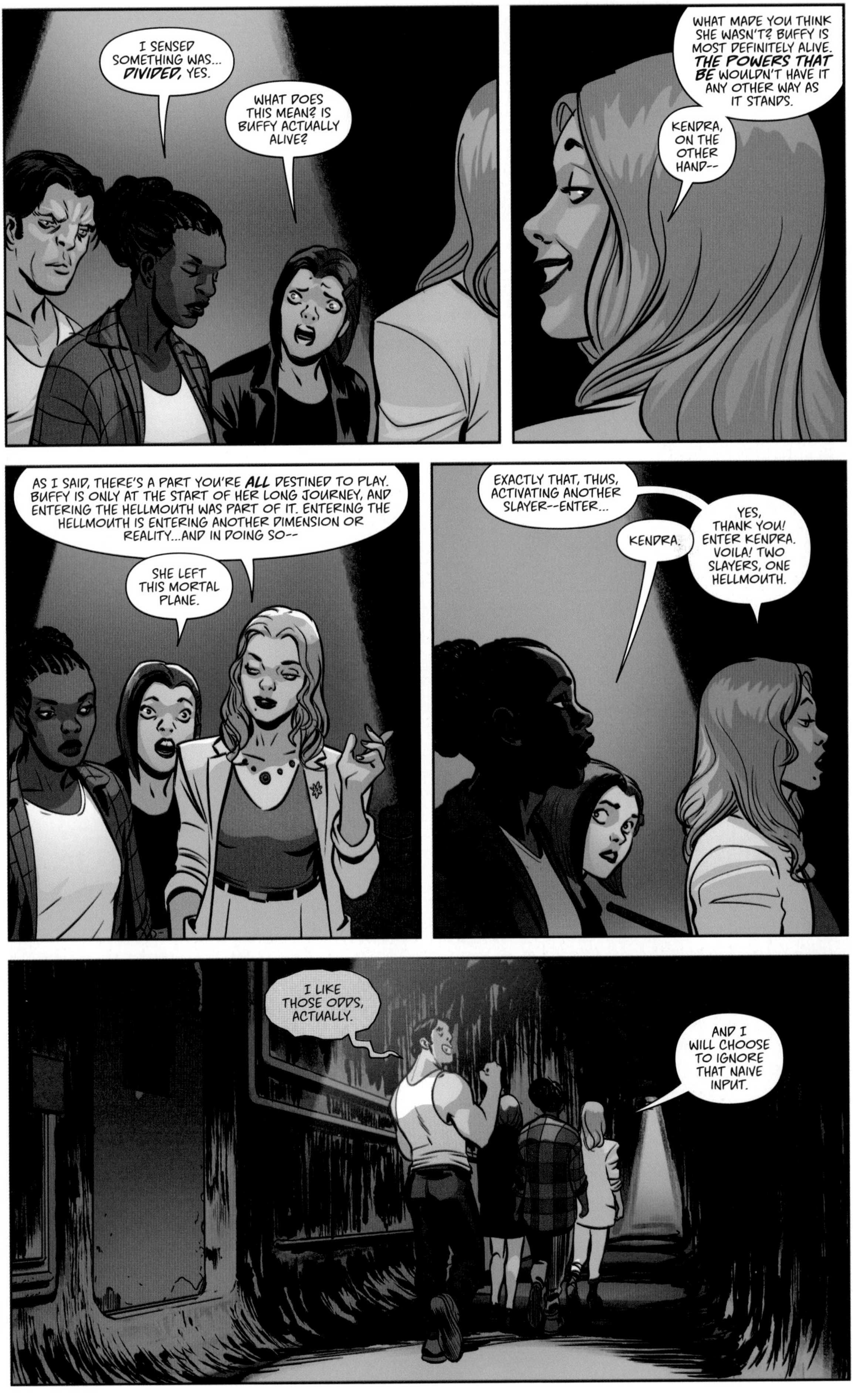
I SENSED SOMETHING WAS... DIVIDED, YES.
WHAT DOES THIS MEAN? IS BUFFY ACTUALLY ALIVE?
WHAT MADE YOU THINK SHE WASN'T? BUFFY IS MOST DEFINITELY ALIVE. THE POWERS THAT BE WOULDN'T HAVE IT ANY OTHER WAY AS IT STANDS.
KENDRA, ON THE OTHER HAND--
AS I SAID, THERE'S A PART YOU'RE ALL DESTINED TO PLAY. BUFFY IS ONLY AT THE START OF HER LONG JOURNEY, AND ENTERING THE HELLMOUTH WAS PART OF IT. ENTERING THE HELLMOUTH IS ENTERING ANOTHER DIMENSION OR REALITY...AND IN DOING SO--
SHE LEFT THIS MORTAL PLANE.
EXACTLY THAT, THUS, ACTIVATING ANOTHER SLAYER--ENTER...
KENDRA.
YES, THANK YOU! ENTER KENDRA. VOILA! TWO SLAYERS, ONE HELLMOUTH.
I LIKE THOSE ODDS, ACTUALLY.
AND I WILL CHOOSE TO IGNORE THAT NAIVE INPUT.

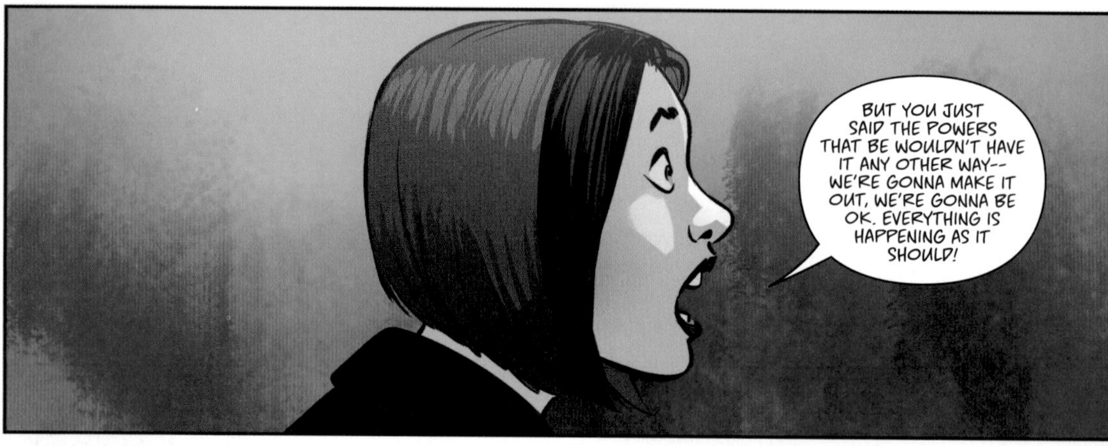
BUT YOU JUST SAID THE POWERS THAT BE WOULDN'T HAVE IT ANY OTHER WAY-- WE'RE GONNA MAKE IT OUT, WE'RE GONNA BE OK. EVERYTHING IS HAPPENING AS IT SHOULD!

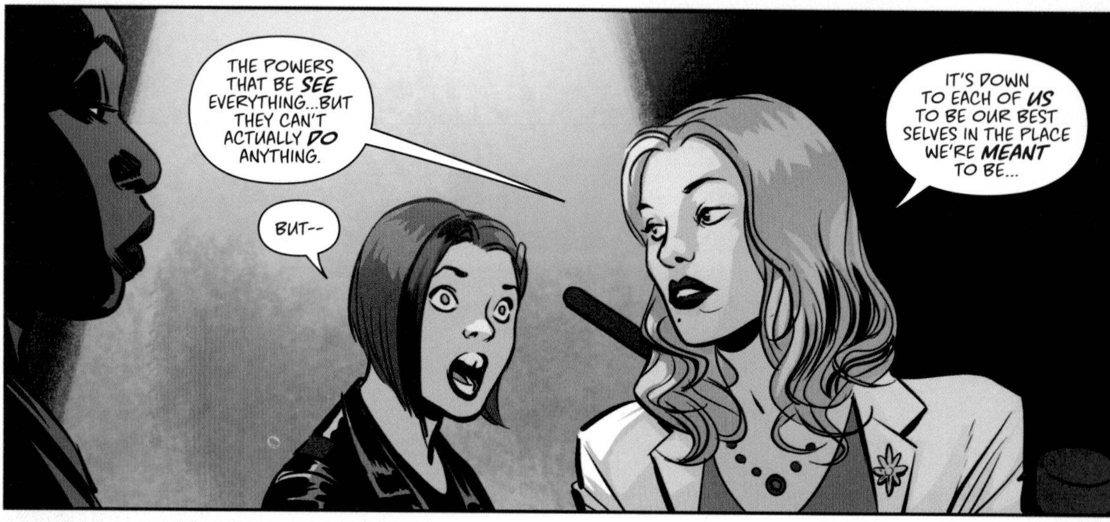
THE POWERS THAT BE SEE EVERYTHING...BUT THEY CAN'T ACTUALLY DO ANYTHING.
BUT--
IT'S DOWN TO EACH OF US TO BE OUR BEST SELVES IN THE PLACE WE'RE MEANT TO BE...

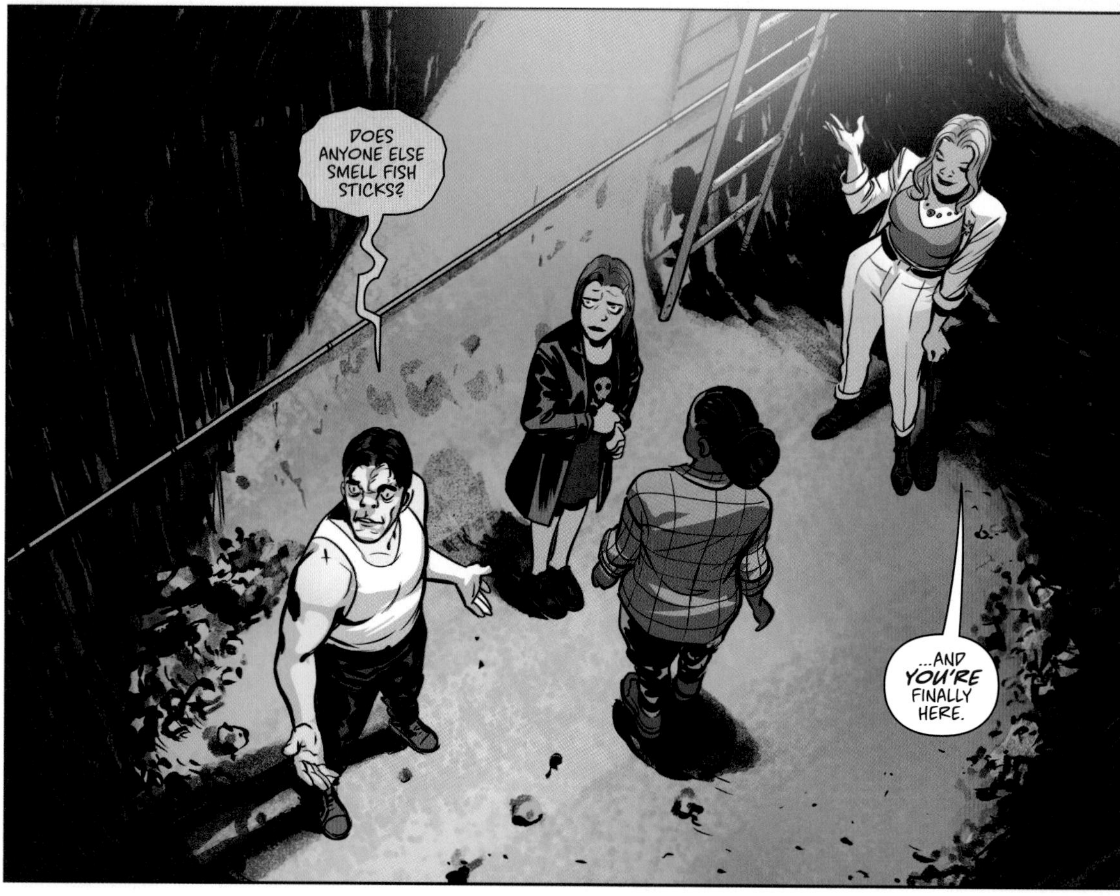
DOES ANYONE ELSE SMELL FISH STICKS?
...AND YOU'RE FINALLY HERE.

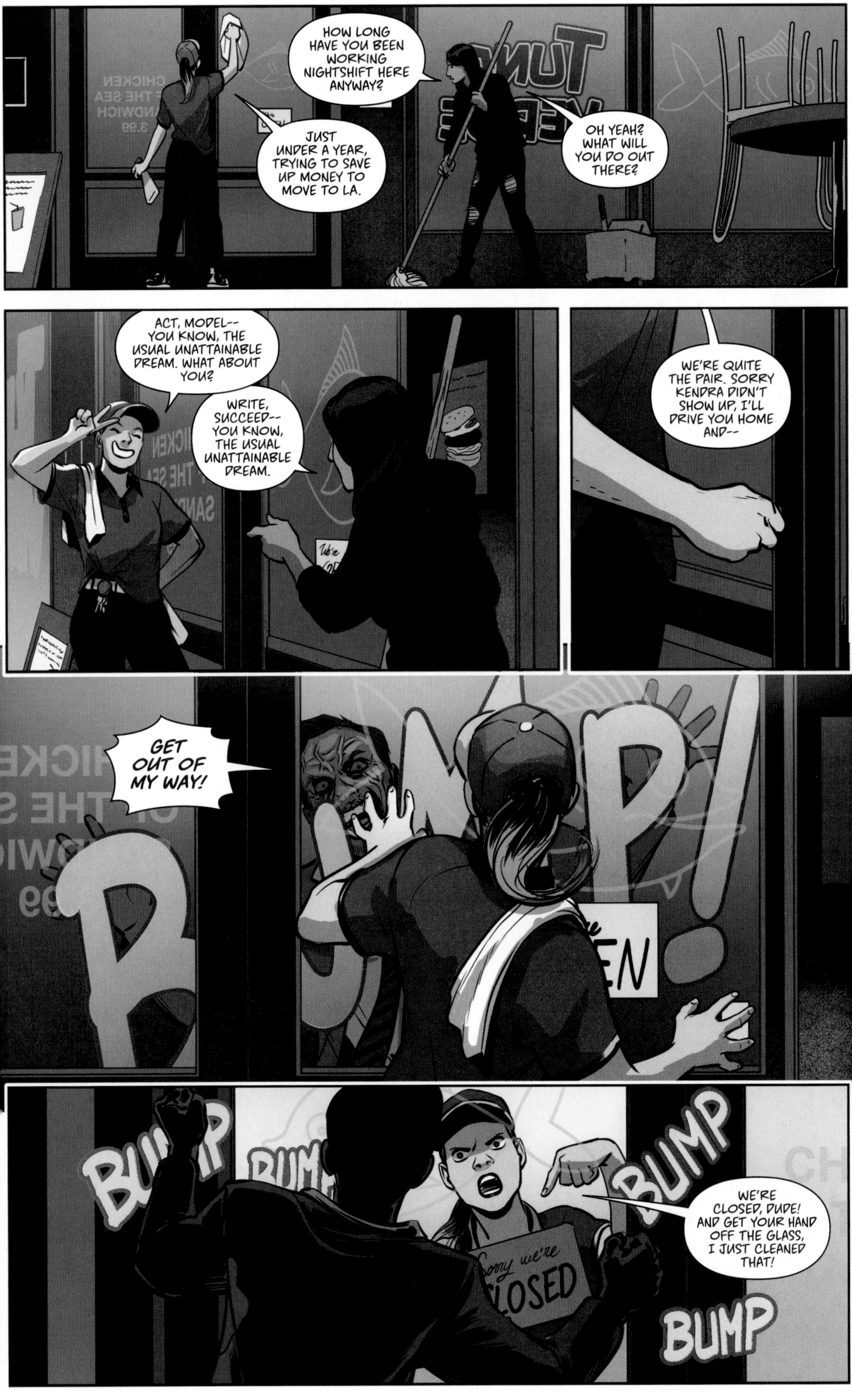
HOW LONG HAVE YOU BEEN WORKING NIGHTSHIFT HERE ANYWAY?
JUST UNDER A YEAR, TRYING TO SAVE UP MONEY TO MOVE TO LA.
OH YEAH? WHAT WILL YOU DO OUT THERE?
ACT, MODEL-- YOU KNOW, THE USUAL UNATTAINABLE DREAM. WHAT ABOUT YOU?
WRITE, SUCCEED-- YOU KNOW, THE USUAL UNATTAINABLE DREAM.
WE'RE QUITE THE PAIR. SORRY KENDRA DIDN'T SHOW UP, I'LL DRIVE YOU HOME AND--
GET OUT OF MY WAY!
WE'RE CLOSED, DUDE! AND GET YOUR HAND OFF THE GLASS, I JUST CLEANED THAT!
BUMP
BUMP
BUMP
BUMP
Sorry we're CLOSED

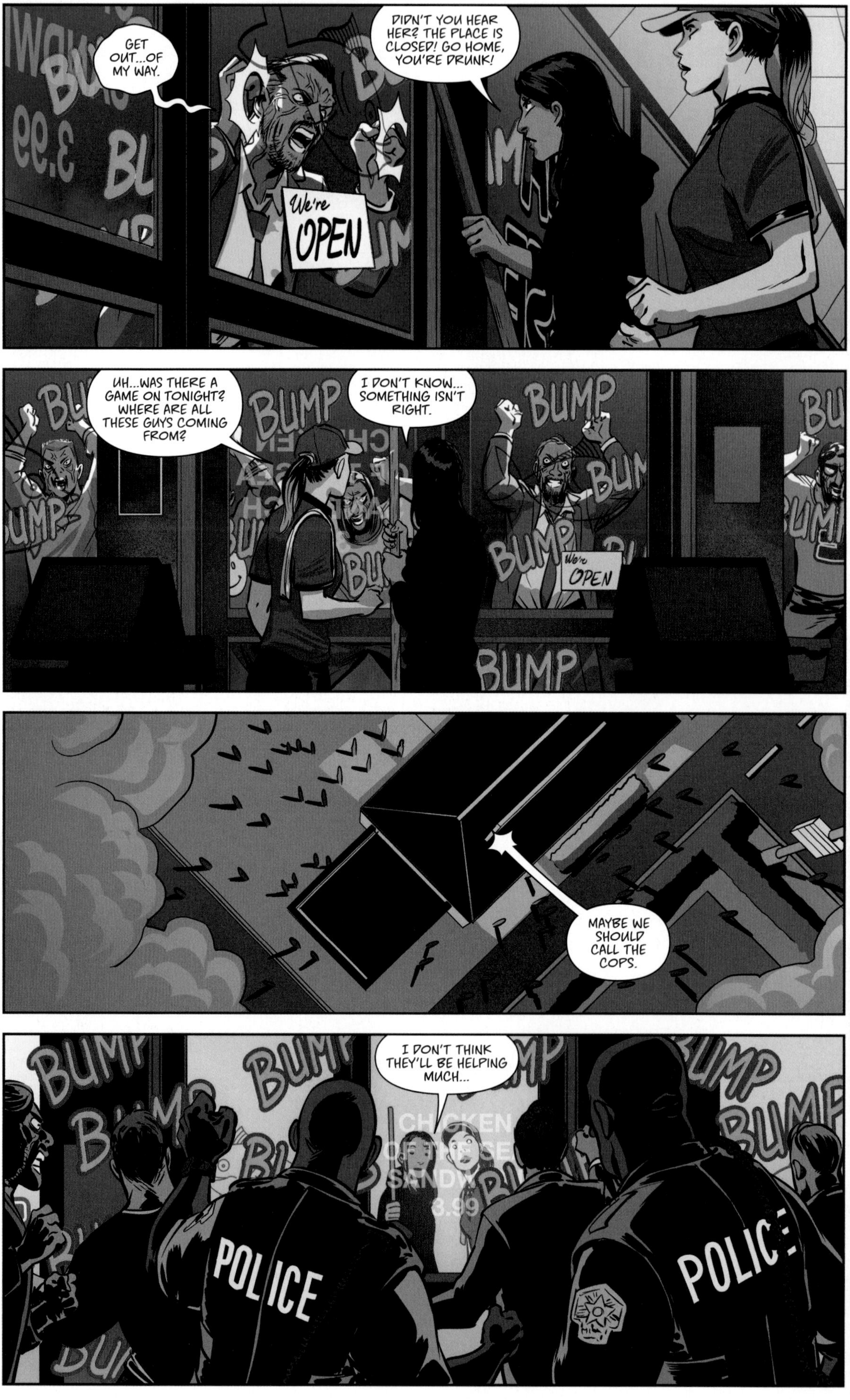
GET OUT...OF MY WAY.
DIDN'T YOU HEAR HER? THE PLACE IS CLOSED! GO HOME, YOU'RE DRUNK!
We're OPEN
UH...WAS THERE A GAME ON TONIGHT? WHERE ARE ALL THESE GUYS COMING FROM?
I DON'T KNOW... SOMETHING ISN'T RIGHT.
BUMP
BUMP
BUMP
We're OPEN
BUMP
MAYBE WE SHOULD CALL THE COPS.
I DON'T THINK THEY'LL BE HELPING MUCH...
BUMP
BUMP
POLICE
POLICE

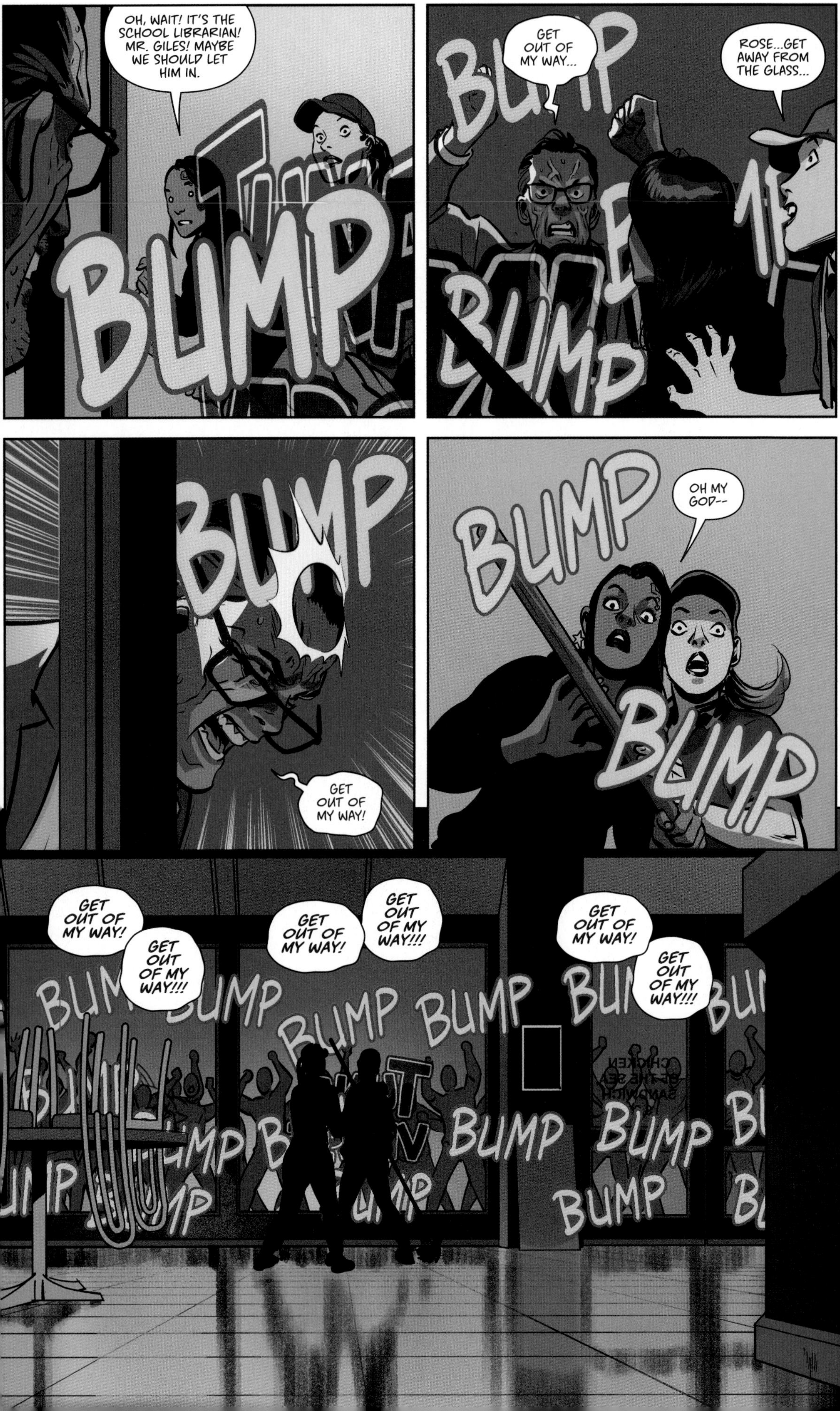
OH, WAIT! IT'S THE SCHOOL LIBRARIAN! MR. GILES! MAYBE WE SHOULD LET HIM IN.
BUMP
BUMP
GET OUT OF MY WAY...
ROSE...GET AWAY FROM THE GLASS...
BUMP
BUMP
BUMP
GET OUT OF MY WAY!
BUMP
OH MY GOD--
BUMP
GET OUT OF MY WAY!
GET OUT OF MY WAY!!!
GET OUT OF MY WAY!
GET OUT OF MY WAY!!!
GET OUT OF MY WAY!
GET OUT OF MY WAY!!!
BUMP BUMP BUMP BUMP
BUMP BUMP BUMP
BUMP

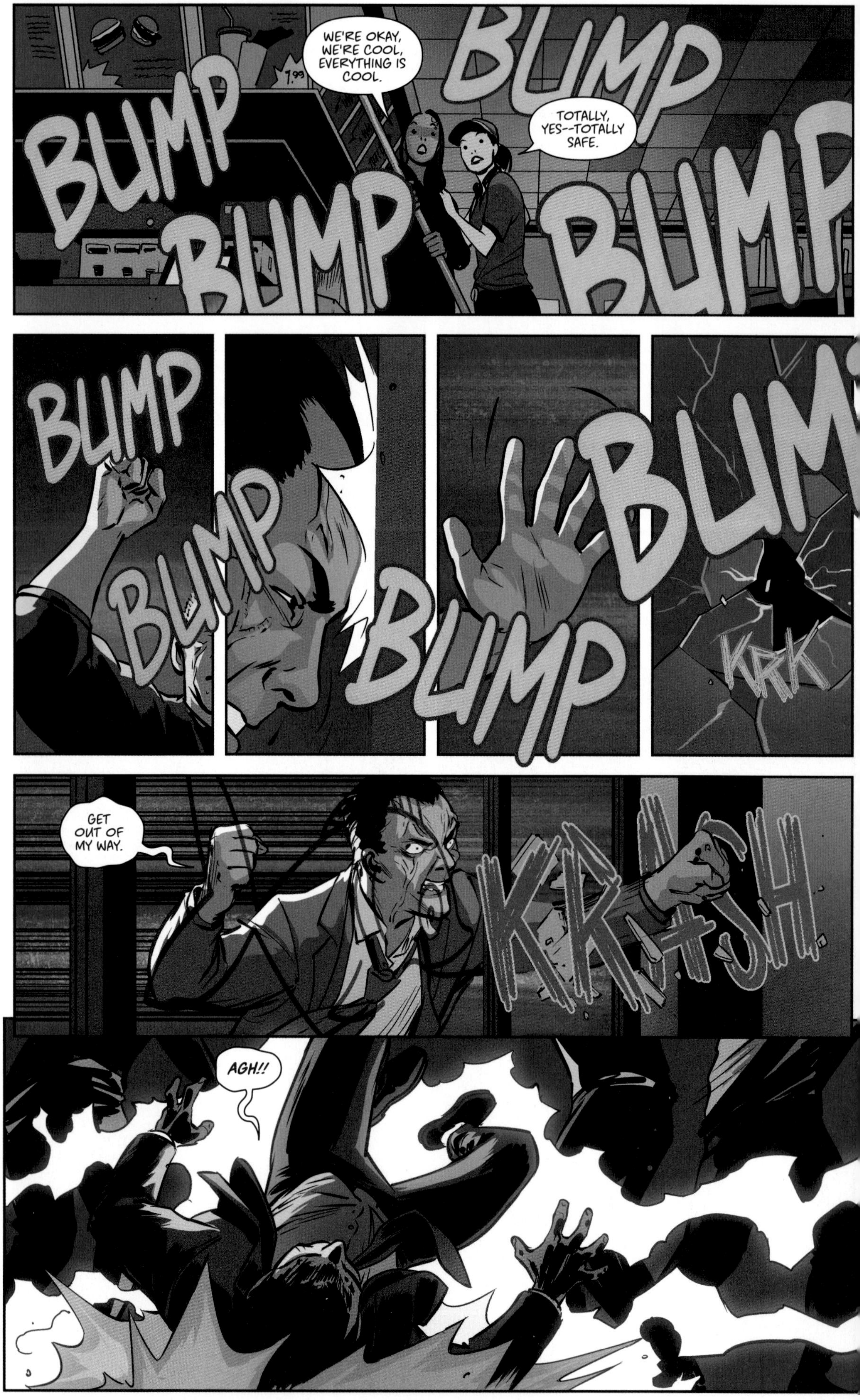
WE'RE OKAY, WE'RE COOL, EVERYTHING IS COOL.
BUMP
TOTALLY, YES--TOTALLY SAFE.
BUMP
BUMP
BUMP
BUMP
BUMP
BUMP
BUMP
BUM
KRK
GET OUT OF MY WAY.
KRASH
AGH!!

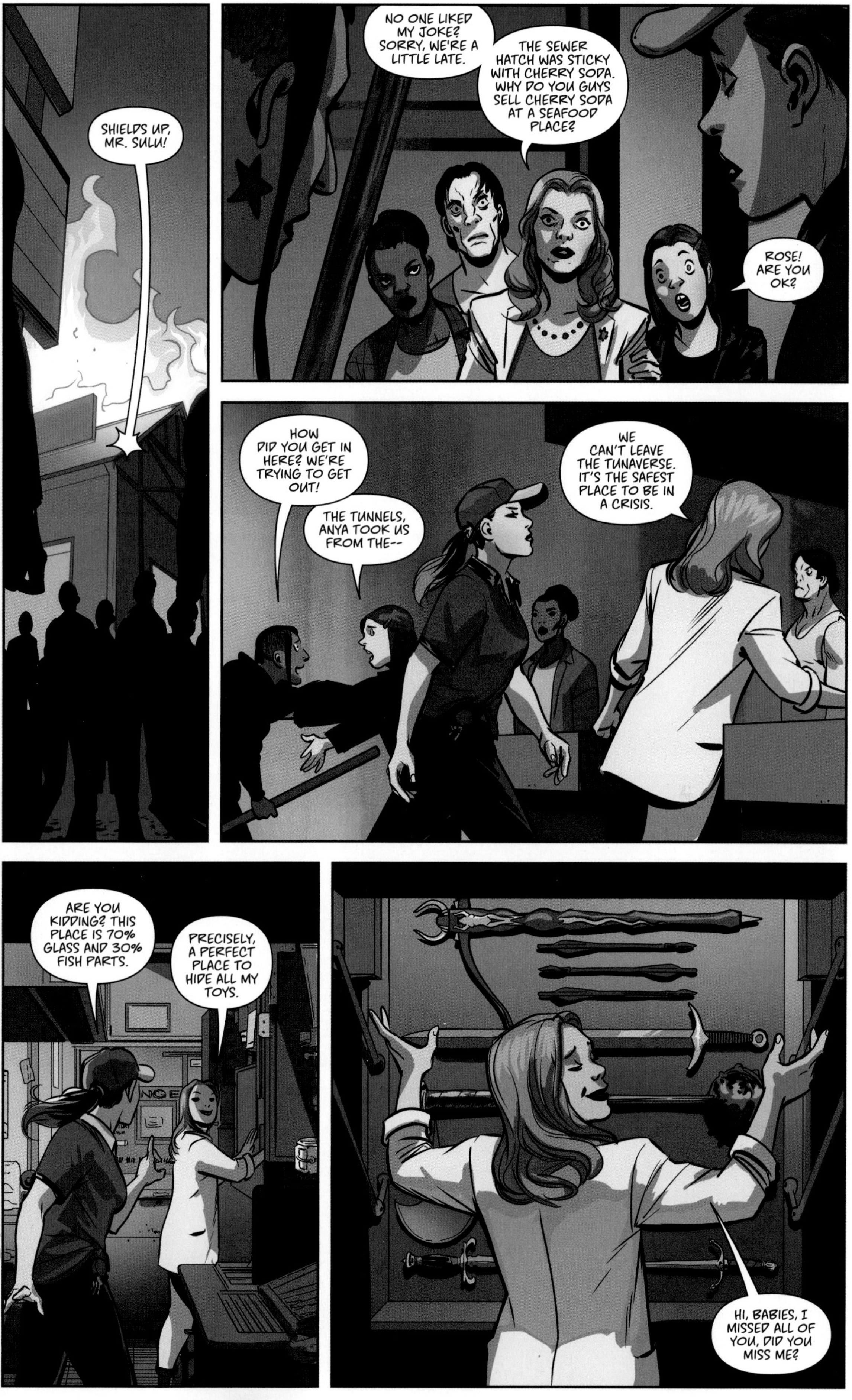
SHIELDS UP, MR. SULU!
NO ONE LIKED MY JOKE? SORRY, WE'RE A LITTLE LATE.
THE SEWER HATCH WAS STICKY WITH CHERRY SODA. WHY DO YOU GUYS SELL CHERRY SODA AT A SEAFOOD PLACE?
ROSE! ARE YOU OK?
HOW DID YOU GET IN HERE? WE'RE TRYING TO GET OUT!
THE TUNNELS, ANYA TOOK US FROM THE--
WE CAN'T LEAVE THE TUNAVERSE. IT'S THE SAFEST PLACE TO BE IN A CRISIS.
ARE YOU KIDDING? THIS PLACE IS 70% GLASS AND 30% FISH PARTS.
PRECISELY, A PERFECT PLACE TO HIDE ALL MY TOYS.
HI, BABIES, I MISSED ALL OF YOU, DID YOU MISS ME?

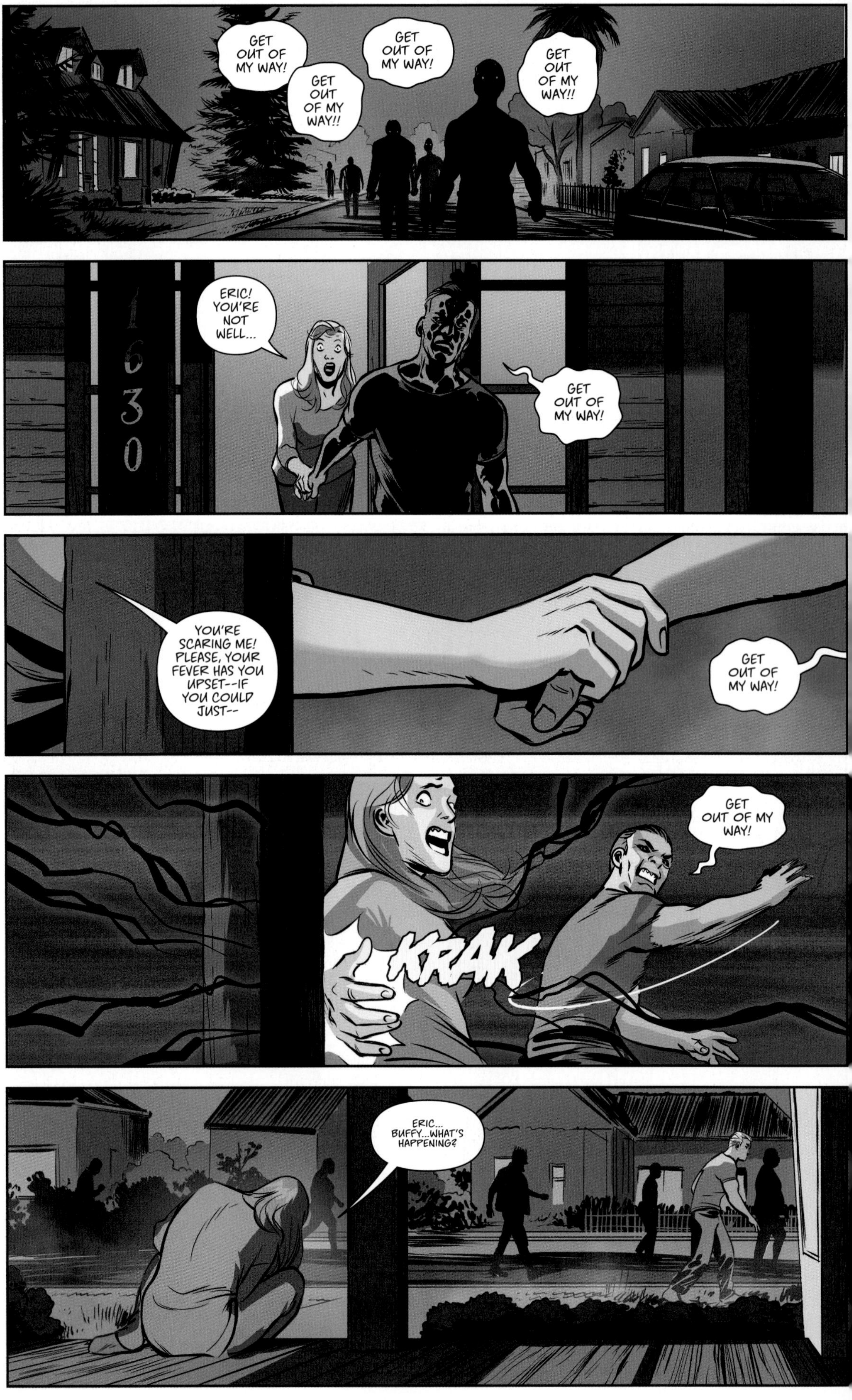
GET OUT OF MY WAY!
GET OUT OF MY WAY!!
GET OUT OF MY WAY!
GET OUT OF MY WAY!!
ERIC! YOU'RE NOT WELL...
GET OUT OF MY WAY!
YOU'RE SCARING ME! PLEASE, YOUR FEVER HAS YOU UPSET--IF YOU COULD JUST--
GET OUT OF MY WAY!
GET OUT OF MY WAY!
KRAK
ERIC... BUFFY...WHAT'S HAPPENING?

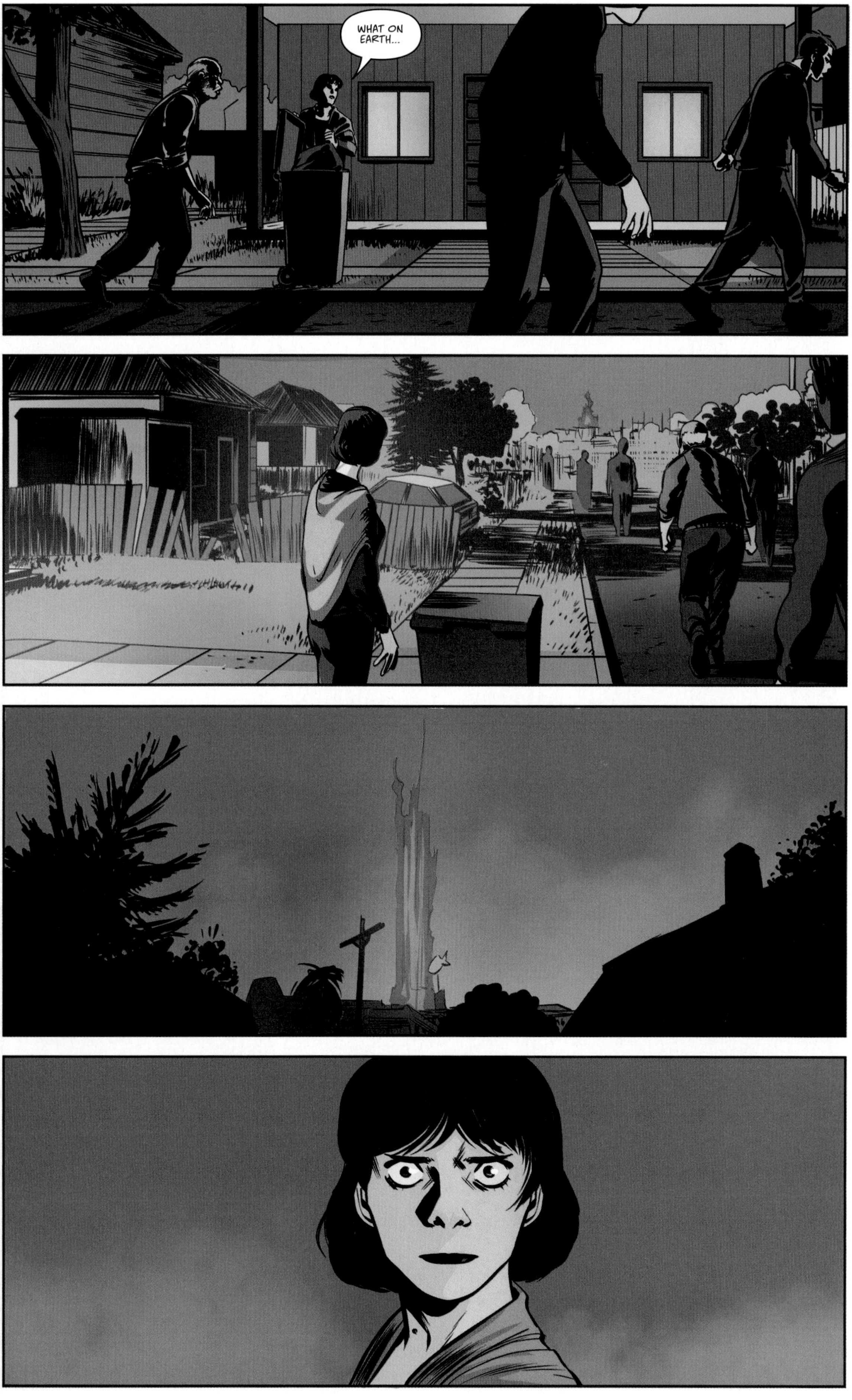
WHAT ON EARTH...

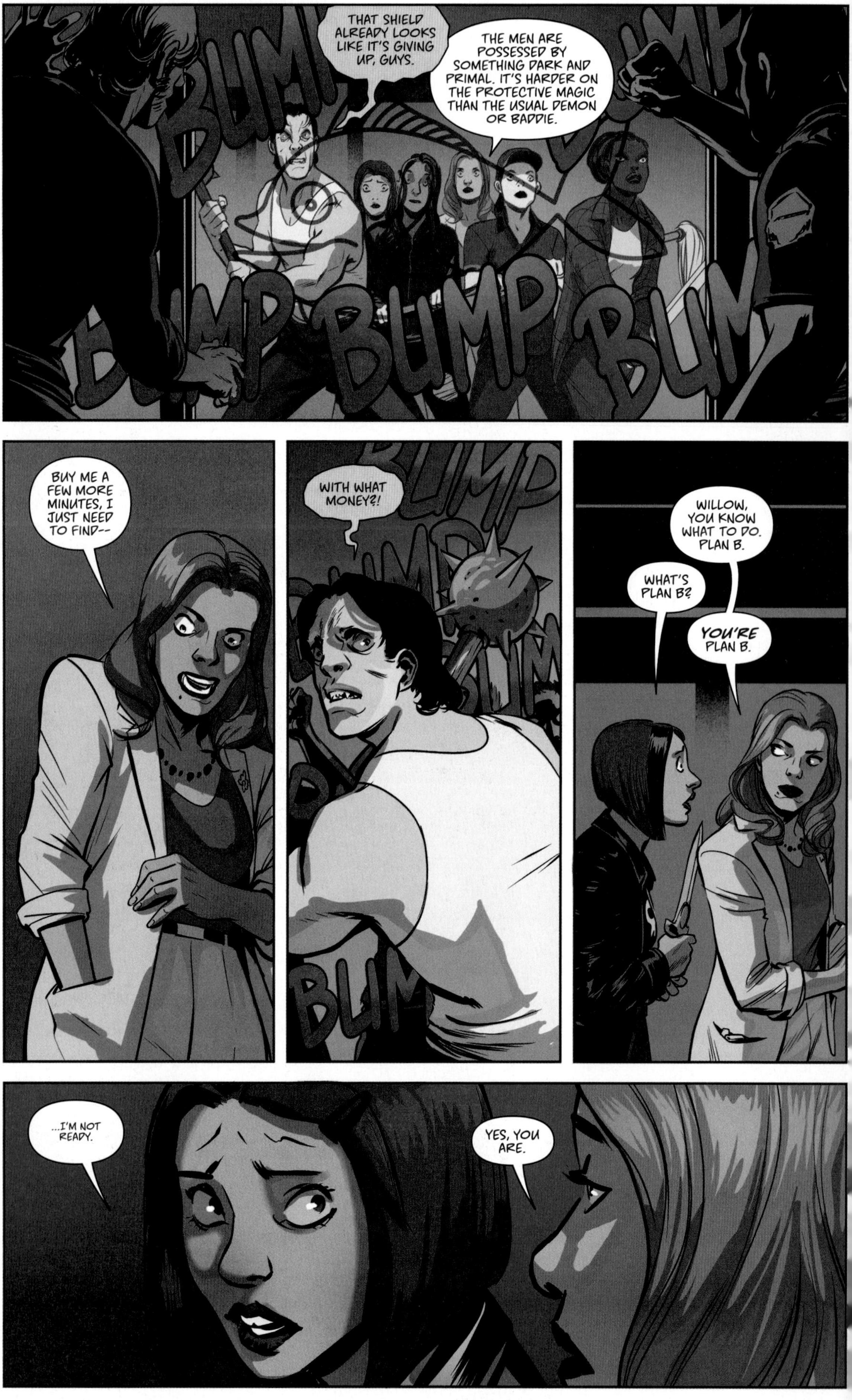
THAT SHIELD ALREADY LOOKS LIKE IT'S GIVING UP, GUYS.
THE MEN ARE POSSESSED BY SOMETHING DARK AND PRIMAL. IT'S HARDER ON THE PROTECTIVE MAGIC THAN THE USUAL DEMON OR BADDIE.
BUMP BUMP BUMP BUMP
BUY ME A FEW MORE MINUTES, I JUST NEED TO FIND--
WITH WHAT MONEY?!
BUMP
WILLOW, YOU KNOW WHAT TO DO. PLAN B.
WHAT'S PLAN B?
YOU'RE PLAN B.
...I'M NOT READY.
YES, YOU ARE.

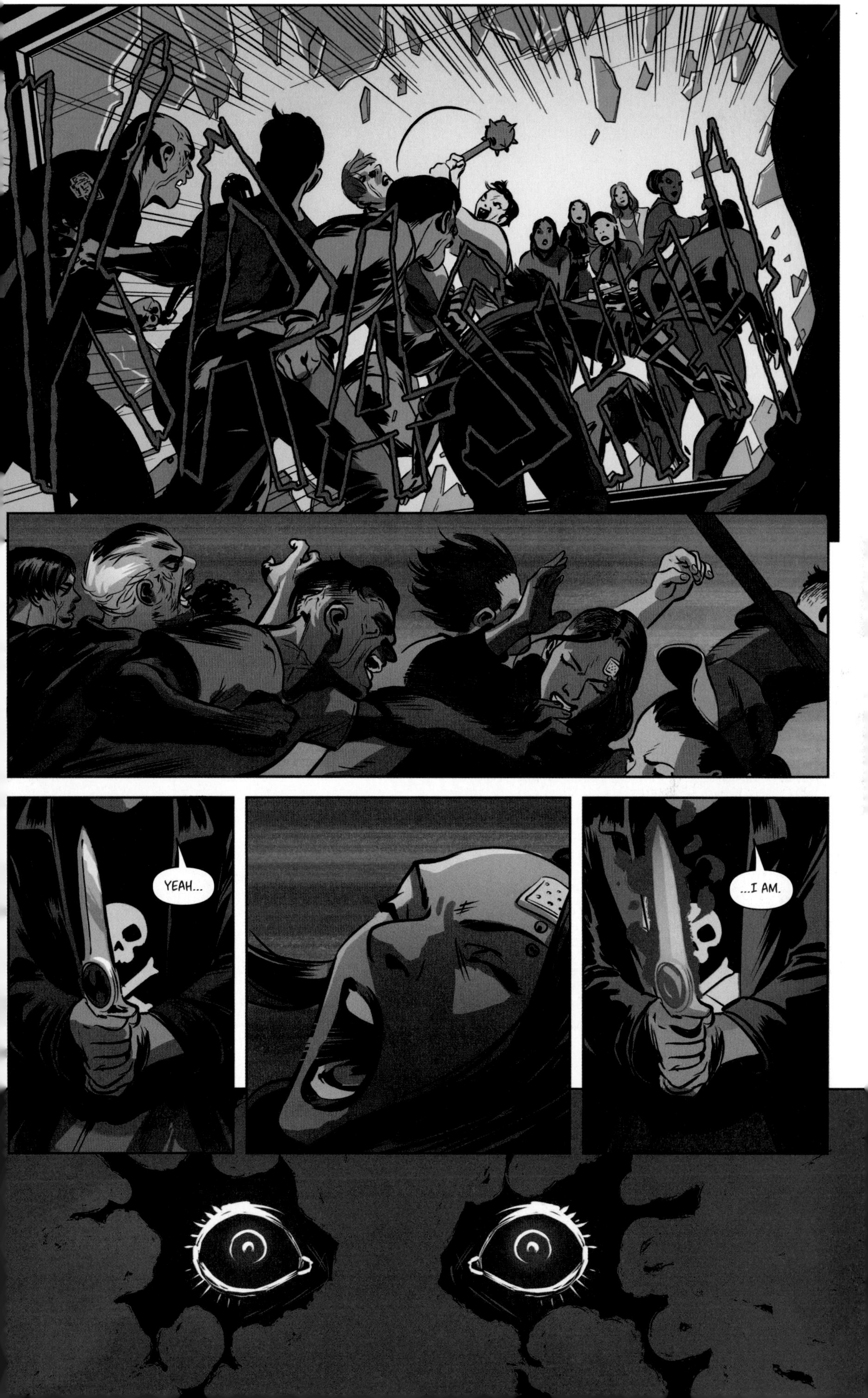
YEAH...
...I AM.

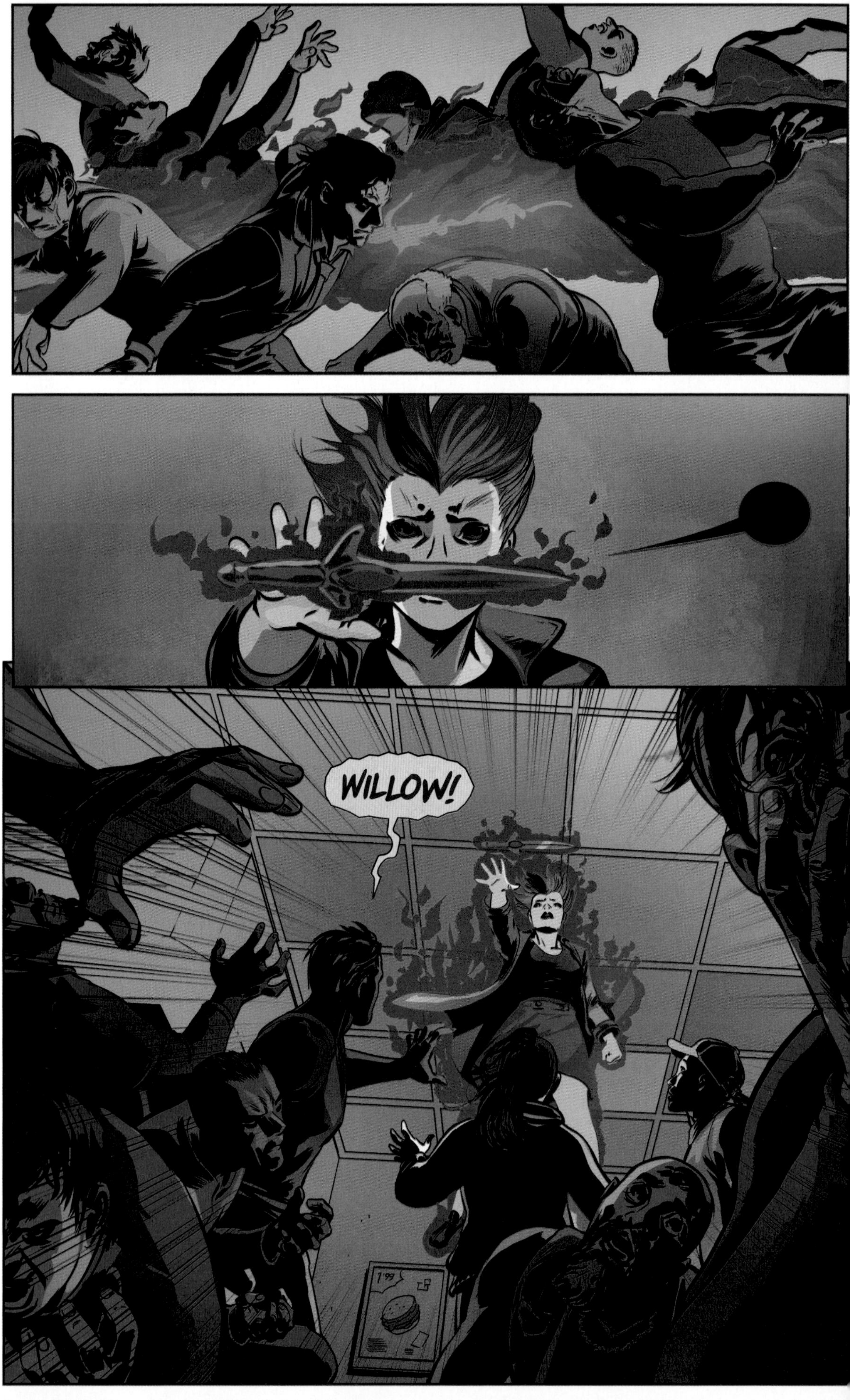
WILLOW!

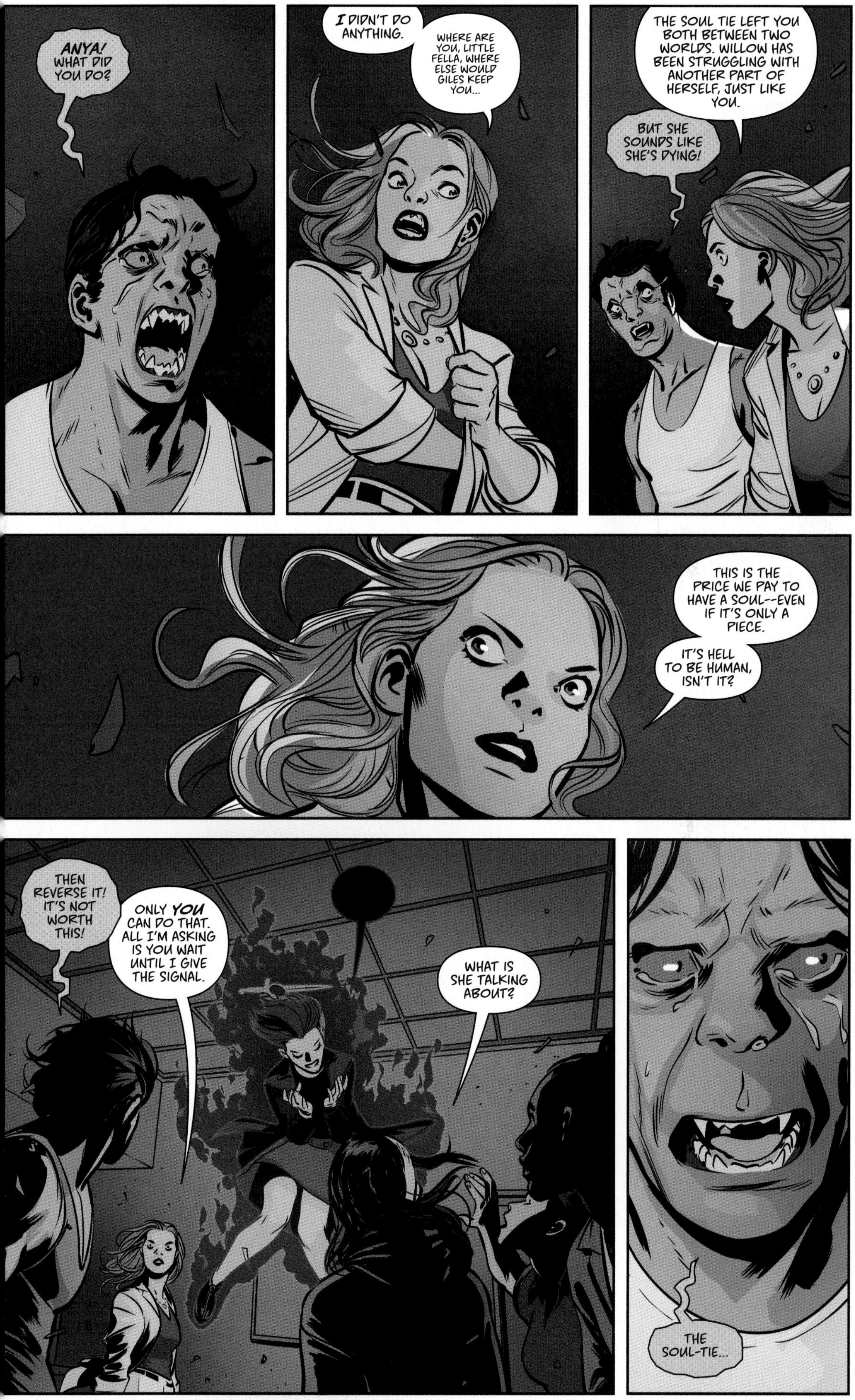
ANYA! WHAT DID YOU DO?
I DIDN'T DO ANYTHING.
WHERE ARE YOU, LITTLE FELLA, WHERE ELSE WOULD GILES KEEP YOU...
THE SOUL TIE LEFT YOU BOTH BETWEEN TWO WORLDS. WILLOW HAS BEEN STRUGGLING WITH ANOTHER PART OF HERSELF, JUST LIKE YOU.
BUT SHE SOUNDS LIKE SHE'S DYING!
THIS IS THE PRICE WE PAY TO HAVE A SOUL--EVEN IF IT'S ONLY A PIECE.
IT'S HELL TO BE HUMAN, ISN'T IT?
THEN REVERSE IT! IT'S NOT WORTH THIS!
ONLY YOU CAN DO THAT. ALL I'M ASKING IS YOU WAIT UNTIL I GIVE THE SIGNAL.
WHAT IS SHE TALKING ABOUT?
THE SOUL-TIE...

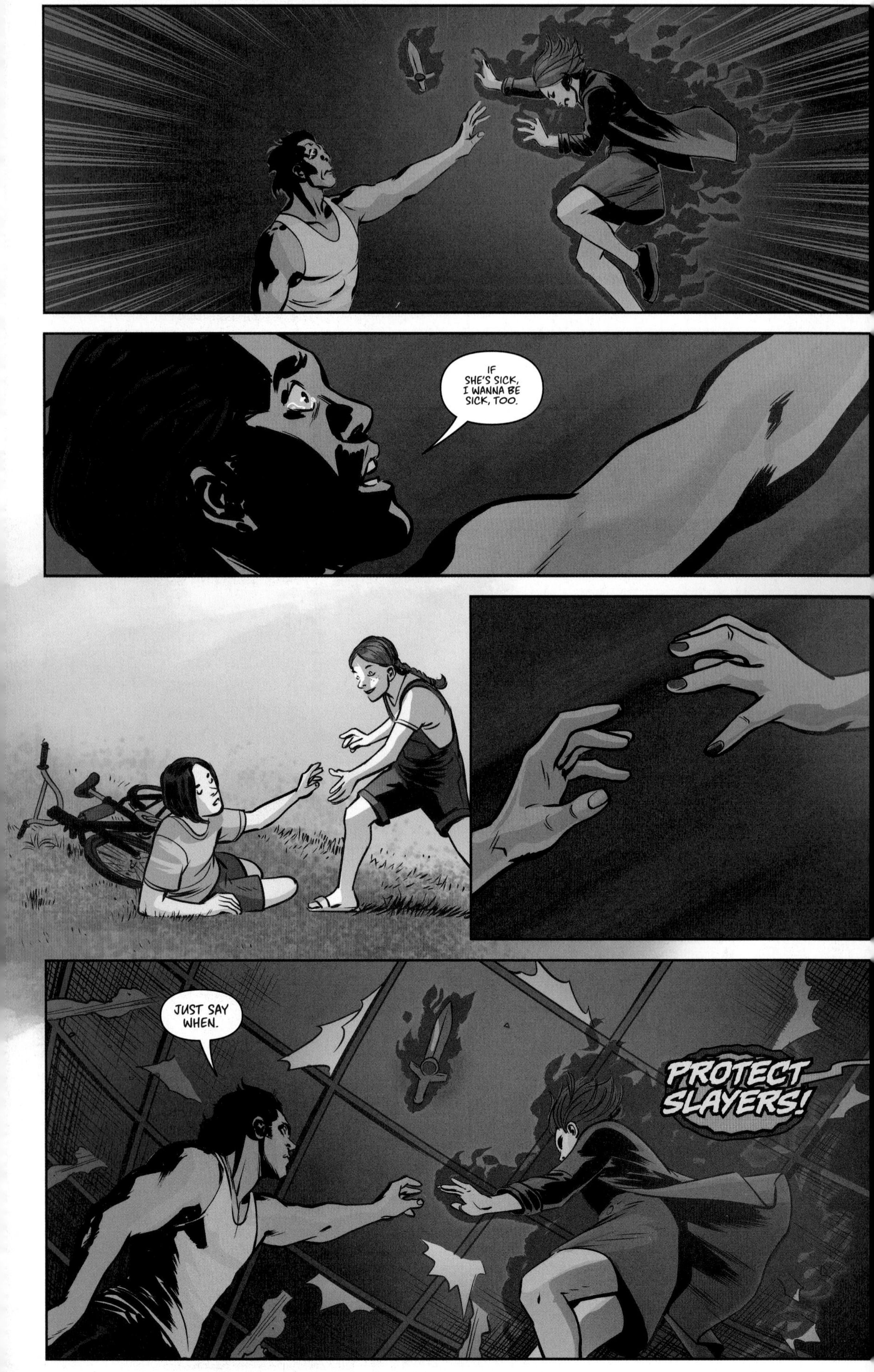
IF SHE'S SICK, I WANNA BE SICK, TOO.
JUST SAY WHEN.
PROTECT SLAYERS!

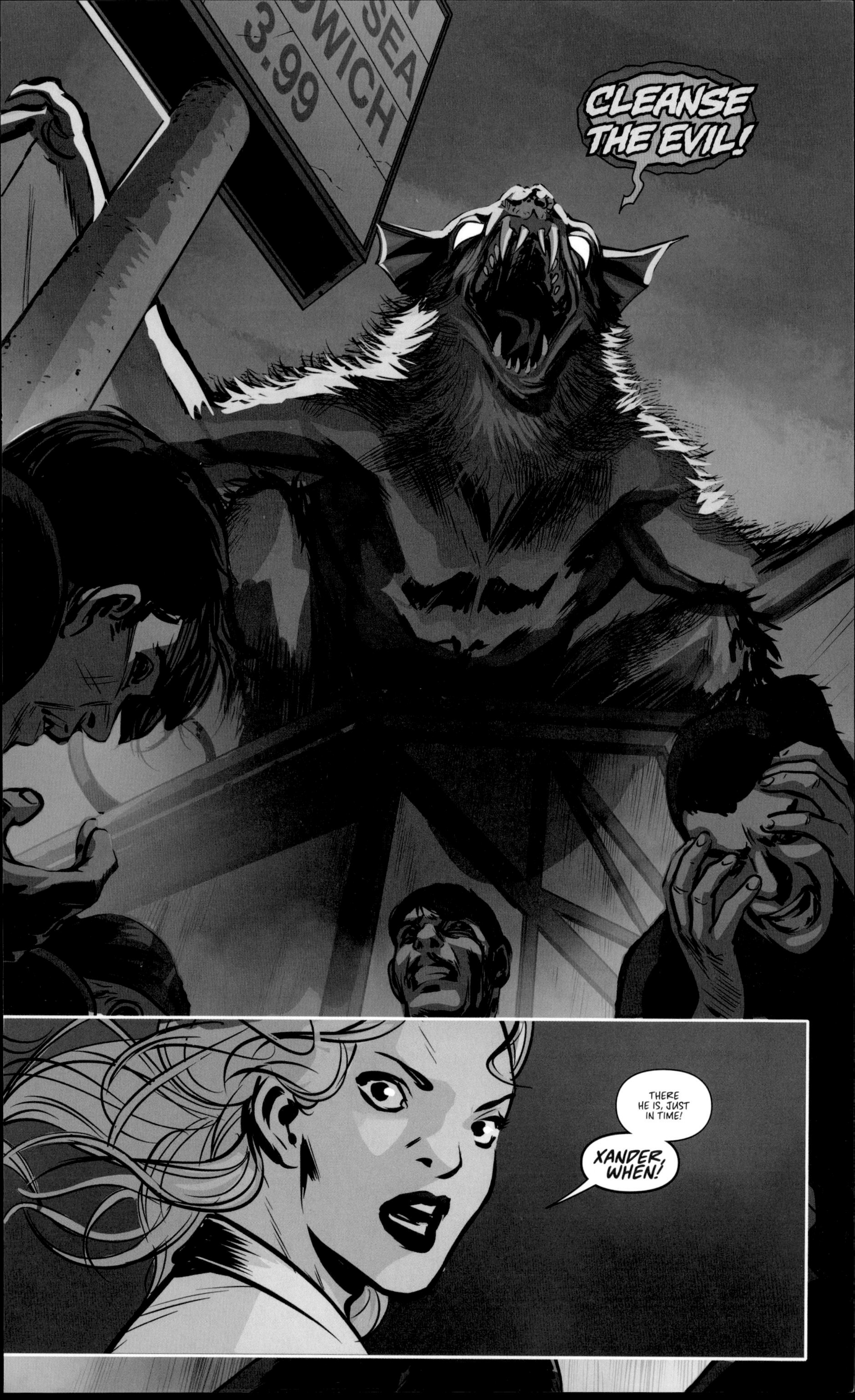
CLEANSE THE EVIL!
THERE HE IS, JUST IN TIME!
XANDER, WHEN!

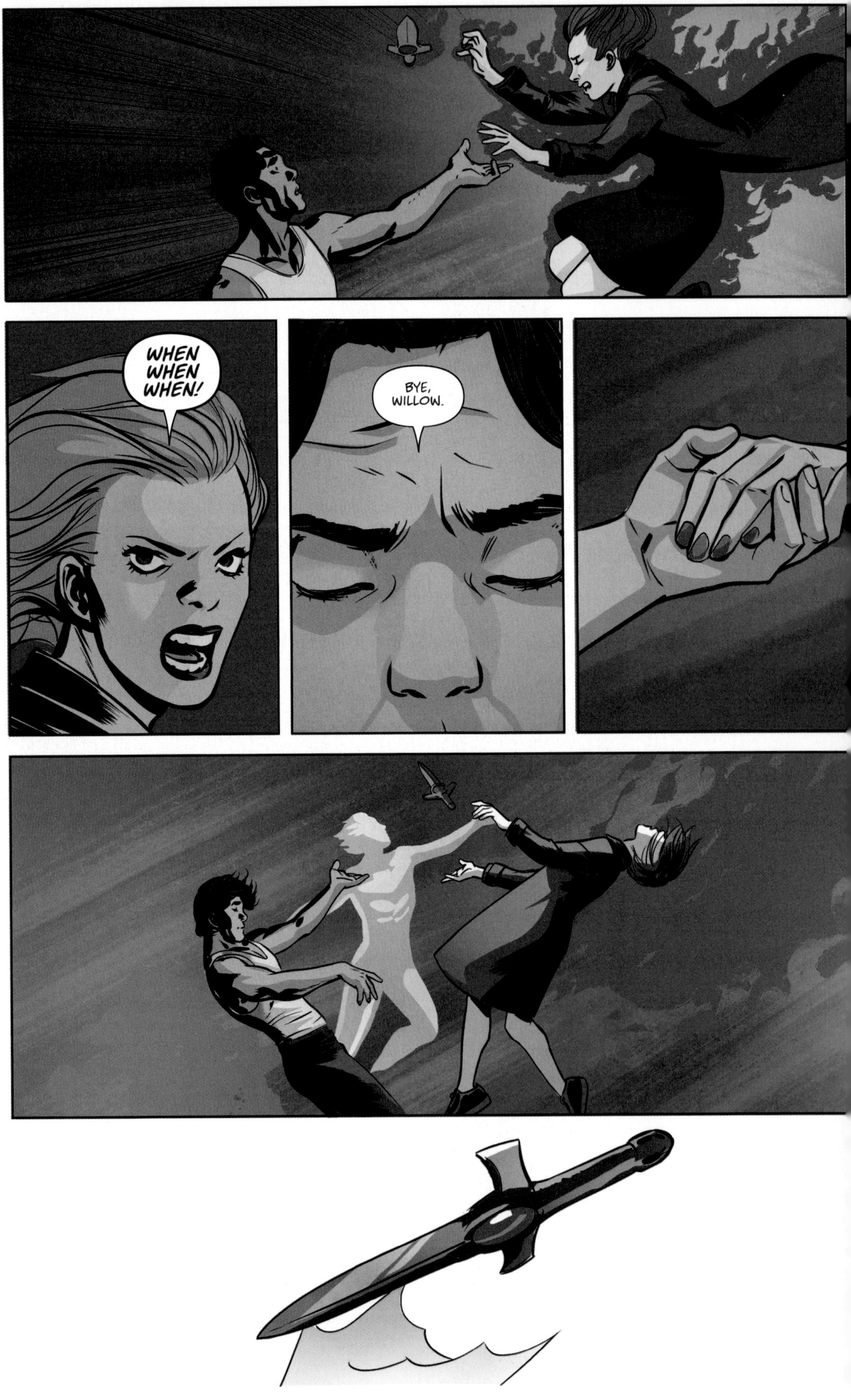
WHEN WHEN WHEN!
BYE, WILLOW.

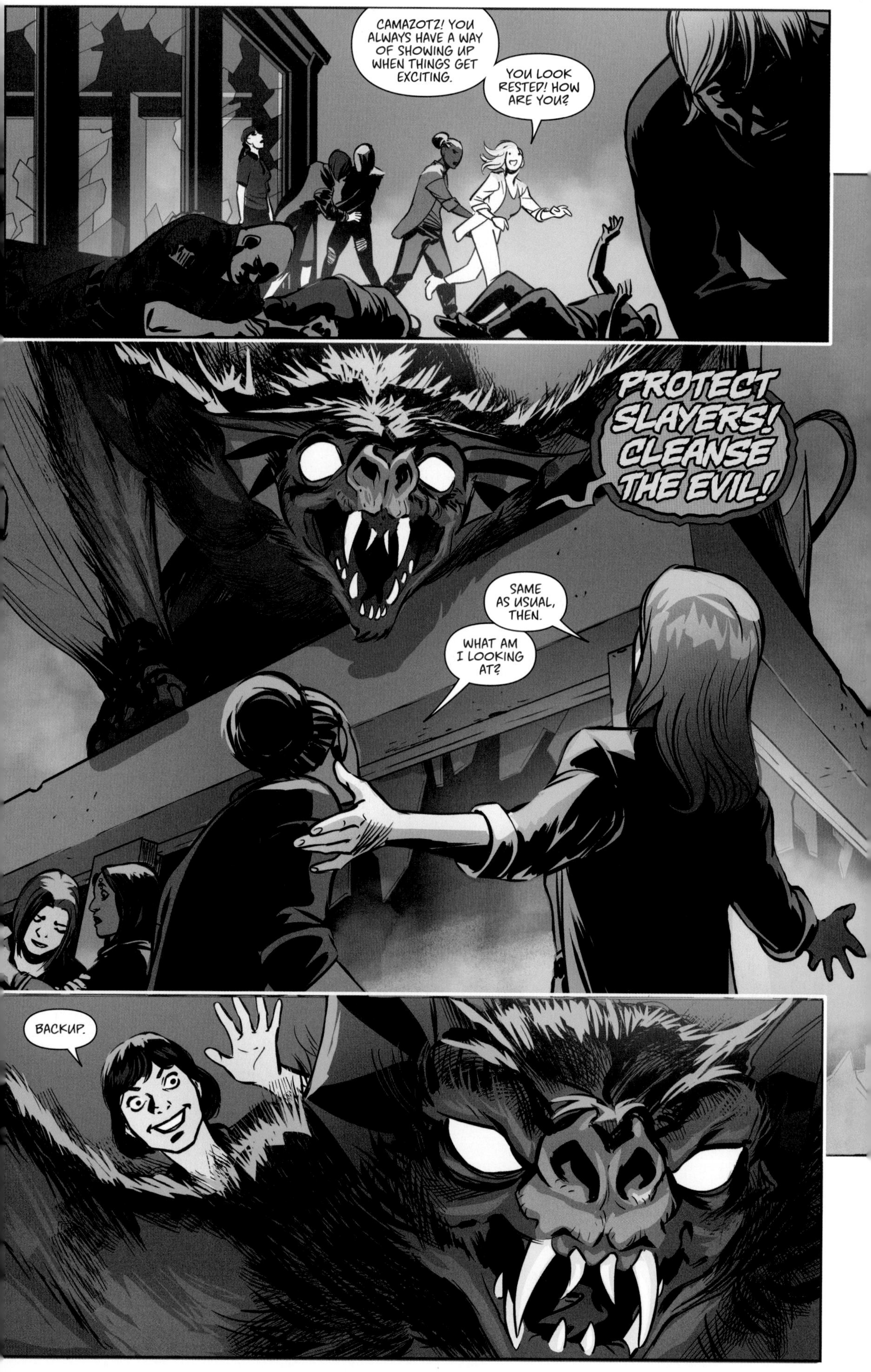
CAMAZOTZ! YOU ALWAYS HAVE A WAY OF SHOWING UP WHEN THINGS GET EXCITING.
YOU LOOK RESTED! HOW ARE YOU?
PROTECT SLAYERS! CLEANSE THE EVIL!
SAME AS USUAL, THEN.
WHAT AM I LOOKING AT?
BACKUP.

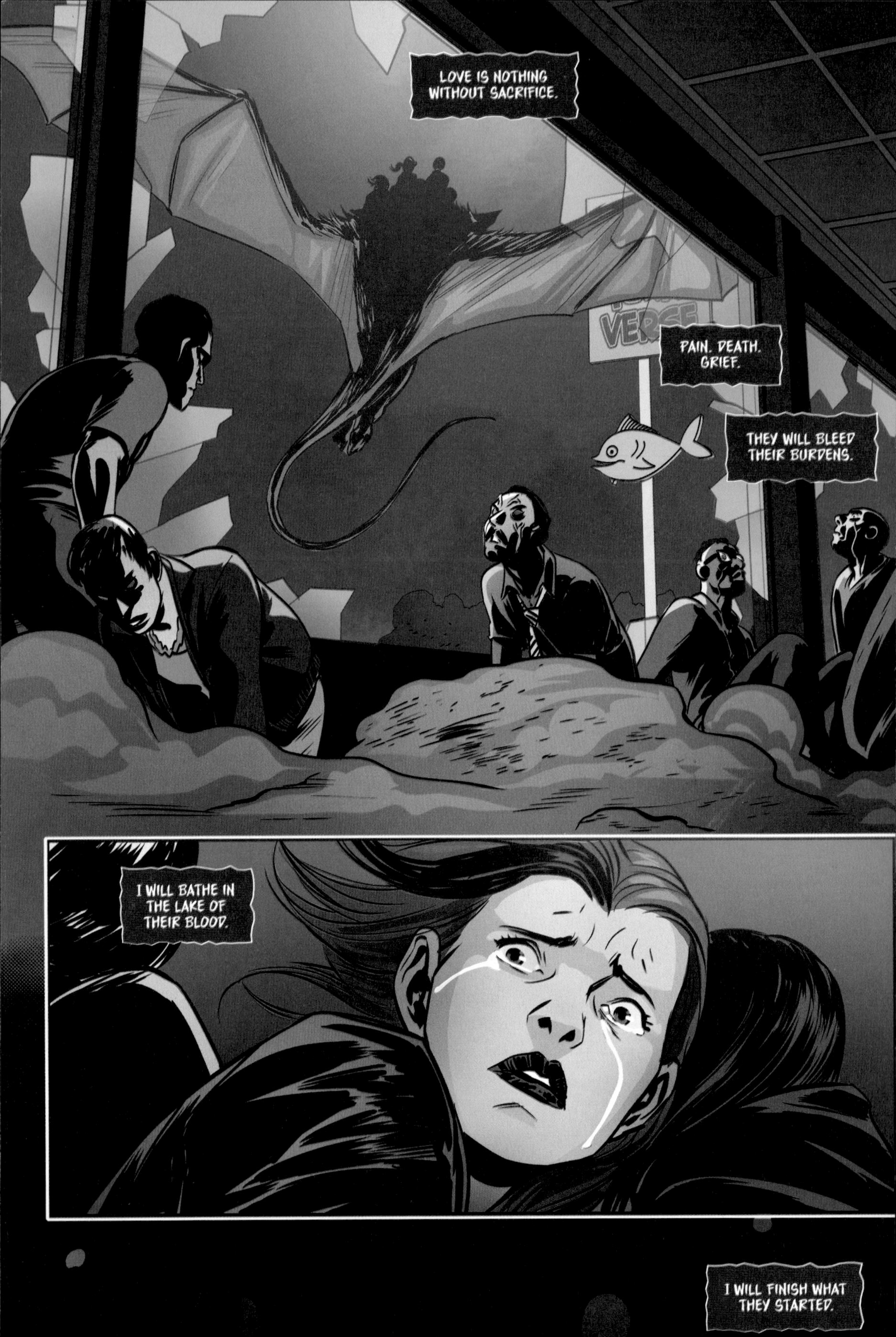
LOVE IS NOTHING WITHOUT SACRIFICE.
PAIN. DEATH. GRIEF.
THEY WILL BLEED THEIR BURDENS.
I WILL BATHE IN THE LAKE OF THEIR BLOOD.
I WILL FINISH WHAT THEY STARTED.

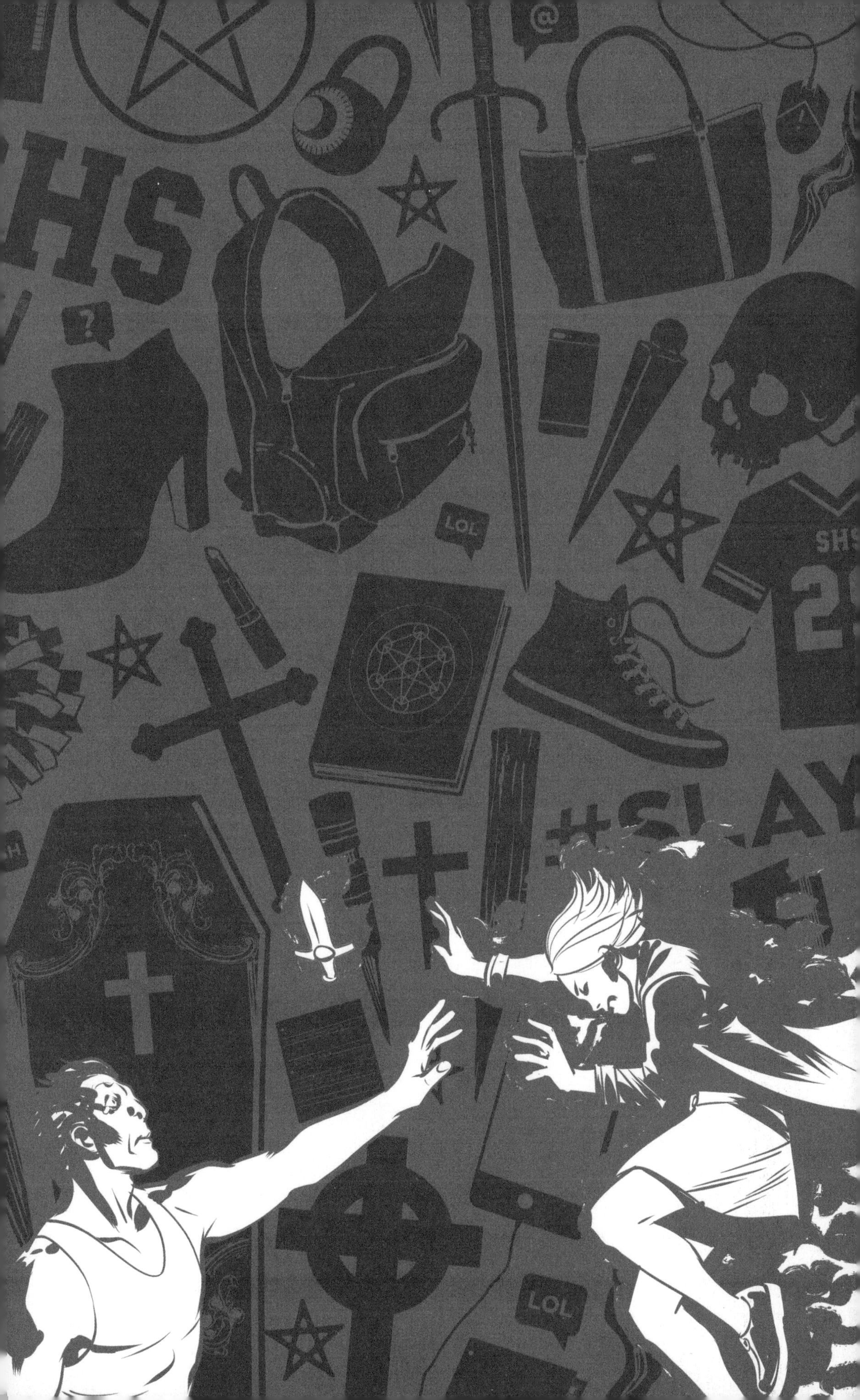
SHS
LOL
LOL

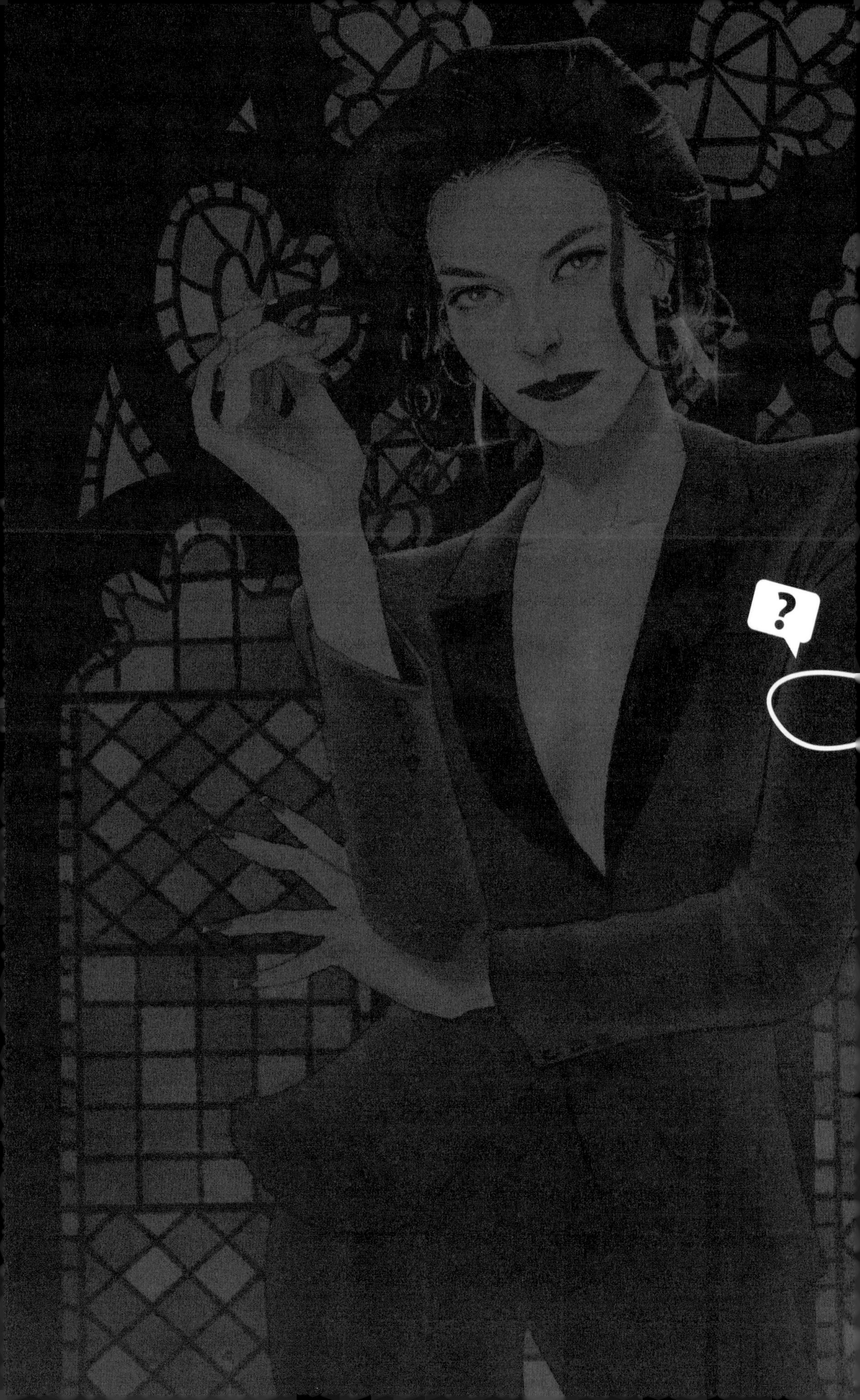

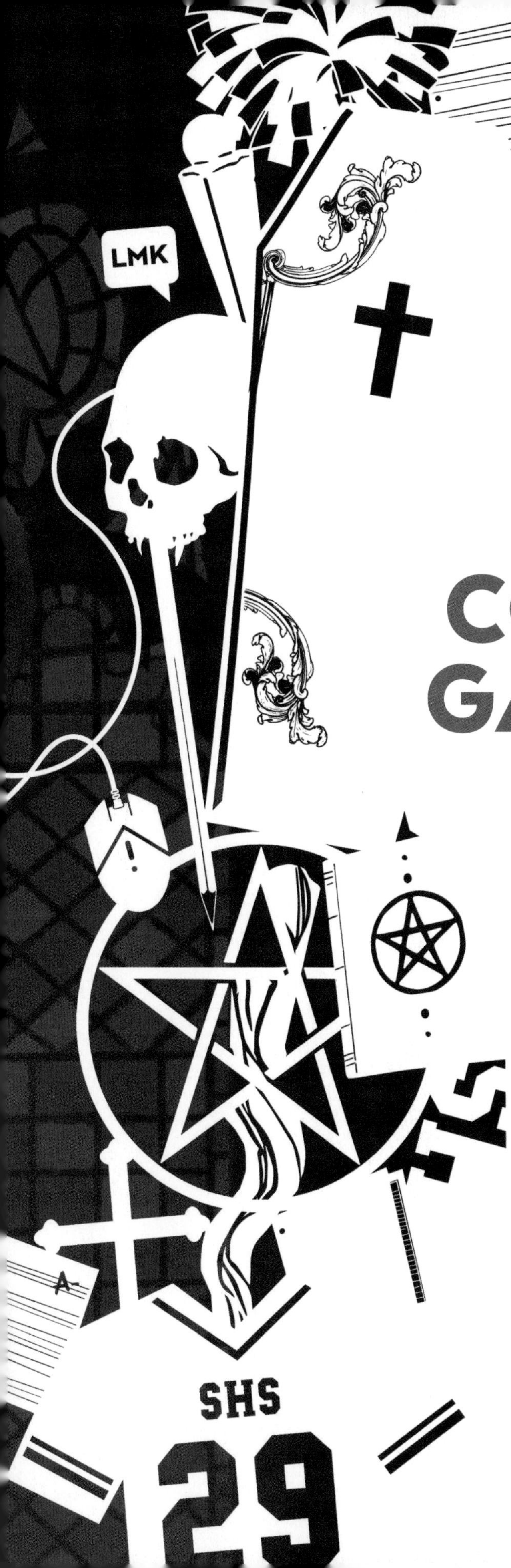
LMK
SHS
29

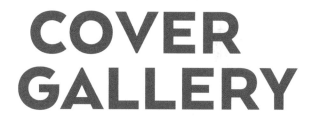

COVER GALLERY

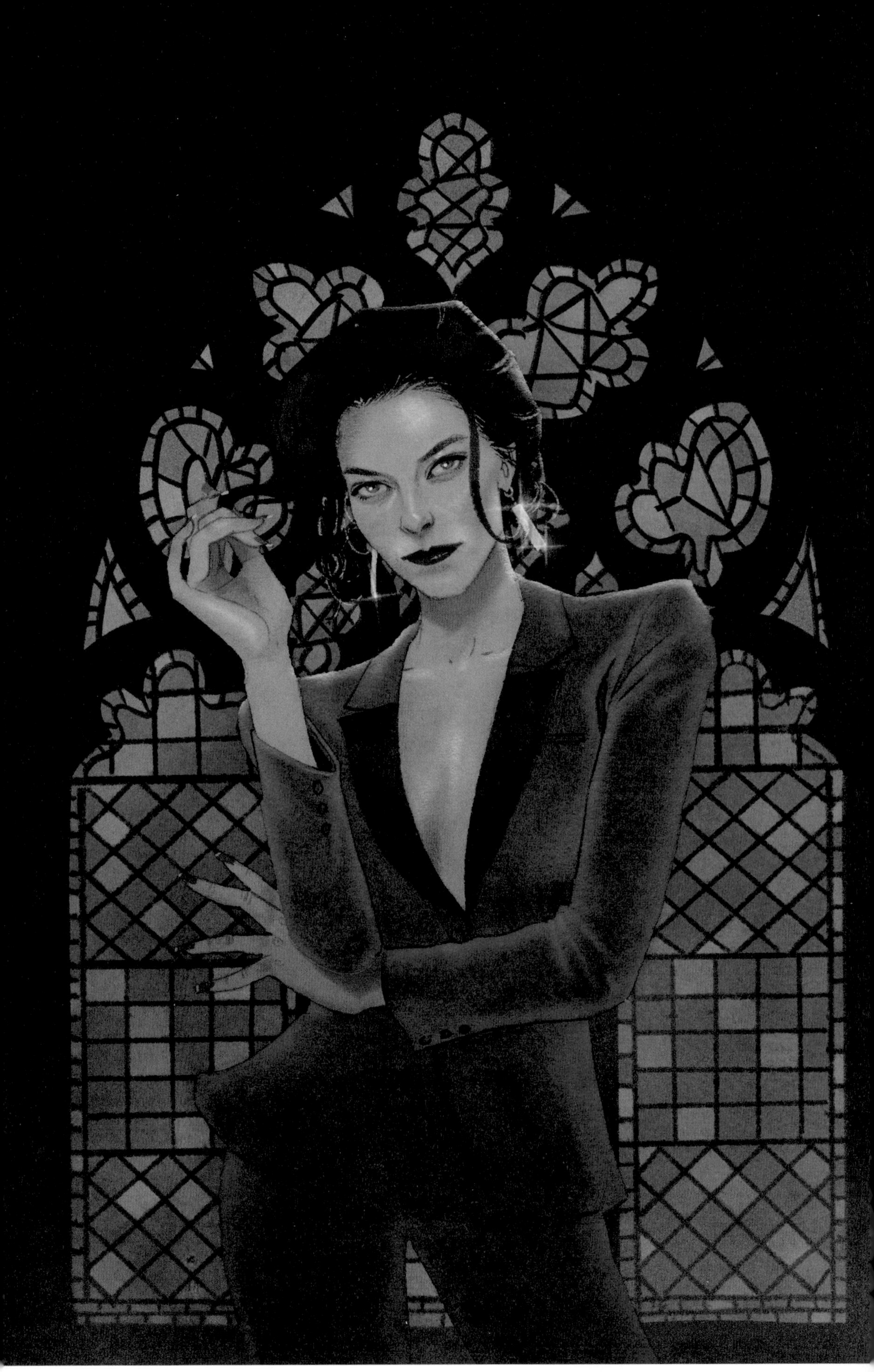

Issue Nine Spotlight Variant by **Kevin Wada**

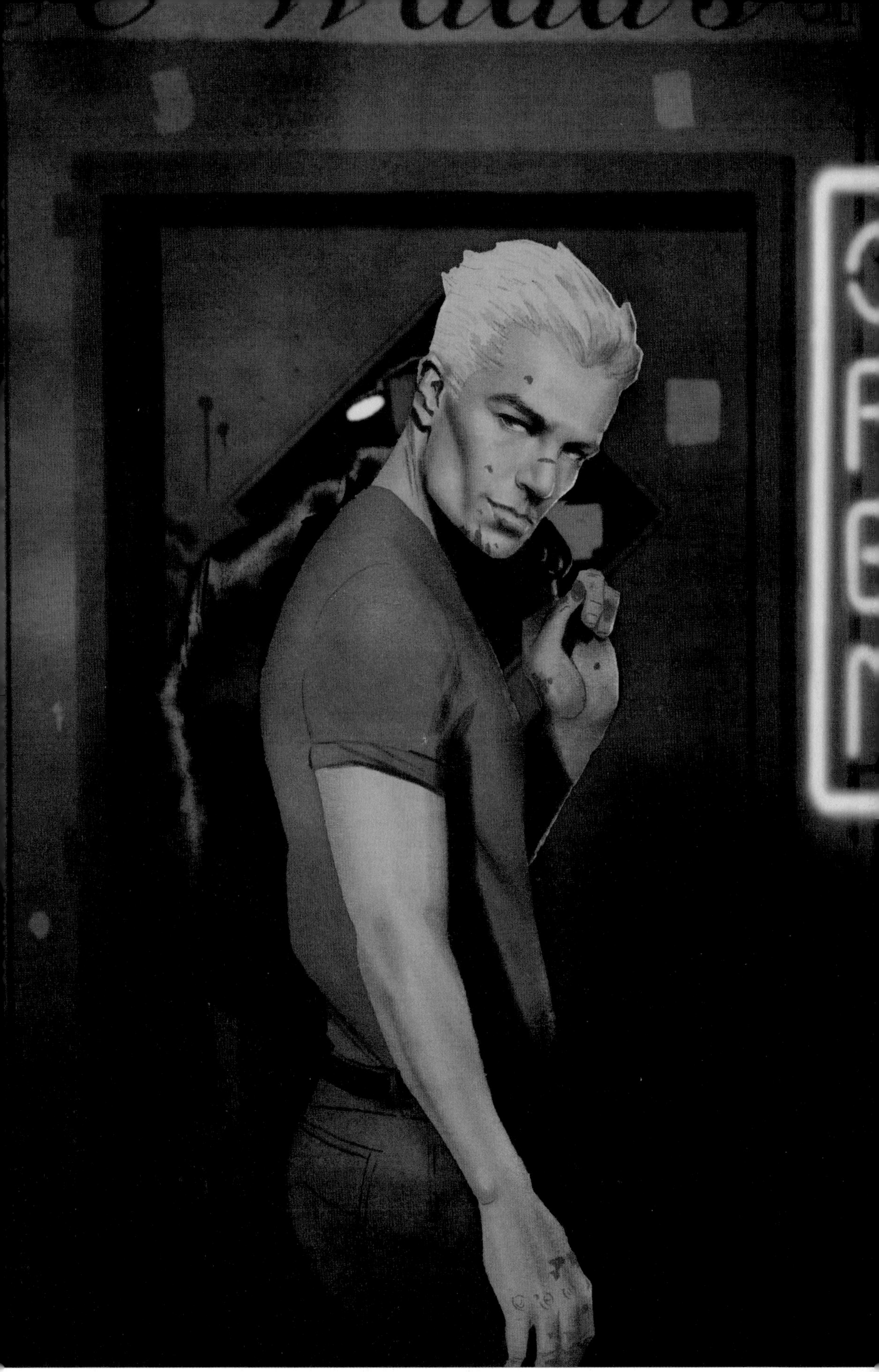

Issue Ten Spotlight Variant by **Kevin Wada**

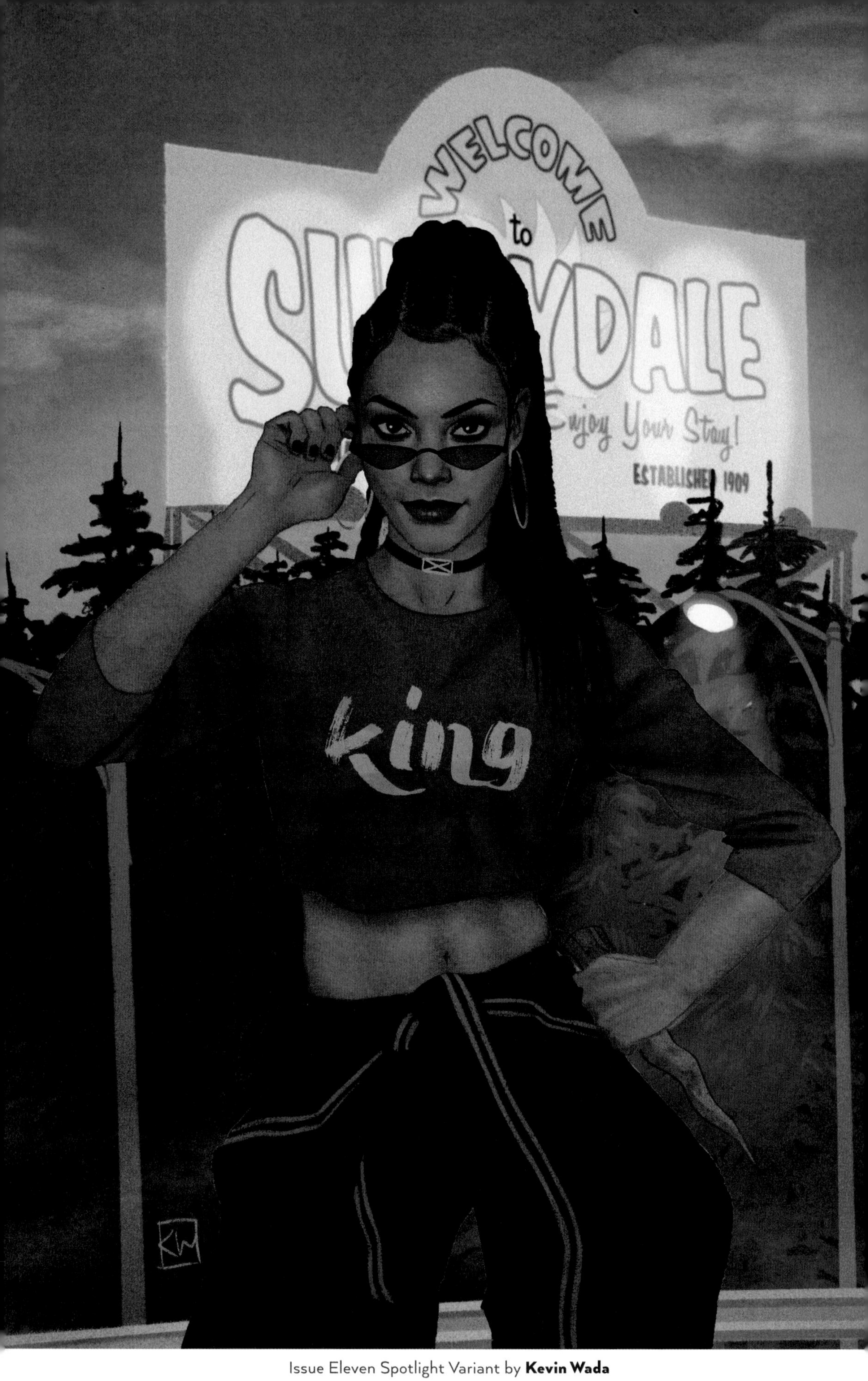
WELCOME
to
Enjoy Your Stay!
1909
king

Issue Eleven Spotlight Variant by **Kevin Wada**

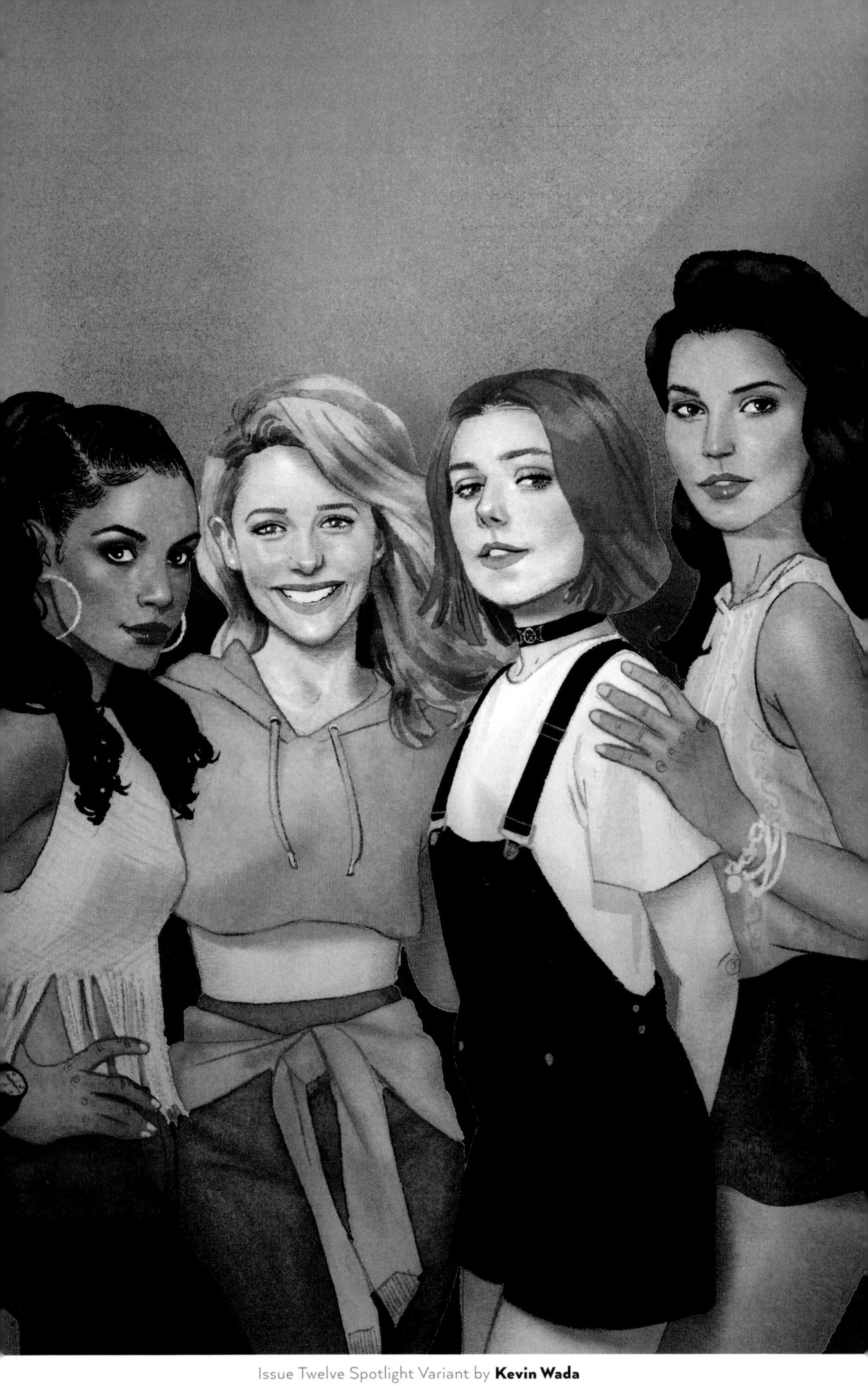

Issue Twelve Spotlight Variant by **Kevin Wada**

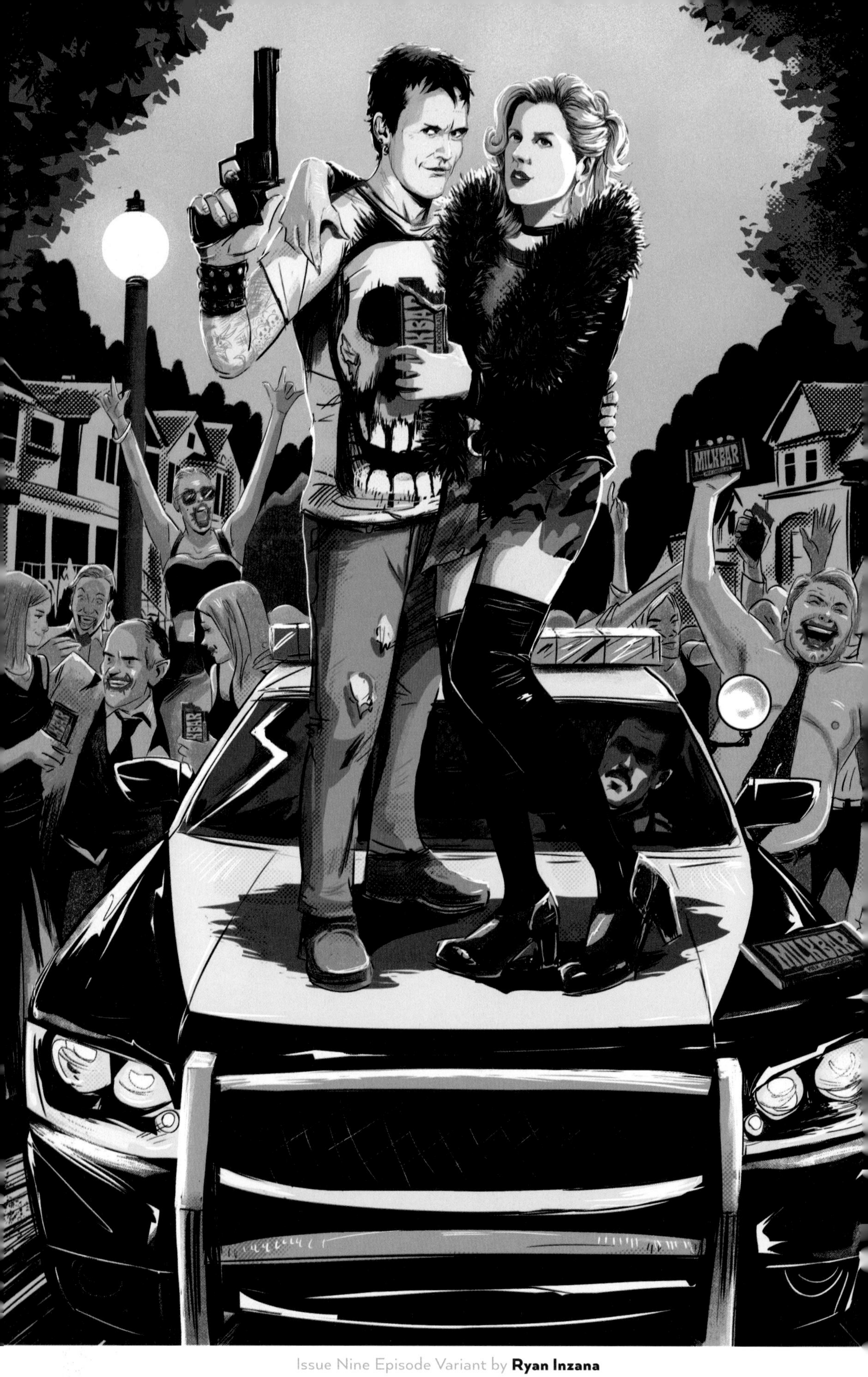
MILKBAR
MILKBAR

Issue Nine Episode Variant by **Ryan Inzana**

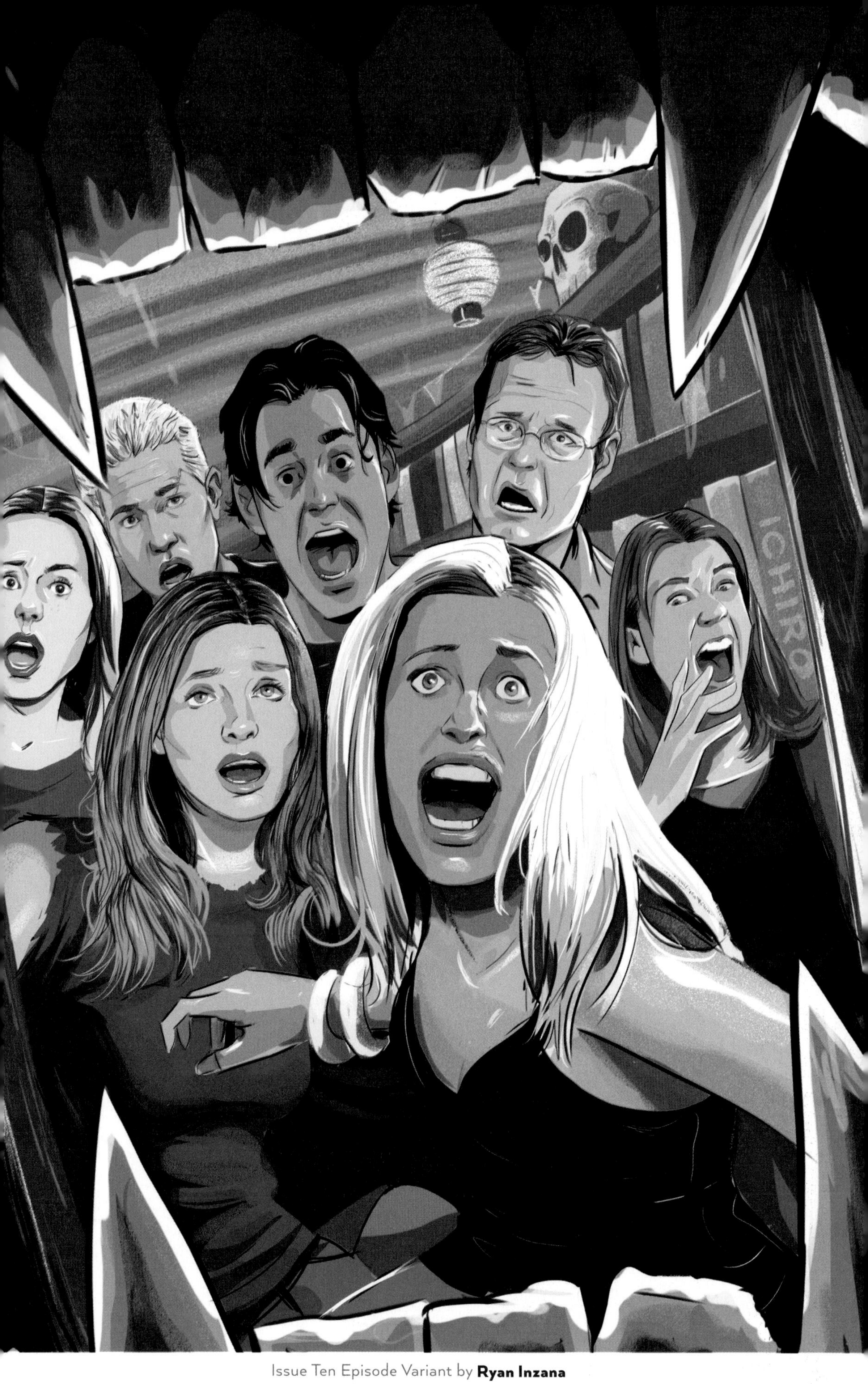
ICHIRO

Issue Ten Episode Variant by **Ryan Inzana**

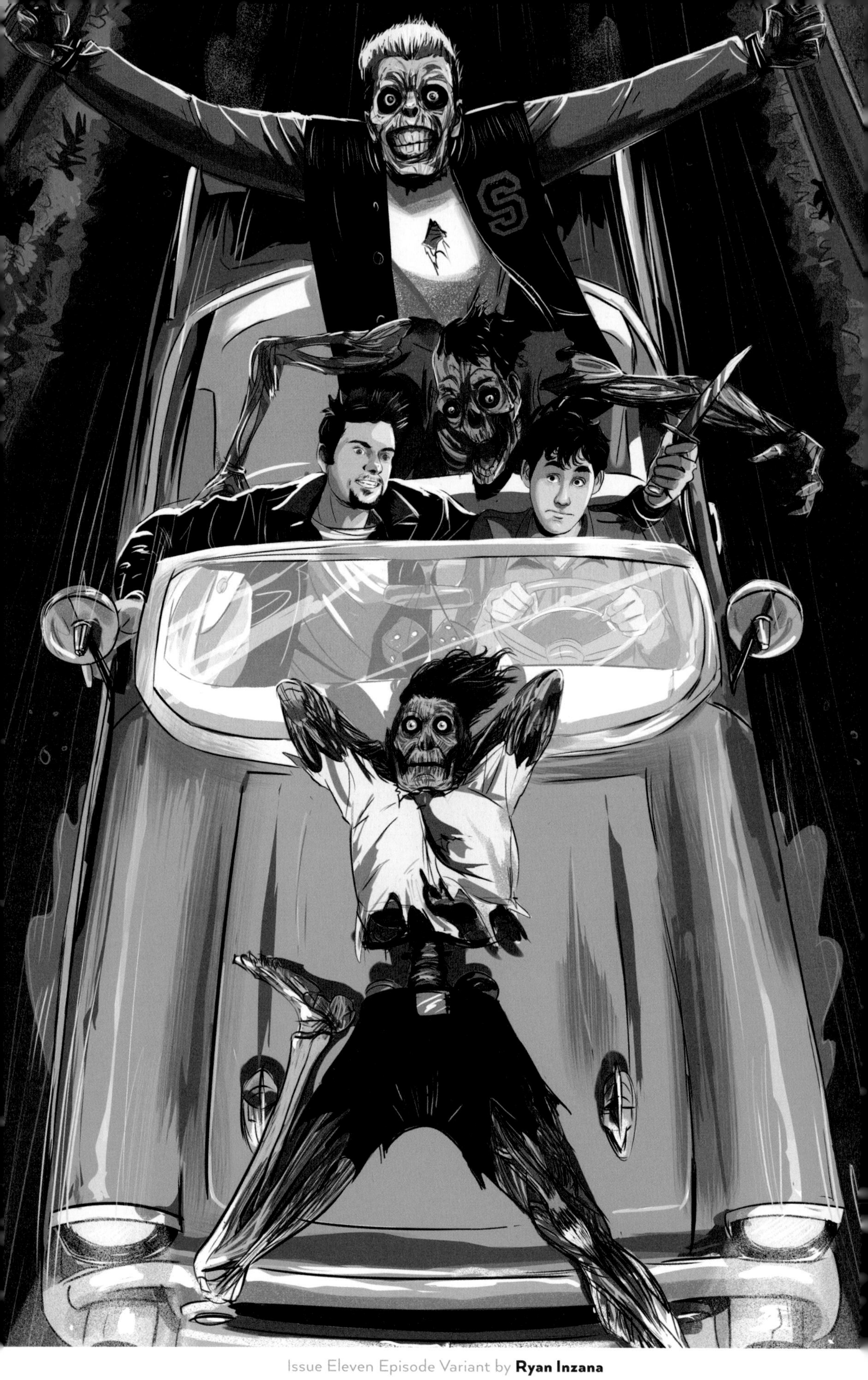
S

Issue Eleven Episode Variant by **Ryan Inzana**

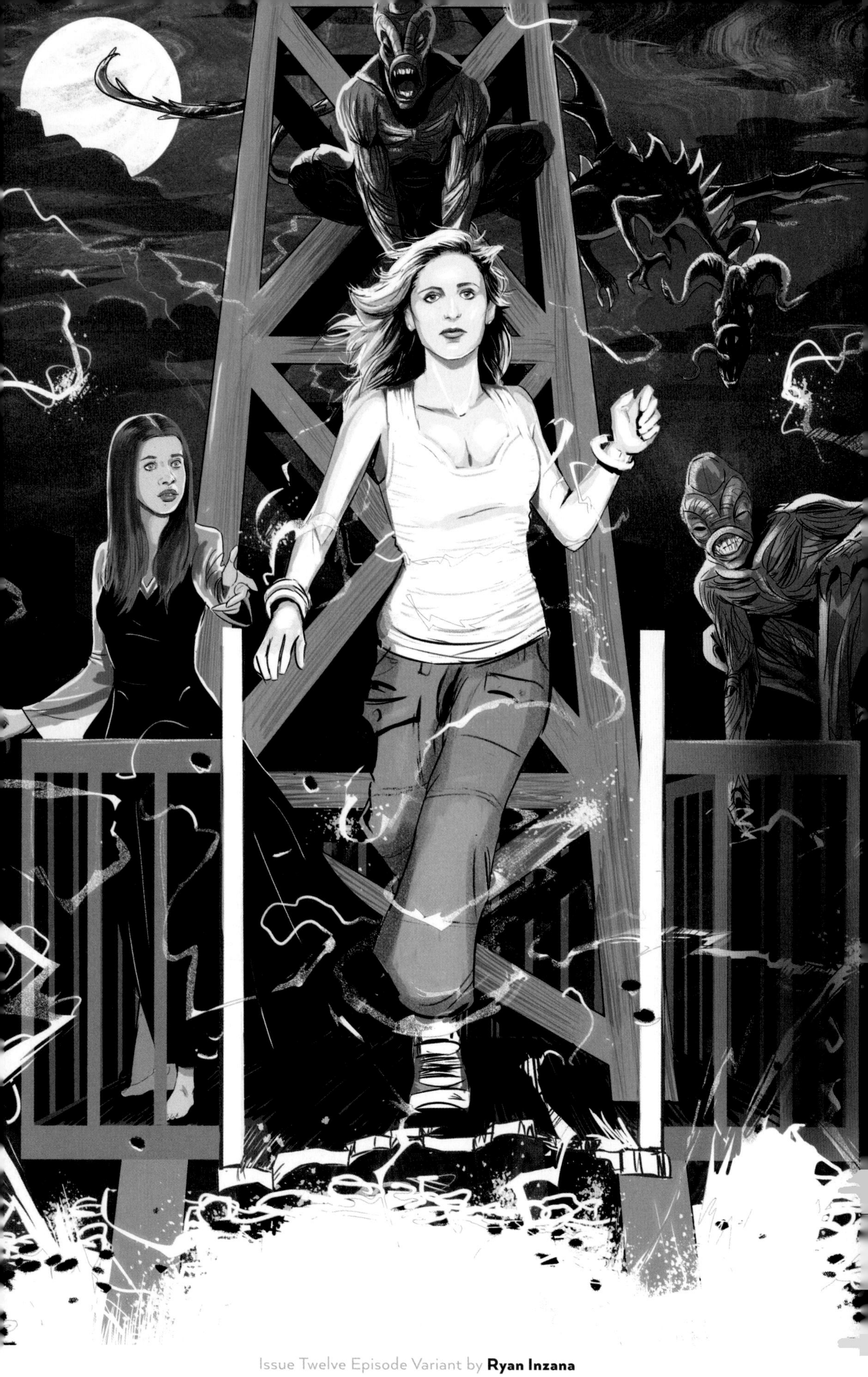

Issue Twelve Episode Variant by **Ryan Inzana**

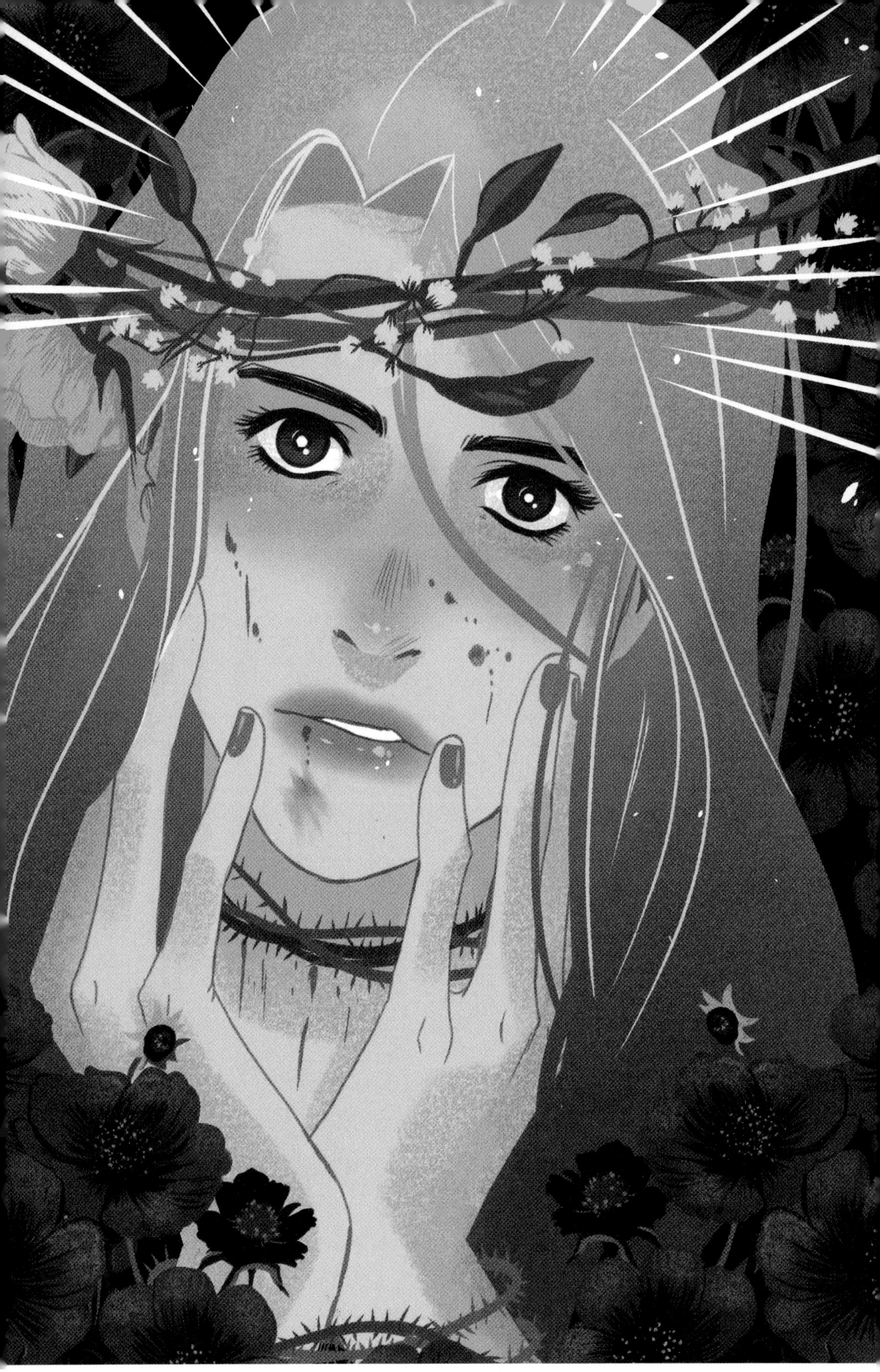

Issue Nine Incentive Cover by **Cara McGee**

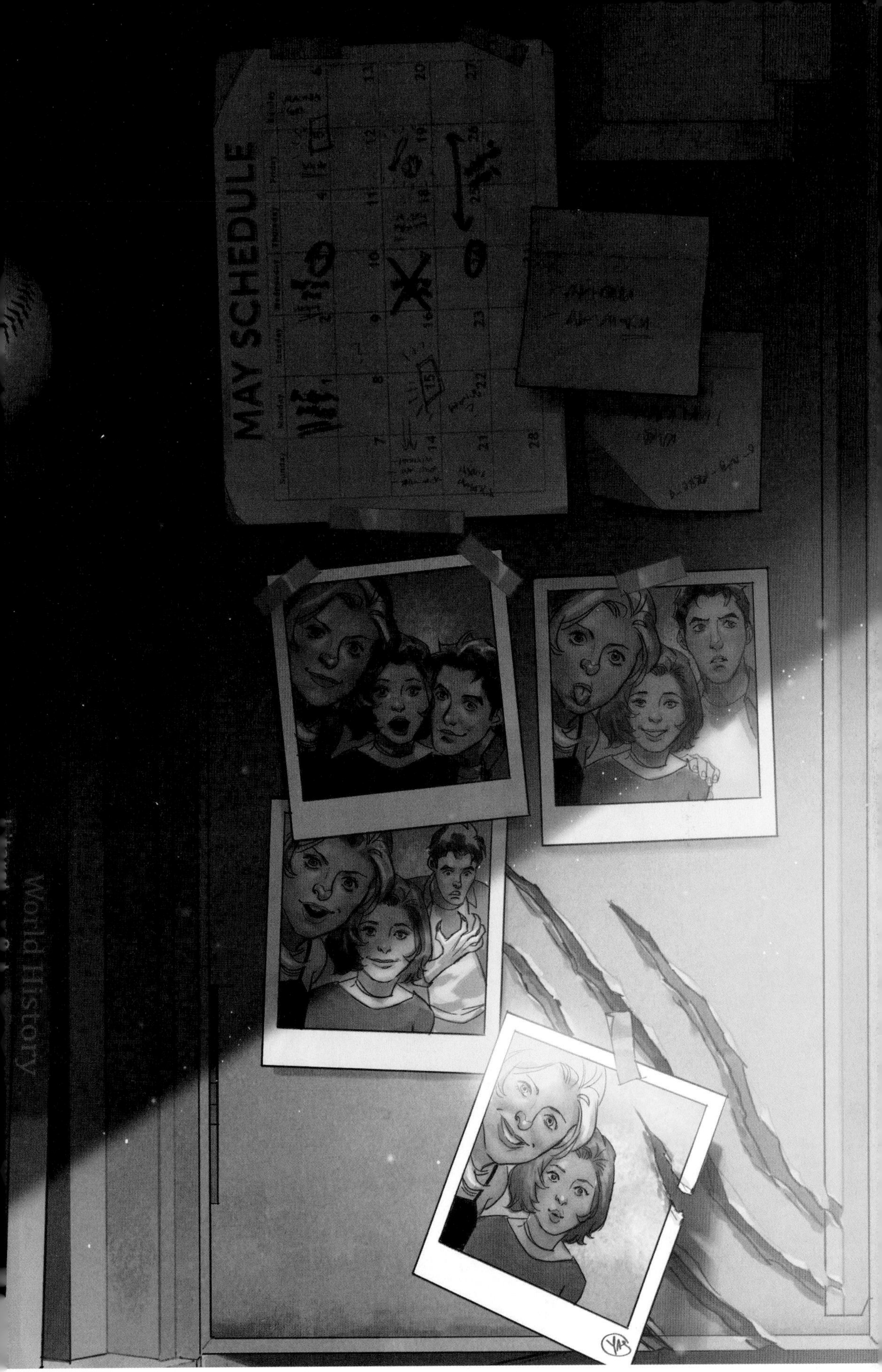
MAY SCHEDULE
World History

Issue Ten Incentive Cover by **Yasmine Putri**

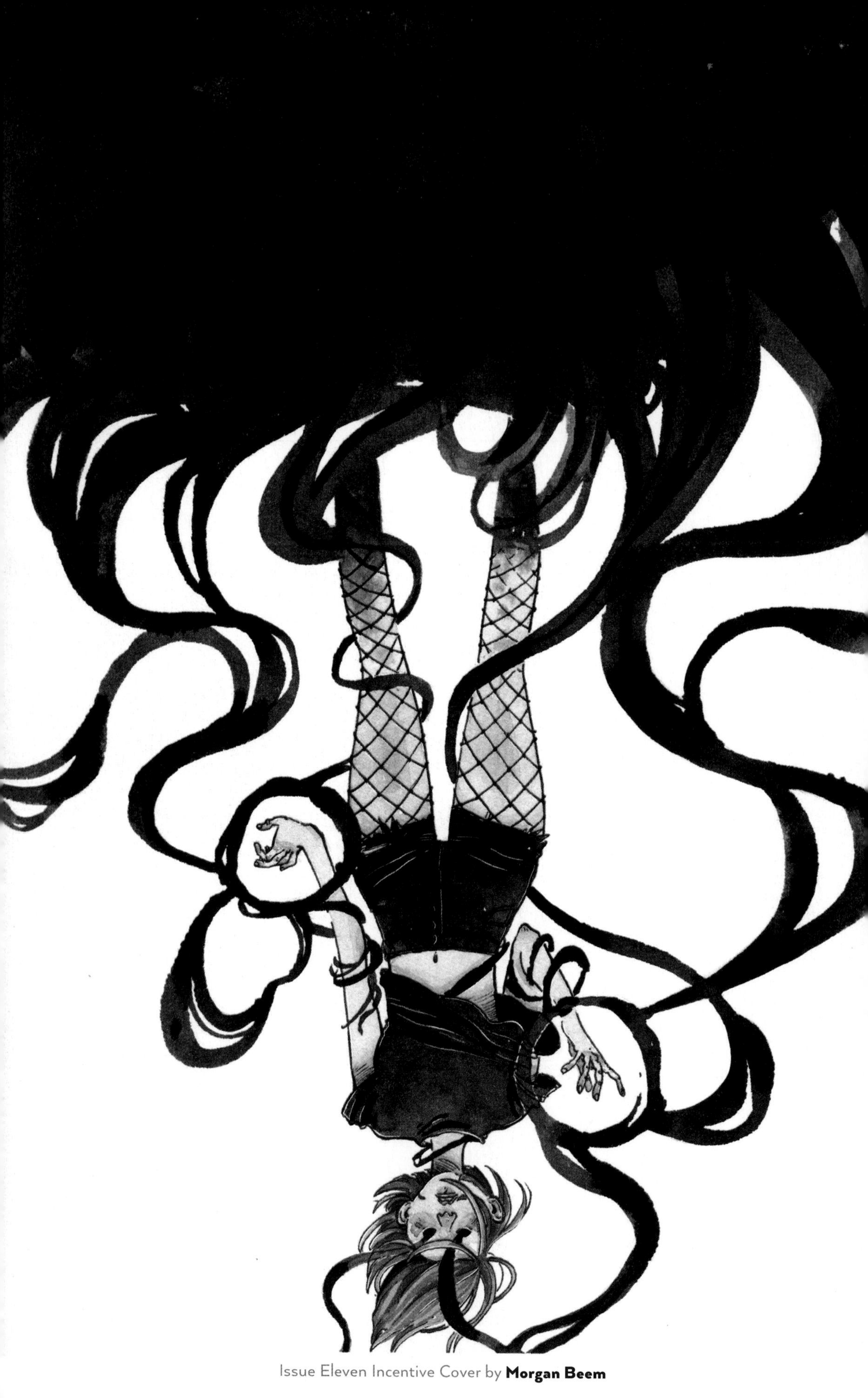

Issue Eleven Incentive Cover by **Morgan Beem**

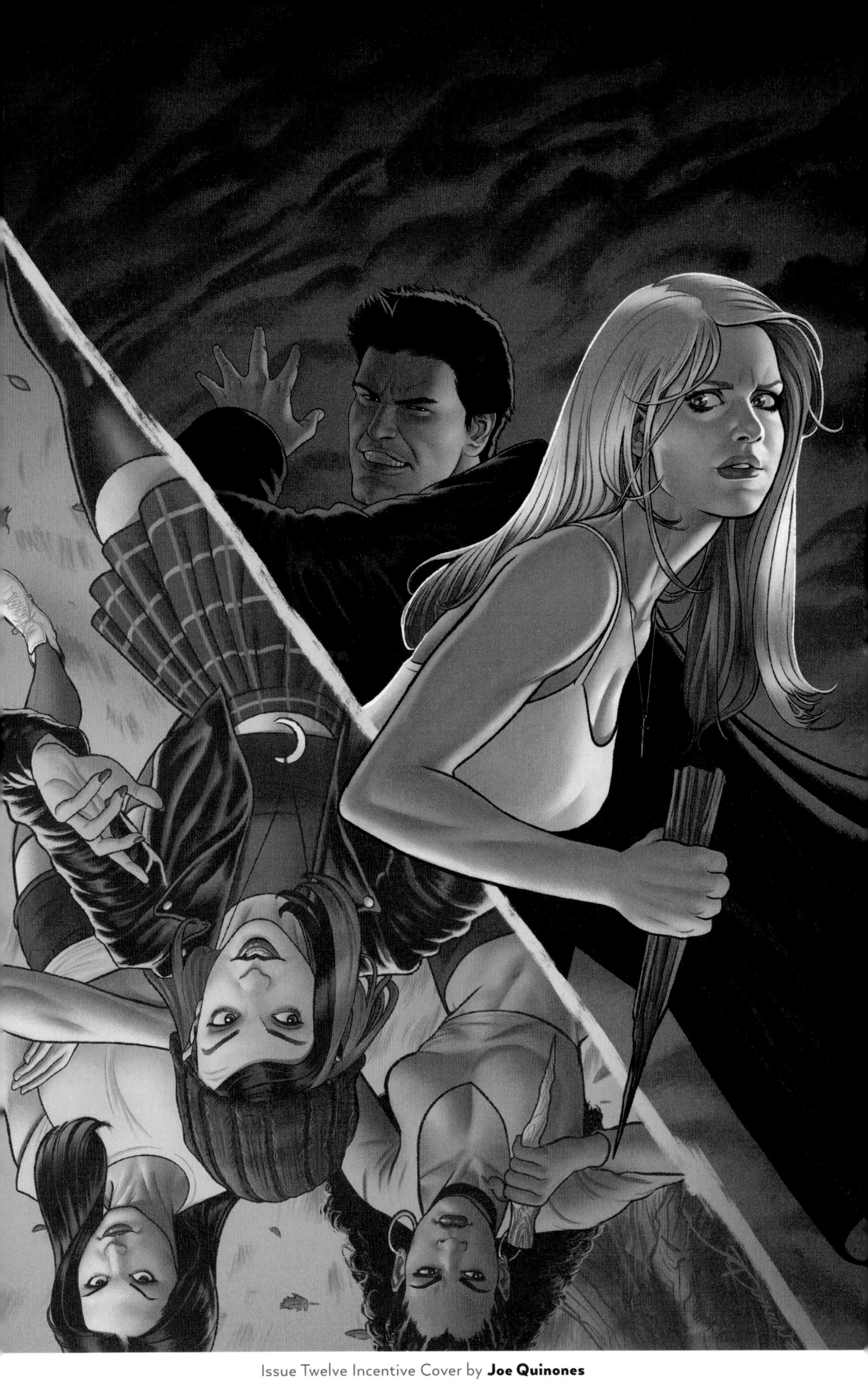

Issue Twelve Incentive Cover by **Joe Quinones**

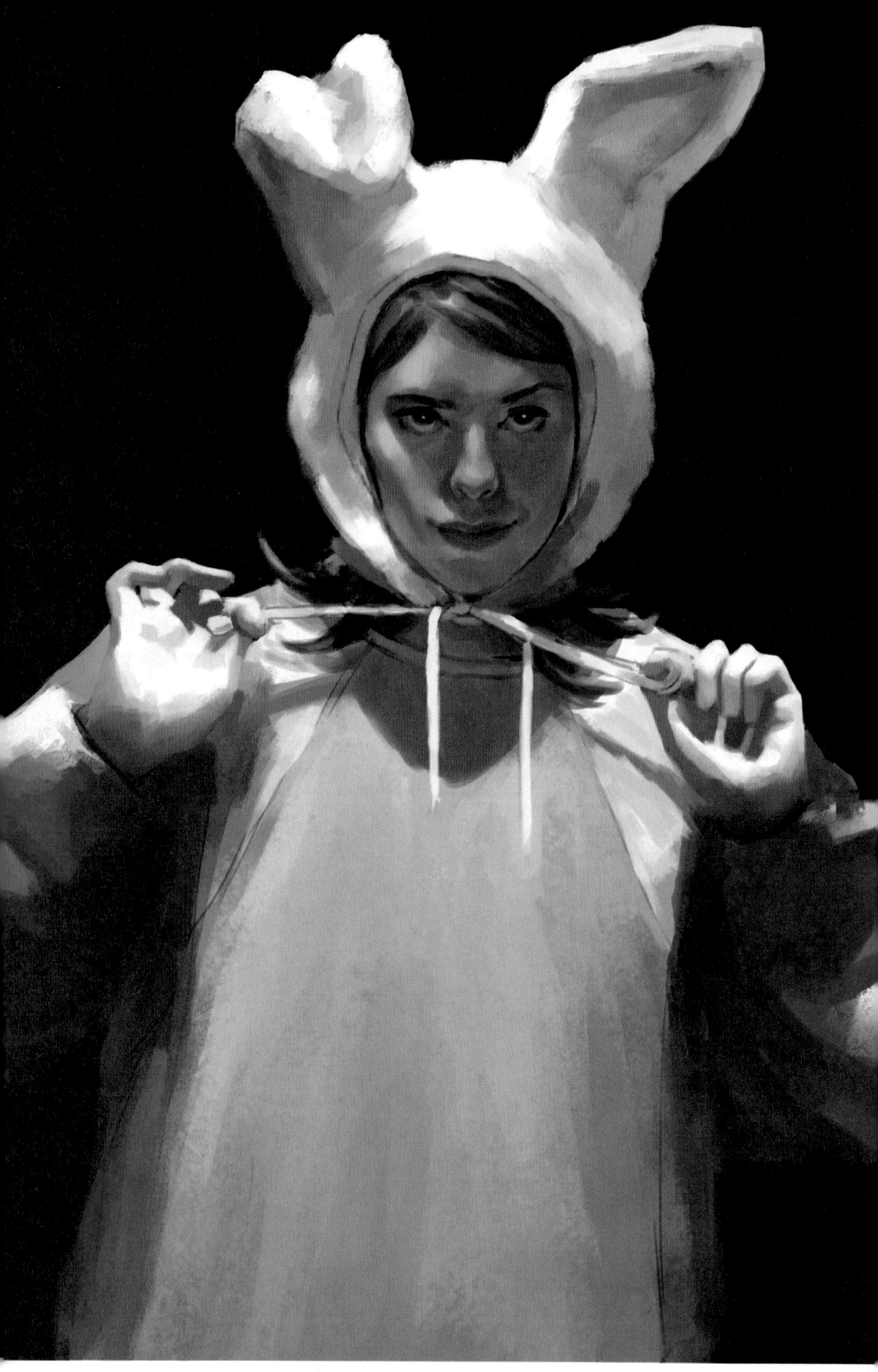

Issue Nine Choose Your Side Slayer Variant by **Miguel Mercado**

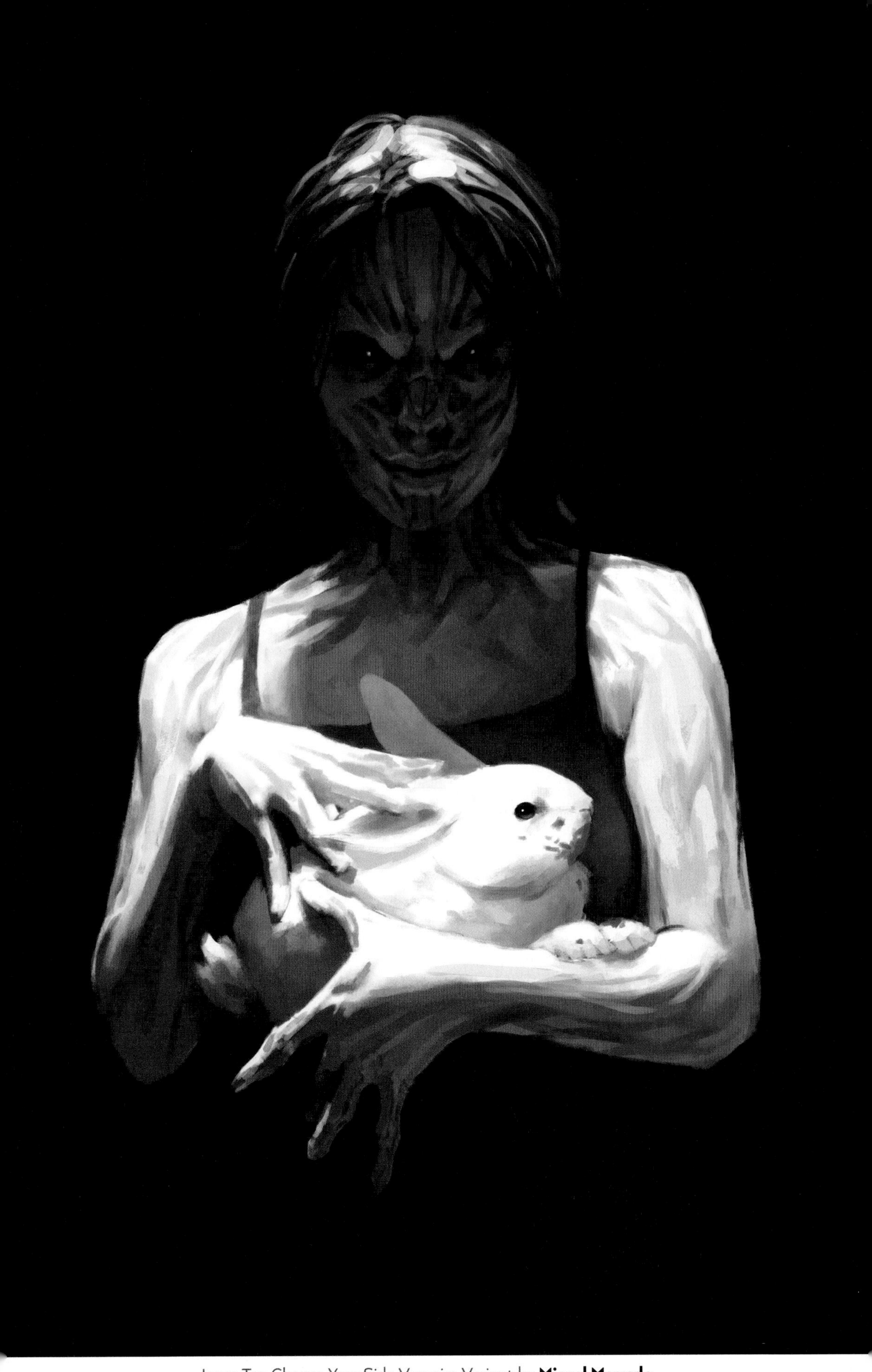

Issue Ten Choose Your Side Vampire Variant by **Miguel Mercado**

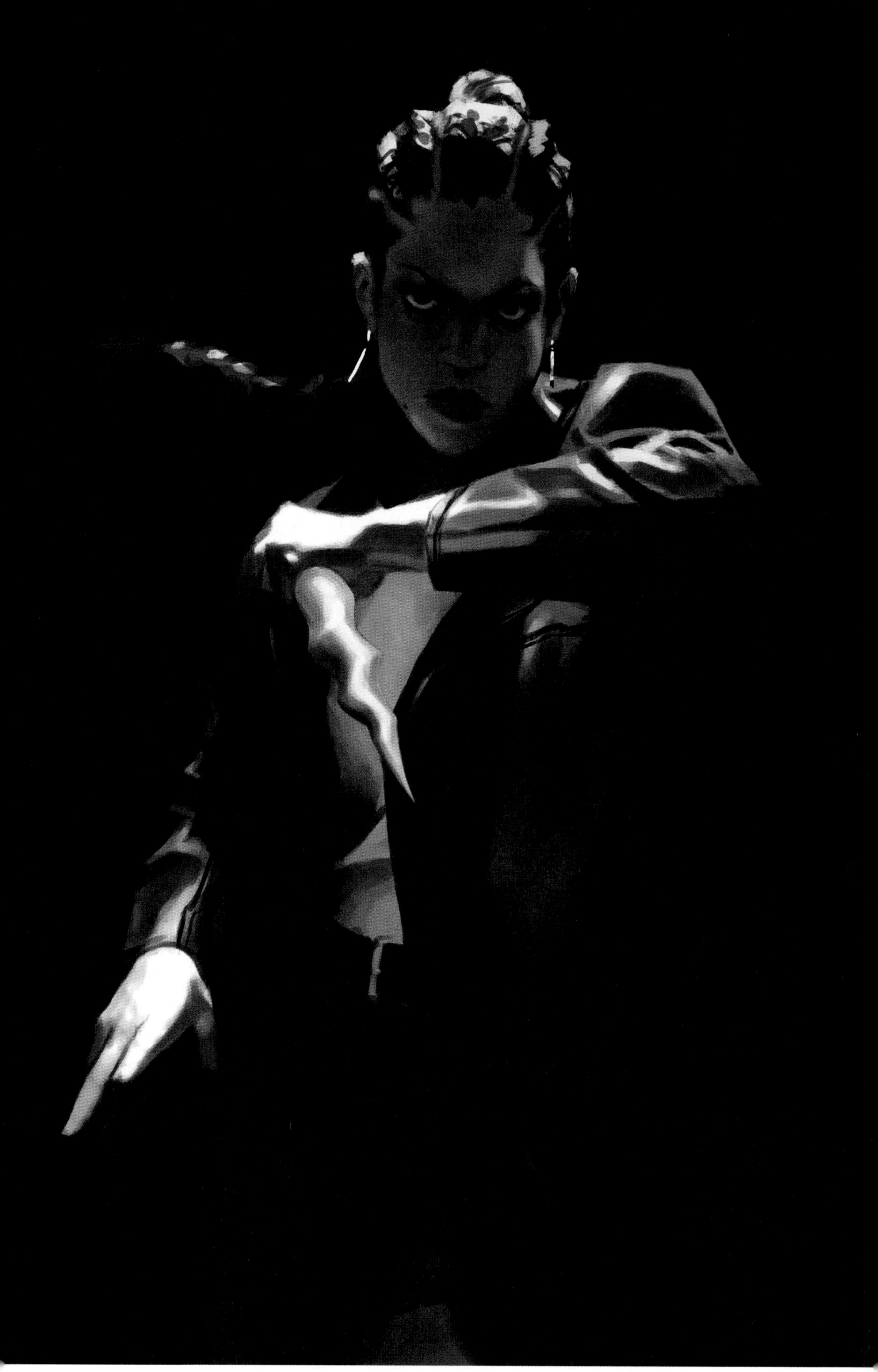

Issue Eleven Choose Your Side Slayer Variant by **Miguel Mercado**

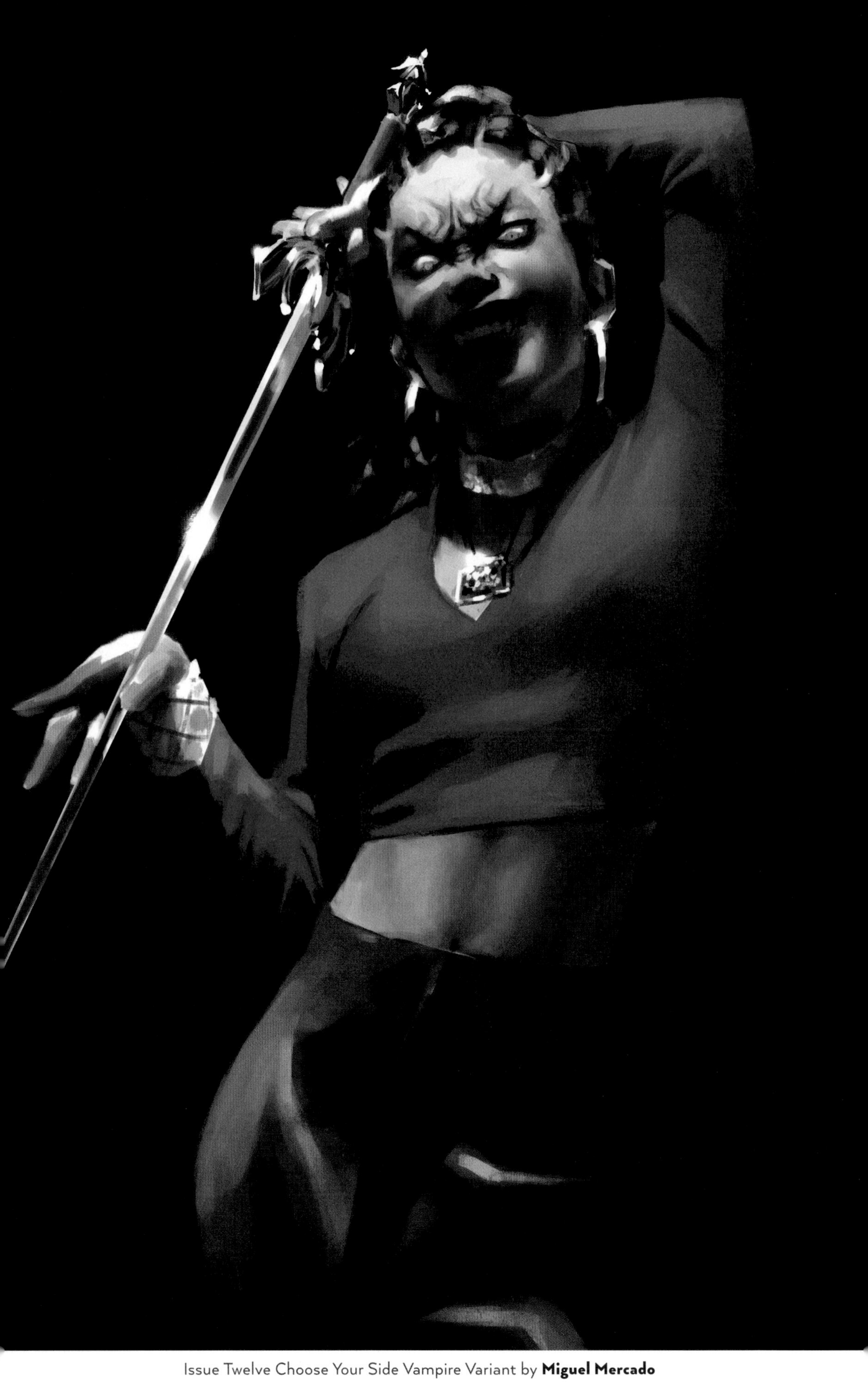

Issue Twelve Choose Your Side Vampire Variant by **Miguel Mercado**

CHARACTER DESIGNS
AND SKETCHES

by **David López**

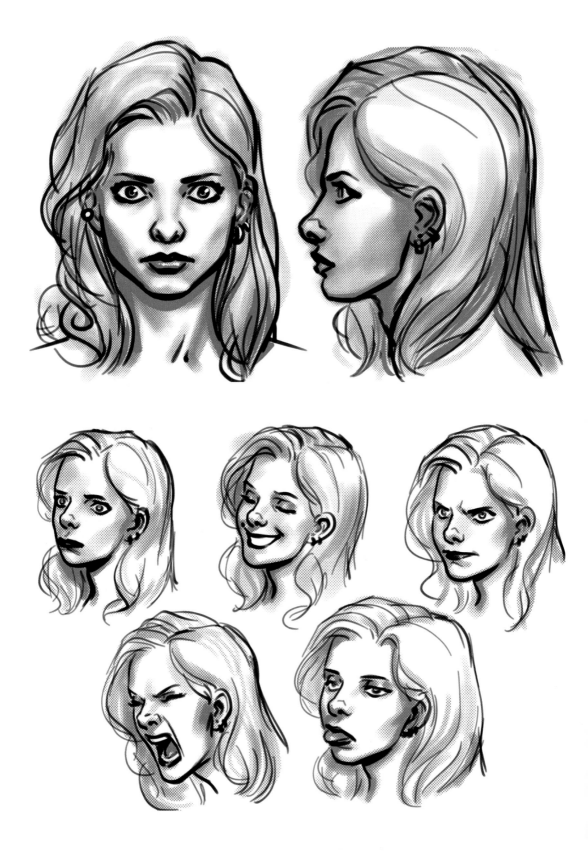

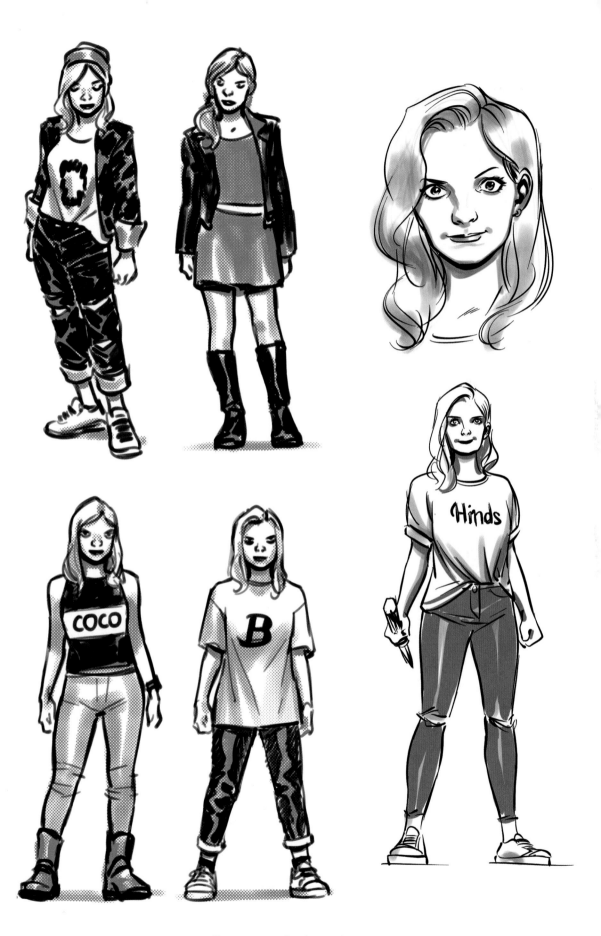

Buffy Summers Sketches and Designs

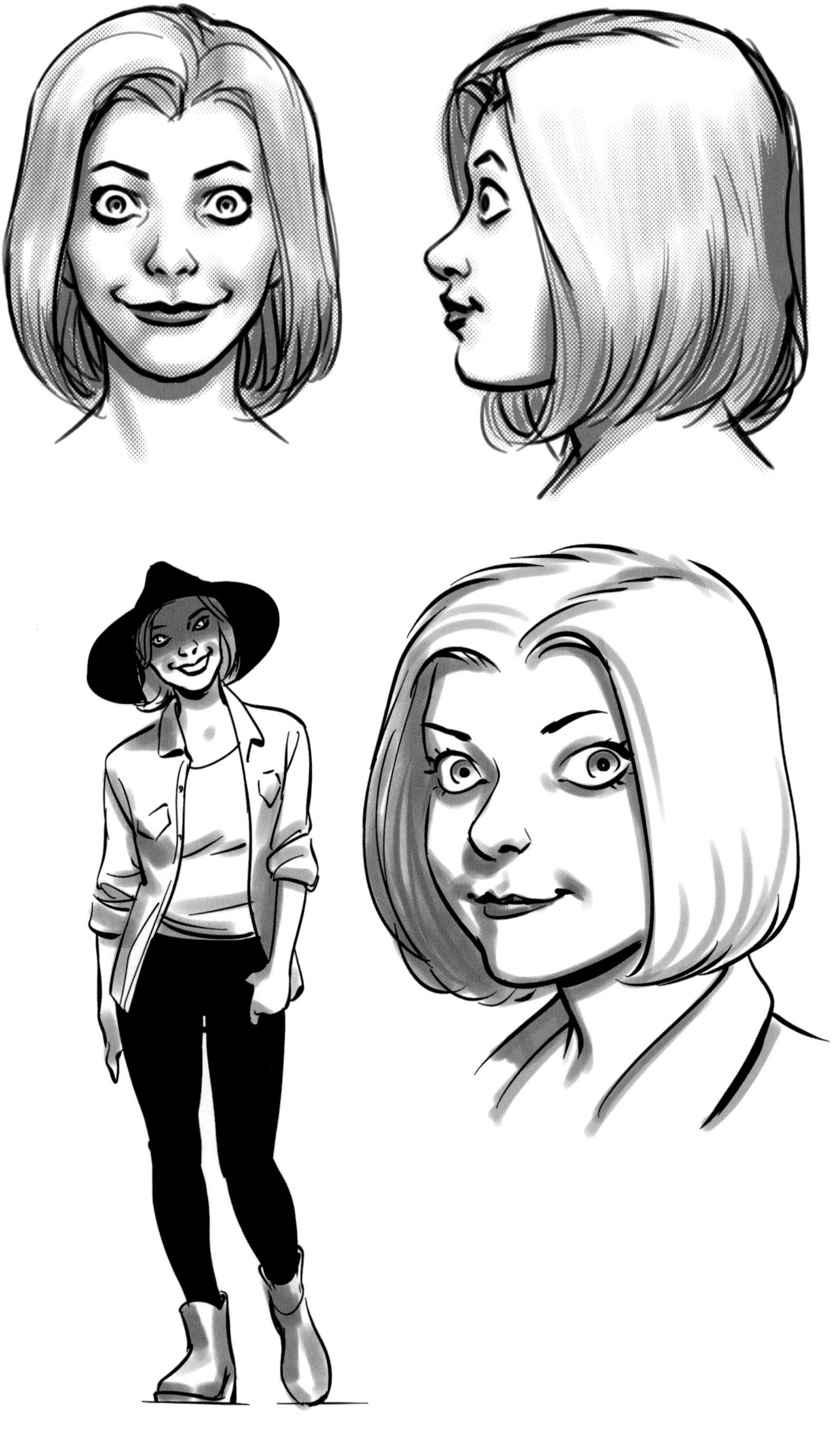

Willow Rosenberg Sketches and Designs

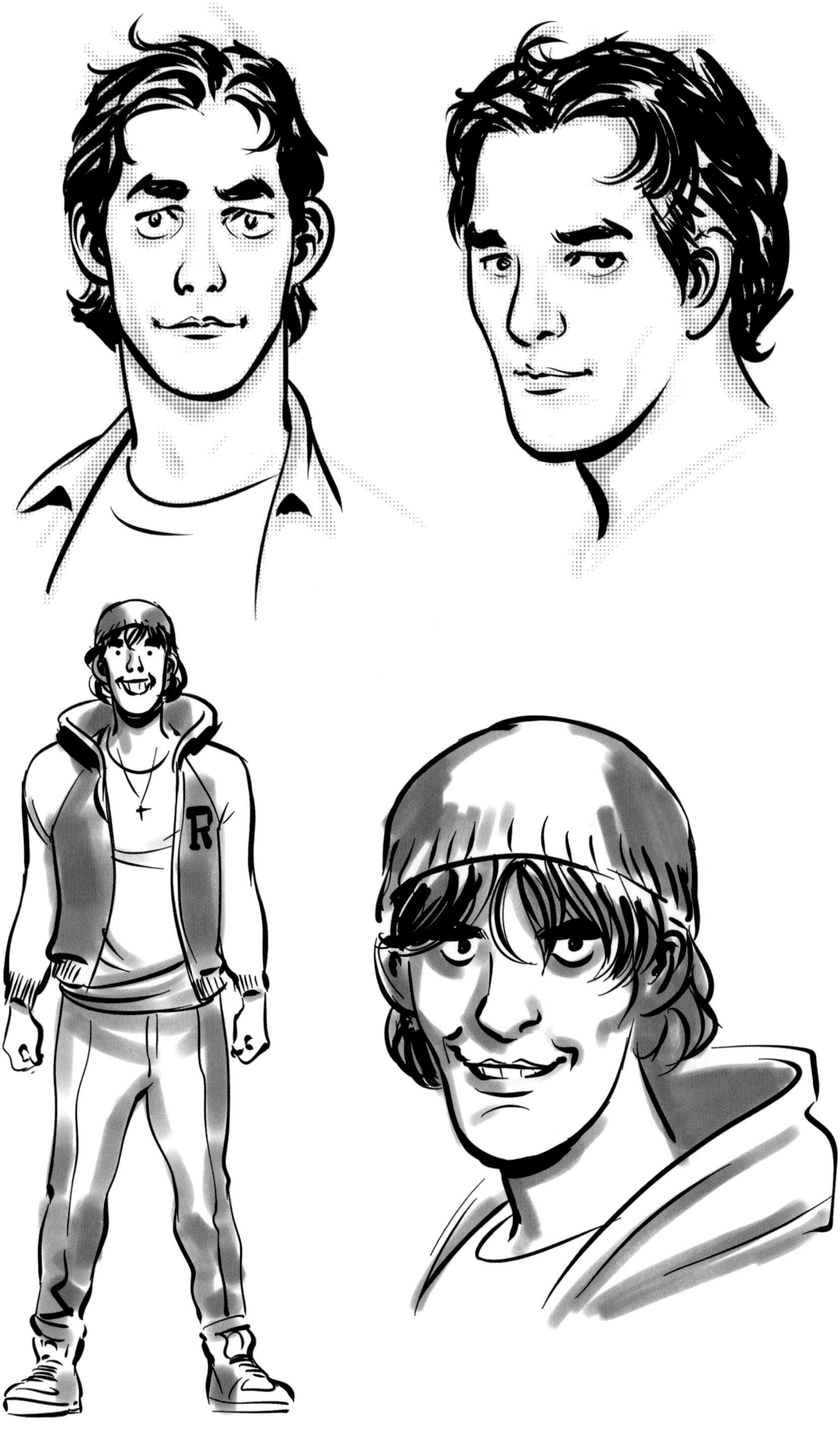
R

Xander Harris Sketches and Designs

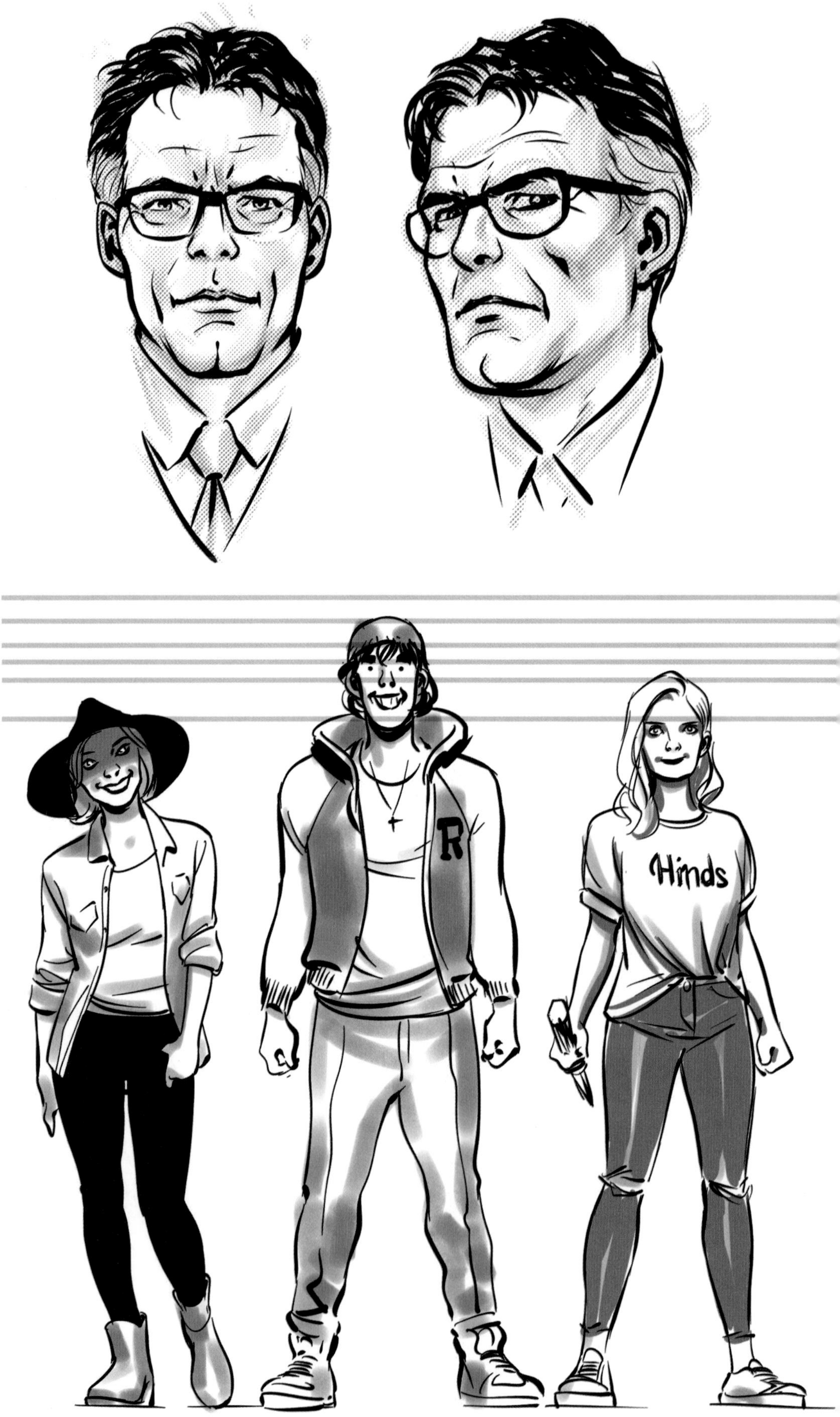
R
Hinds

Above: Cordelia, Spike, and Giles Sketches

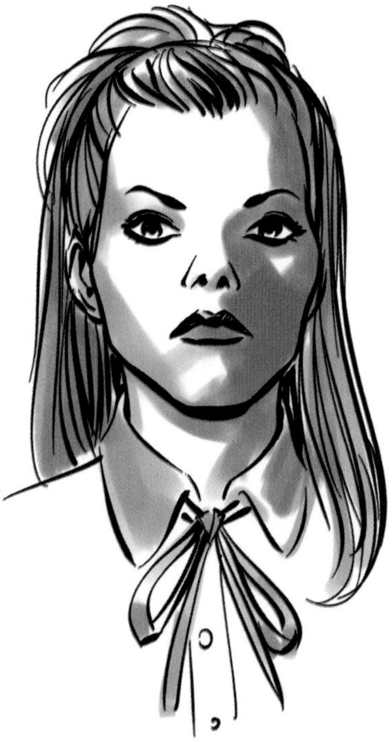
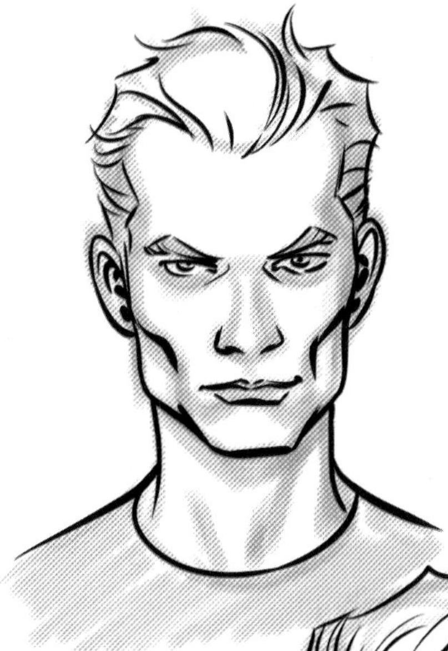
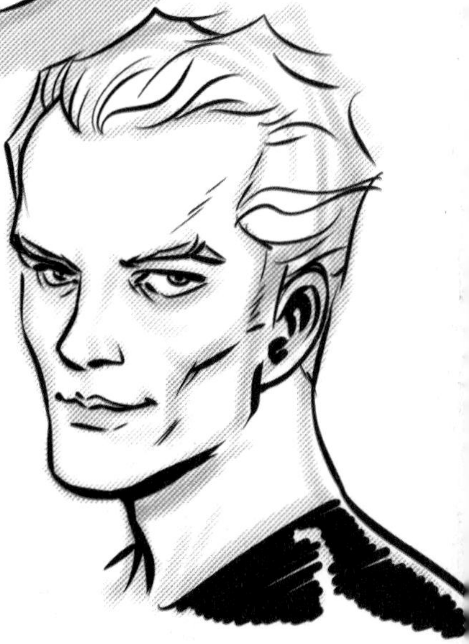
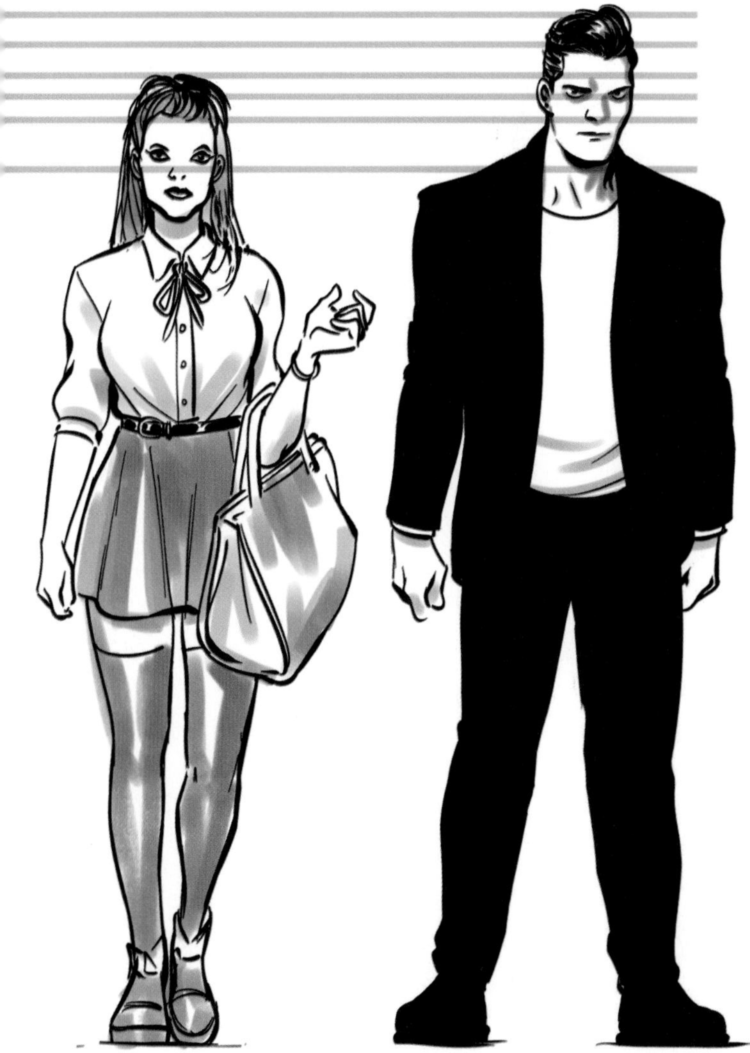

Below: Character Model Sketches

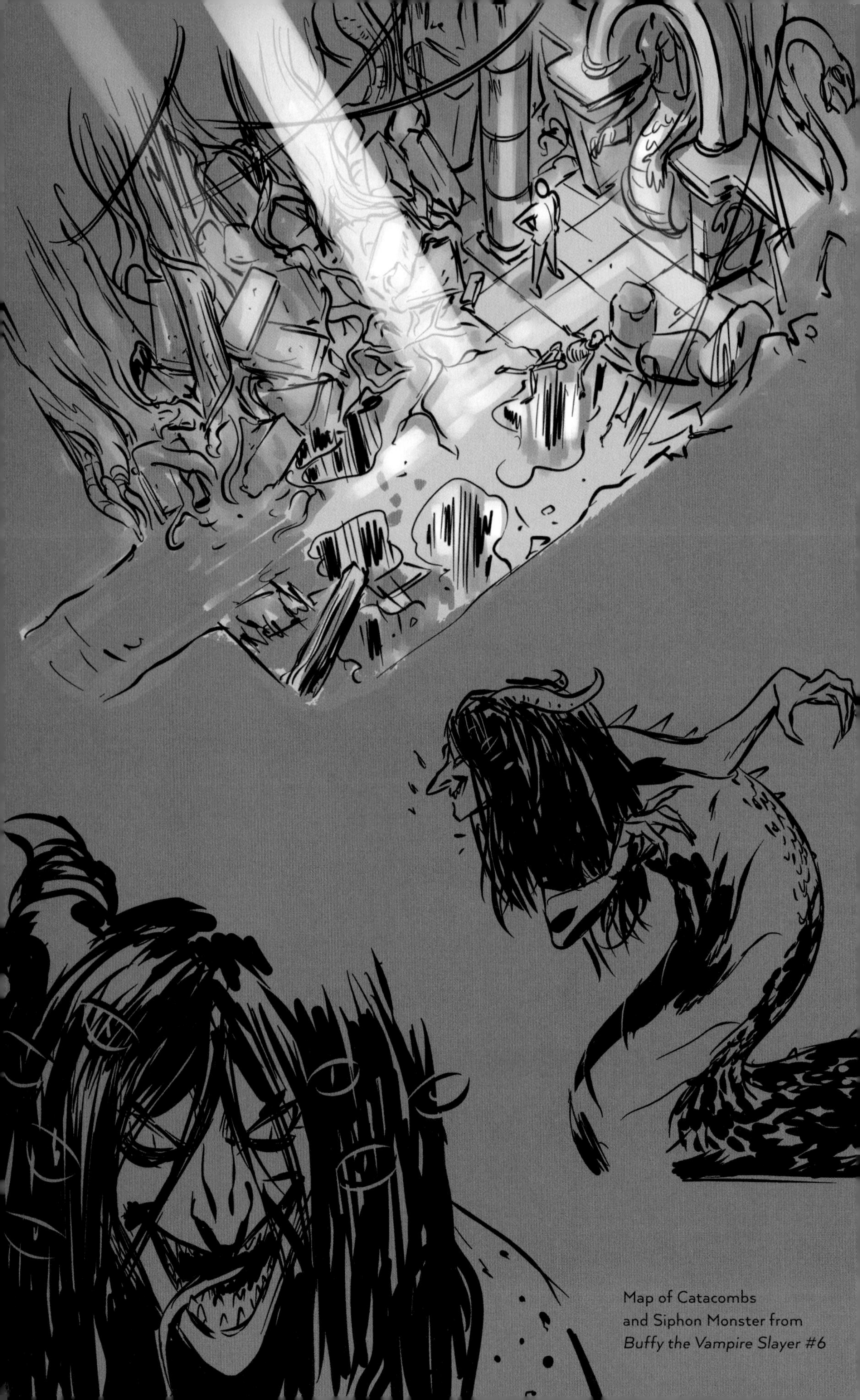

Map of Catacombs
and Siphon Monster from
Buffy the Vampire Slayer #6

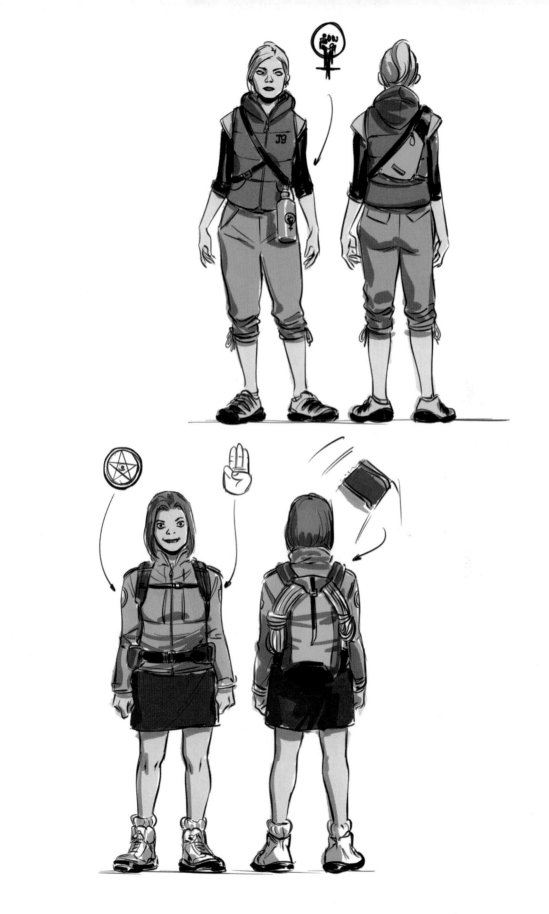

Buffy & Willow outdoor design from *Buffy the Vampire Slayer #6*

DISCOVER
VISIONARY CREATORS

THE WOODS
JAMES TYNION IV • MICHAEL DIALYNAS
VOL. 1
THE ARROW

"The Spire is fantastic! My kind of genre free-for-all."
—BRIAN K. VAUGHAN (Saga)
THE SPIRE
SIMON SPURRIER
JEFF STOKELY
ANDRÉ MAY

MARK WAID • PETER KRAUSE
IRREDEEMABLE
AFTERWORD BY GRANT MORRISON

MARK WAID • JEAN DIAZ
INCORRUPTIBLE

MICHAEL ALAN NELSON
DAN MORA
GABRIEL CASSATA
HEXED
THE HARLOT & THE THIEF VOLUME ONE

ABNETT • CULBARD
WILD'S END
FIRST LIGHT

BOOM!™ STUDIOS

AVAILABLE AT YOUR LOCAL COMICS SHOP AND BOOKSTORE

To find a comics shop in your area, visit www.comicshoplocator.com

WWW.**BOOM-STUDIOS**.COM

James Tynion IV

The Woods

Volume 1

ISBN: 978-1-60886-454-6 | $9.99 US

Volume 2

ISBN: 978-1-60886-495-9 | $14.99 US

Volume 3

ISBN: 978-1-60886-773-8 | $14.99 US

The Backstagers

Volume 1

ISBN: 978-1-60886-993-0 | $14.99 US

Simon Spurrier

Six-Gun Gorilla

ISBN: 978-1-60886-390-7 | $19.99 US

The Spire

ISBN: 978-1-60886-913-8 | $29.99 US

Weavers

ISBN: 978-1-60886-963-3 | $19.99 US

Mark Waid

Irredeemable

Volume 1

ISBN: 978-1-93450-690-5 | $16.99 US

Volume 2

ISBN: 978-1-60886-000-5 | $16.99 US

Incorruptible

Volume 1

ISBN: 978-1-60886-015-9 | $16.99 US

Volume 2

ISBN: 978-1-60886-028-9 | $16.99 US

Michael Alan Nelson

Hexed The Harlot & The Thief

Volume 1

ISBN: 978-1-60886-718-9 | $14.99 US

Volume 2

ISBN: 978-1-60886-816-2 | $14.99 US

Day Men

Volume 1

ISBN: 978-1-60886-393-8 | $9.99 US

Volume 2

ISBN: 978-1-60886-852-0 | $9.99 US

Dan Abnett

Wild's End

Volume 1: First Light

ISBN: 978-1-60886-735-6 | $19.99 US

Volume 2: The Enemy Within

ISBN: 978-1-60886-877-3 | $19.99 US

Hypernaturals

Volume 1

ISBN: 978-1-60886-298-6 | $16.99 US

Volume 2

ISBN: 978-1-60886-319-8 | $19.99 US

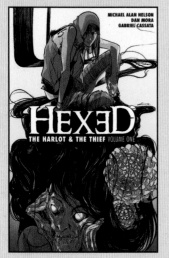